THE ARA PACIS OF AUGUSTUS AND MUSSOLINI

Wayne Andersen

THE ARA PACIS OF AUGUSTUS AND MUSSOLINI

An Archeological Mystery

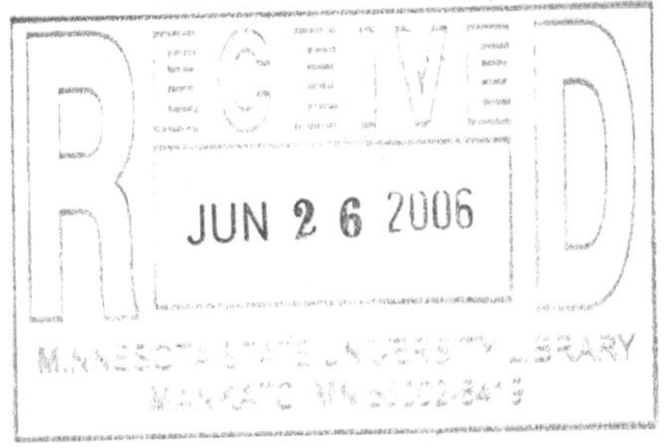

ÈDITIONS FABRIART
Geneva and Boston

Typesetting by Fabriart S. A., Geneva. Book Antiqua 10/14.

10 9 8 7 6 5 4 3 2 1

Library of Congress Cataloging-in-Publications Data

Andersen, Wayne V., 1928 –
The Ara Pacis of Augustus and Mussolini / Wayne Andersen
p. cm.
Includes bibliographical references.

ISBN 0-9725573-1-8 (trade paper)

1. Ara Pacis. Augustus, 63 BC - AD 14. 2. Octavian, 63 BC – AD 14. 3. Mussolini, Benito, 1883 - 1945 — Art History 4. Roman sculpture. 5. Roman architecture. 6. Fascist architecture — Italy. 1. Title.

COVER IMAGE
Based on a photograph by Diane Conlin

FRONTISPIECE
Based on the marble Augustus of Prima Porta in the Boston Museum of Fine Arts and a photograph of Benito Mussolini.

Dedicated to the memory of two great teachers

Daryl Amyx and *Otto Brendel*

BOOKS BY THE SAME AUTHOR

Cézanne's Portrait Drawings
American Sculpture in Process
Gauguin's Paradise Lost
My Self (Autobiography)
Scenario for an Artist's Apocalypse
Freud, Leonardo, and the Vulture's Tail
Picasso's Brothel: Les Demoiselles d'Avignon
The Dirtfarmer's Son (autobiography)
Little Sister (novel writtm as a screenplay)

FORTHCOMING

The Youth of Cézanne and Zola: Notoriety at its Source
Cézanne and the Eternal Feminine
The Picnic and the Prostitute: Manet's
Art of the 1860s
Picasso and the Alien Oilcloth (essays)

CONTENTS

PREFACE

To the extent that I'm known in the academic world, considering my several publications on Cézanne, Gauguin, Manet, and Picasso, it's as a specialist in nineteenth and twentieth-century art history. How I know myself is quite another matter. When a while back it became known that I was undertaking a book on the Ara Pacis, I was assaulted with disbelief, as if fearing I would crash the Romanist art field, tread on the lilies and poach nymphs. One most eminent Romanist asked me in a letter, "Why are you venturing into an area that has been so thoroughly covered by Roman historians?"

Well, how to respond to that question? I did not undertake this extensive bout with research and write this book for Roman historians, but for unfettered people like me who walk through fences. If by no other right than academic freedom or artistic license, I think and write about what interests me. Like Noah's dove finding a place to roost, every book I've written has found its own audience. On release from my hands, I did not tell them in which direction they should fly. To aim a book at an audience is to snub those who don't have tickets to the performance.

My writing and lecturing is for the world. If that's what a public intellectual is, so be it. I am not pretending to be a Romanist scholar, just a compulsively curious intellectual trying to make the most out of his brain and its unruly talents. Supporters for my effort are not individual Romanists but rather their labors and publications from which I've benefited, especially, in alphabetical order, books by Richard Brilliant, David Castriota, Diane Conlin, Georges Dumézil, Niels Hannestad, Karl Galinsky, Diane Kleiner, Ann Kuttner, William McDonald, Jerome Pollitt, Mario Torelli, and Paul Zanker, not to mention Cato, Vitruvius, Titus Lucretius, Cicero, Tacitus,

Livy, and Suetonius. And I am particularly indebted to Marvin Tameanko, fellow architect and notable expert on Roman coins, for his kind assistance when working my way through coin imagery as it relates to the Ara Pacis and associated altars.

Like other books I've written, this one is disputatious. My natural implulse is to question whatever I read. In that sense, I am academically unattached. No advance in knowlege has come about through agreement in the reciprocal courtship of peerage. In a 1988 lecture entitled "Approaches to Art History," the eminent art historian, Ernst Gombrich, argued that for the historian, the rejection of false explanations is as important as formulations of better ones. "We must clear the ground of rubbish before we can build," he said. The metaphor is apt for more reasons than one: archeology and the historical practice that assembles its findings deal essentially with dug up rubbish. When engaging ancient art and architecture, about all one has to work with is detritis found in land fills, sunken ships, and tombs. Commensurately, one must deal with acacademic rubbish—not to dig it up but to bury it.

This book is not about archeology in general, or Roman history in general, but about the vissitudes of one monument, the *ara Pacis Augustae.* This most complete of Roman artifacts was fabricated at a relatively certain time and demolished at an uncertain time. Its foundation and rubble became landfill in a marshy place, the Campus Martius, with some parts salvaged and set aside in a cellar, possibly for reuse. In time, the cellar, too, was buried. Over some four hundred years, many of its parts were recovered. Under the aupices of Mussolini and the Italian Faschist Empire, it was reassembled for our time at the bi-millennial celebration of Augustus' birth—an altar of peace ironically reconstituted at the onset of World War II.

Some aspects of this book are derived from my other profession: architect and founding head of Vesti Design International (Vesti is my middle name, used when performing as an architect so I don't get confused over who I am from one moment to the next). Pertinent to this book are my projects in Saudi Arabia, which include the mirhab for the the King Abdulazziz Airport mosque at Jeddah, partial re-design of the interior of the Royal Reception Pavilion at Jeddah, the interior of the great King Khaled mosque at Riyadh (see the supplemental reproductions at the end of this book), the ceiling domes of the Community mosque at Riyadh, the Royal Terminal landscape at the King Fahd International Airport in the Eastern Provinces, the landscape design for the Eastern Provinces International Airport, and inspector for the Visitors' Palace at Riyadh. These projects were realized over the years 1976 to 1988. In 1984, with Leslie Chabot as co-producer, we produced for the Saudi government a film on Vesti's work for the King Khaled Mosque in Riyadh. The film was featured for several months as a cabin movie on Saudia Airline flights when approaching the kingdom. Some of my work in the Middle East has been published: *Riyadh,* ed. Nicholas Drake (London, 1988) pp. 72-76, and J. Graham, "A Modern Statement in Islamic Art," in *Arts, The Islamic World,* II, No. 1 (Spring 1984).

Over the final weeks of preparing this book for publication, I enjoyed the assistance and pleasurable company of two young scholars, John Ulrich and Robert Chavez. If any errors now lurk in the text, they resulted from my messing with the manuscript after they had finished their work. I also wish to acknowledge here the affectionate friendship in Paris of Parry Jubert and Jacques Jubert, who, at every opportunity have supported my writings. Publication of this book was made possible by the generosity of my friends at Èditions Fabriart of Geneva, who published two of my books in 1990 when I resided in France: *Scenario for an Artist's Apocalypse,* and, with the collaboration of Presses Universitaires de France, *MY SELF.*

Wayne Andersen
Boston, January 1, 2003

AN ODE TO AUGUSTUS'S SAFE RETURN THAT INITIATED THE ARA PACIS

Child of kind gods, good guardian
Of the Roman people, you are too long away,
Return since you promised your return
And bring us day.
Good leader, give light back to your country:
It will be spring when your good face will seem
To shine on the people, days will go cheerfully
And suns will gleam.

....

You will sing happy days and this city
At public play at last and you will tell
The return of brave Augustus, the courts free
With no quarrel.
Then my voice too if I may say something
Will join the shouting and will cry O Sun
Of beauty, son of praises! I shall sing
He's home, we've won.
We shan't say it just once , Io Triumphe!
As your procession passes, Io Triumphe!
All the city with incense smoke from seven
hills up to heaven.
Ten bulls and ten heifers from you will pass.
A tender calf from me sniffing calm airs
Just free from its mother, eating
fine grass to express my prayers.

....

HORACE

Passages from Peter Levi, *Horace: A Life.*

[1] The *Ara Pacis Augustae*, Rome. West entrance into the shrine.

1
THE MYSTERY

Two millennia ago, the ancient Roman senate decreed a sacrificial altar, the *ara Pacis Augustae* (*ara* meaning "altar," *pacis* meaning "peace"), to give thanks for the safe return of Augustus *imperator* (victorious general) from the northern provinces, Spain and Gaul. Over a three-year absence from Rome, he'd been there to settle outbreaks of affairs that threatened the Empire's economic health. It is broadly believed that the enshrined Ara Pacis now standing in Rome between the Mausoleum of Augustus and the Tiber River is that monument, its corner stone laid in 13 BC, it's said, and after three-and-a-half years of construction, dedicated in 9 BC, it's also said. In this book, I venture to bet against all odds that, while it is indeed an *ara Pacis Augustae,* it is not the structure that existed on either of those dates.

The smoking gun to which my evidence will return fire is a lesser detail than a cigarette butt that could lead Hercule Poirot to solve an impossible murder. Mine is a 1 ¾ -inch disparity in riser height of one step (*crassitudo*) in a short stair run that moves up from the altar's floor to the platform on which priests would have stood when performing sacrificial rituals. Along with use of other evidence, including a missing segment of molding that the aforesaid anomaly prompted me to discover, I will bring my case against the Ara Pacis' reconstruction to trial. Because one cannot prove one's convictions simply by pointing, to show respect for rules of evidence I will lay considerable groundwork. In my profession, combining architectural practise and art history, this means providing on-site drawings and some pertinent history.

The Augustan altar of peace served an uplifting purpose in Rome's ancient history, as it would for Mussolini and the Italian Fascist government in the 1930s when formulating imperial ambitions to reestablish the Roman Empire. Mussolini's conduct in office over the 1920s and early '30s—promoting benevolent social policies, programs of public works, maintenance of laws, and a conciliatory policy toward religion—was uncannily like Augustus'. Even Mussolini's title *Il duce,* meaning "leader," recapitulated Augustus' title *princeps,* meaning "principal" or "head man." And like Augustus becoming emperor, *Il duce* soon became *Il dittatore.*

Mussolini set about to recapitulate his forebear's success by creating an empire that once again might dominate the Mediterranean and the Adriatic.[1] Like Augustus, to whom the ancient Romans looked to bring about an age of renewal, Mussolini's furthest goal was to return strife-torn and economically depressed Italy to a state of peace and plenty. But to achieve peace he needed first to attain the plenty, which meant taking rule over other nations that would provide economic resources—foodstuffs, minerals, lumber, and other raw materials—that the Italian peninsula lacked and had lacked as well during the Augustan era.

Augustus had been similarly motivated when taking command of the far-flung Roman Empire after the civil wars—the murder of Julius Caesar and the war with Antony and Cleopatra. Italy was depleted of lumber trees needed for structural beams, ship planking and masts, was perennially short of wheat, vegetable oils, and ores, and dependent on slavery to fill out manpower needs without which aggressive agriculture and road-building industries couldn't manage. Mussolini would adopt Julius Caesar and Augustus' strategy to restrict northern defenses to the Danube River, forge trade alliances rather than booty-yielding wars, and colonize less developed nations in support of a politically and economically integrated empire. In 1935, Mussolini sent an army to invade farm produce-rich Ethiopia, while threatening France and England to forestall economic sanctions and military intervention. The following year saw the Fascist Italian Empire officially proclaimed. Mussolini then extended his ambitions to influence Spain by supporting Franco, and made a move to confederate Italy and Germany, despite Hitler's overtaking of Austria that long ago had been part of the Roman Empire and still played a substantial role in Italy's economy. By forming an alliance with Germany, the vast medieval, eleventh-century German-Roman territory would be recharged.

The Italian Fascist Empire lavishly sponsored the 1937 bimillennial ceremony of Augustus' reign. A vast exhibition installed for the event is aptly described by the historian of fascist architecture, Spiro Kostof, as not intended for a scholarly show of Roman history but overtly for propaganda, a didactic display of the ancient Empire's achievements staged to renew national pride and inspire loyalty to Mussolini as the custodian of Italy's illustrious traditions.[2] An enormous meaning then came into focus on this relatively small monument dwarfed by Augustus' mausoleum—ironically, an altar of peace reconstituted at the onset of a great war.

Mussolini's empire building was a windfall in support of Italian archeology. The Forum of Augustus, his mausoleum, and the Theater of Marcellus were reconstructed in the 1930s to stand as monumen-

[2] Mussolini and his entourage inspecting the Ara Pacis reconstruction.

tal reminders of Italy's glorious past. Mussolini's delight would be the Altar of Augustan Peace, the subject of this book. Many of its parts had accumulated over years of excavations, reaching back to the sixteenth century, and were in storage in the Museo Nazionale Romano, with exceptional pieces in the Museo delle Terme, the Vatican Museum, and the Louvre [3].

In the nineteenth century the altar's foundation had been found six meters underground in the still swampy Campus Martius (Field of Mars), northwest of the city's edge and about one mile from the *pomerium*, the religious boundary of the ancient city. Centuries earlier this expansive field was Tarquinian grazing land. When driven out by the Romans, the acres were retained as parkland and military exercise fields. It took the name Campus Martius in conjunction with an altar to Mars erected there, Mars being the god of war. The altar's footprint thus established as to dimensions and layout, hypothetical reconstructions could be drawn up from time to time, but only by completing a jigsaw of actual pieces would a picture emerge telling what the Ara Pacis looked like two thousand years ago.

[3] Fragments in storage in the Museo Nazionale Romano, Rome.

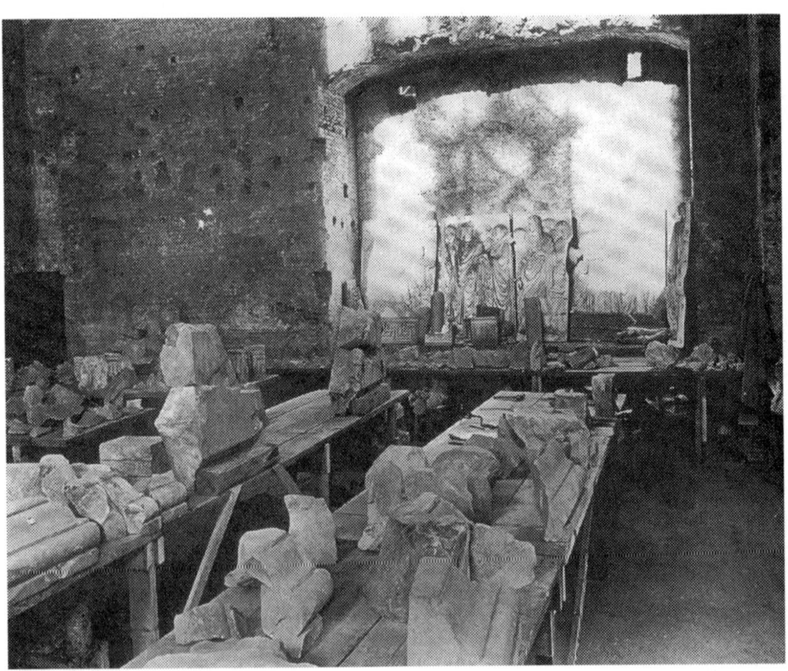

Under the direction of distinguished archeologists Guiseppe Moretti and Antonio Gatti, a team of archeologists was put to the task of reconstituting the altar at a new location within the city, alongside the Tiber, the original site having been built over by modern structures. This new location had been until 1900 the eighteenth-century river port, the Porta di Ripetta, which had been leveled and covered over when the Tiber River walls and the river road, the Lungotevere, were constructed. By mid-1937, the Ara Pacis was reborn, its final salvageable parts extracted from the ancient swamp after refrigeration pipes were installed all around the dig to freeze the mud and hold it back until excavators found all they could identify as potential Ara Pacis remnants.

Five years later, the Italian Fascist regime collapsed, but Hitler had *Il duce* quickly restored to power in northern Italy. In 1945, Mussolini's own military officers murdered him, echoing Julius Caesar's fate at the hands of senatorial assassins headed by the generals Brutus and Cassius. Mussolini's bullet-riddled corpse was hung by its feet in a public square for all to see—as Leonardo da Vinci might have envisioned it, the Florentine painter having said, "To illustrate defeat, draw a tree with its roots in the air."

Italy became a republic in 1946, and the Ara Pacis stood naked of relevance in its glass house—just another tourist magnet and not a dazzling one at that. Not until Italy's fascist past had faded with the death of its generation did the Italian government give the monument much thought. In 1997, in anticipation of the new millennium, Richard Meier, best known as the architect of the Getty Museum in Los Angeles, was commissioned to design a building to replace the transparent box and revitalize the sorry state of the Piazzale Augusto Imperatore, an area that featured as well Augustus' mausoleum and the church of S. Rocco. Construction is scheduled to begin October 2002 with an anticipated completion date 2005-06.[3]

[6] Left: The steel and glass protective enclosure of the Ara Pacis before its destruction.

Below: Architect's rendering of the new enclosure and the Ara Pacis Museum. Photo courtesy Richard Meier and Partners, Architects.

2

THE AUTHOR'S AUGURY

Relative to the years of my life, this book is as old as the Augustan Age relative to Roman history. It began in the autumn of 1959 as a seminar report during the first semester of my graduate studies at Columbia University, prepared for oral delivery in the esteemed Otto Brendel's seminar on Roman relief sculpture. My topic focused on the marble relief panels at the east and west side of the Ara Pacis' enclosing walls, especially the Tellus panel [7], and expanded to spell out an iconographic program for the entire altar complex. Professor Brendel didn't have much to say when I'd finished my presentation, but had smiled broadly throughout it while puffing a very long cigar. Anyone blessed with the good fortune to have studied with that seminal classicist and remarkable man will understand why I still see him smiling now, as years later I undertake this book.

He said back then that I may be correct in proposing that the Tellus relief connected to traditions of Egyptian nilotic landscape rendering, that a master trained in Alexandria may have conceived and executed it, and that the other reliefs testified to the handwork of other artisan shops, some Eastern Greek, others Roman. That was about all he said. He was not a man of many words. Later he mentioned how exceptional it was that, to identify the plants in the Tellus relief, I'd visited the herbarium of the New England Botanical Garden, and to ascertain whether the bird in the relief was a goose or a swan, had consulted an ornithologist at the Bronx zoo. Field trips to other than libraries and archives were not normal to academic research at a time when it had taken Meyer Schapiro six years of pleading to get permission to teach a course on French Impressionism at Columbia, and when, shortly before, Lawrence Eitner at Princeton had broken through the barrier at the end of acceptable topics for academic research when he undertook a doctoral dissertation on the early nineteenth-century French painter, Géricault.

In 1965, when I was a start-up professor in the Department of Architecture at the Massachusetts Institute of Technology and invited to deliver an evening lecture at Columbia's Department of Art History and

[7] The Tellus panel on the east facade of the Ara Pacis shrine.

Archaeology on the very non-Roman Paul Gauguin, Professor Brendel took me aside after my presentation to say he'd found my method of interpreting Gauguin's imagery "uncannily similar" to the one I'd developed six years earlier when analyzing the allegorical relief panels on the Ara Pacis. He added that no advance in studies of Roman symbolism had gone beyond what I'd said back then (since then, considerable advance has been made by others).

On an evening four years later, while dining outdoors with Brendel and my wife, Phyllis, in Rome's Piazza Navona, he again brought up the subject matter of my report and asked why I'd not published it. I replied that I'd been up to my gizzard in architecture and modern art, and anyway hadn't understood why what I'd said about the altar was important enough to publish. His reaction registered in the broad smile of a seasoned sage. After a couple of puffs on his iconographic cigar, he said, "You should have published it anyway." Then he turned my attention to the facade of Santa Ignese across the plaza to point out when, at a precise moment in the decline of mid-summer daylight, and only for twenty seconds, the facade would come into perfect silhouette; all surface detail would disappear and a small light would appear in the right bell tower for which no one had discovered a source.

Professor Brendel's sustained interest in the thoughts I'd had about the Tellus panel, and the thematic program of the entire Ara Pacis, prompted me to take a more interested look at the structure. When a few years before I'd made a tourist-type visit to the site, I saw nothing that altered my earlier notions about the reliefs when knowing them only from photographs and as illustrated and described in books. When freshly confronted by the altar complex, walking around it and through it, my architectural eyes felt troubled. After many hours of studying it by just looking at it, much that I'd read about its history and function began to unravel. How could large animal sacrifices have taken place at that altar so confined within its enclosure walls as to allow only a two-person wide corridor around it? Some Romanists say that the procession one sees on the south and north enclosure wall had entered through the west door and *after the ceremony* exited through the east door. Even if that were possible—by no stretch of the imagination could it have been, considering the free interior space is less than that of a prison cell and all of it is corridor—how could the procession depict the altar's consecration in either 13 BC, or its dedication in 9 BC, if the event occurred on either date? If the reliefs on the south and north exterior walls depict the event, how could the event have taken place around and within that enlosure *before* the reliefs were carved? One cannot look at photographs until after they've been shot. A documentary film cannot be made of something that hasn't yet happened.

Even more questionable: how could it have been, as at least one authority claims, that Augustus returned to Rome on the same day the Senate voted him that altar, and on the very same day the corner stone was laid, and on the very same day there occurred a large-animal sacrifice and a celebratory feast? Aside from this collapse of sequence onto one moment, the reliable historian, Suetonius (b. AD 70), tells us that, to avoid a public reception, travel-weary Augustus and his entourage entered the city at night, unannounced![4]

Given that suspicion energizes curiosity and doesn't kill every cat—some of us having nine lives—I allowed myself to suspect that the Ara Pacis was an assemblage of sorts hastily put together by Moretti and his team under the dictatorial eyes of Mussolini, the restorers coerced by a schedule of performance. That thought was not an accusation, but a theory that called for testing.[5]

I had nothing to go on other than a sense of the structure's poor gestalt and the stylistic disparity between the decorative and pictorial elements on the altar proper and those on the exterior of its enclosure, even though precedent denied that condition from being exceptional. On the Parthenon, too, one can observe a range of talent in the reliefs: from the dry academic style of Phidias on the east entrance end, where major deities and personages appear, to evidence of a more vigorous, youthful style on the western backside where the tail of the procession is without major dignitaries. Obviously different workshops were involved when fabricating the Parthenon frieze, with others carving the metope reliefs and the pediment sculpture.[6] Most likely this was also the case with the *ara Pacis Augustae*: one shop more typically Roman doing the altar friezes, one more Eastern Greek or Alexandrian doing the reliefs on the exterior of the enclosure. But I remain troubled as to why, at such an advanced stage of Roman art and architecture, and for a work of such importance to the emperor, a single supervisory eye would have failed to unify the artisanship and thus the style.

By 1986, I had done a great deal of architectural design work on mosque interiors in Saudi Arabia that even involved stone carving at the very site where the Ara Pacis marble was quarried [see my supplementary reproductions on pp. 231-33]. As a design consultant to the Saudi government for the mosque, airport, and royal pavilion in the Eastern Provinces, I formulated and developed programs that wouldn't have differed significantly from the structure of those written for such state monuments as the *ara Pacis Augustae*. For the huge mosque at Riyadh, I had mixed styles to sustain Islamic history within a modern structure:

the *mirhab* (prayer niche) in a very modern design involved carved stone from Italy and ceramics from France and England, but I engaged an Egyptian workshop to execute the mahogany *minbar* (pulpit) with hand tools. Of the many pairs of huge entrance doors for the mosque, one-third I had fabricated in Switzerland using computer-driven cutting machines, another third were hand-carved in Damascus, and the final third carved by Egyptians at a shop set up in Jeddah (like ancient Greek and Alexandrian artisans had done on immigrating to Rome). Political reasons were behind my distribution of commissions to Saudi, Egyptian, and Syrian workshops, just as political motives must surely have stimulated the Roman senators and magistrates to ensure that whoever was in charge of the Ara Pacis' design and construction engage more than one shop to build the monument. The Riyadh mosque represented the whole of Islam, not just Saudi Arabia, while the Ara Pacis referenced Rome but, in addition, its fabrication reflected the Roman Principate sprawled all around the Mediterranean.

By then I'd come to dislike the adjective "eclectic" as characterizing Rome's Republic and Early Empire art, since that label smacks of racial purity and bows to Greek Classical art as standing for artistic purity. It was not that "the Romans" were impure, but that Rome and the Italian peninsula were populated by a mix of what had been at one time, perhaps, pure races constrained, like Galapagos species, by geographical perimeters and tightly circumscribed cultures. So the planners of the Ara Pacis did not draw upon a wide array of "sources" in order to promote Roman "eclecticism" as a national style. The mix of handwork and imaging found on the Ara Pacis resulted not from mixing art but from mixing residual blood-nationalities of artists and stone carvers that resulted in a mix of styles, the mix not intentional as an eclectic style. The tendency to affix style to an ethnic population is faced foursquare by Otto Brendel in his legendary *Prolegomena to the Study of Roman Art*: "New styles of art [other than developmental continuities or internal revolutions] must then come from new races of people." And he adds that efforts to distinguish between national styles in Italy have produced "mere theoretical fictions."[7]

In the summer of 1994, after a span of years living in Paris and about to return to the United States, I went to Rome, as if on unfinished business, armed with a hefty tape measure and calipers to make what in architectural practice we call "measured" or "as built" drawings." I was determined to figure out what it was about that monument to peace that would not leave me in peace. I was even puzzled as to why I was puzzled (a warning sign of a pending mental breakdown). My doubts had by then narrowed down to suspecting that something was wrong with the altar's architecture. Something was wrong with the dimensions. Had the first-century BC architect, Vitruvius, been with me, he might have felt as troubled as I did. Here is what he had to say on the subject:

> Order is the balanced adjustment of the details of the work separately and as to the whole, the arrangement of the proportion with a view to symmetrical result. This is made up of Dimension, which in Greek is called *posotes*. Now Dimension is the taking of modules [units of measurement] from the parts of the work and its dimensions along with a certain quality or character.[8]

That's precisely what I was about to do: take dimensional modules from parts of the monument and interrogate their character.

I had previously studied Moretti's diagrams and noticed, among other oddities, that when giving the width of the ambulatory within the walls and around the altar he did not enter the distance from the face of the lowest stair riser to the base of the enclosure, which would yield the width of the ambulatory, but from midway under the first step [8]. The measurement was 1.28 meters—not an architect's dimension as to positioning the altar base within the enclosure, but a stonemason's dimension for sizing the floor slab. This oddity alone did not signal a major problem, but it offered a proportional measure that, when applied to the width of the ambulatory, yielded 1.0m. Then my suspicions were aroused. Ancient Romans didn't know the metric system. It was invented only in the eighteenth century and not in general use by Italian architects until after 1865. From where did that exact meter come?

Over two sweltering hot days under the quizzical eye of a security guard, I measured every part of the structure while ignoring other dimensions given in official accounts of Moretti's restoration upon

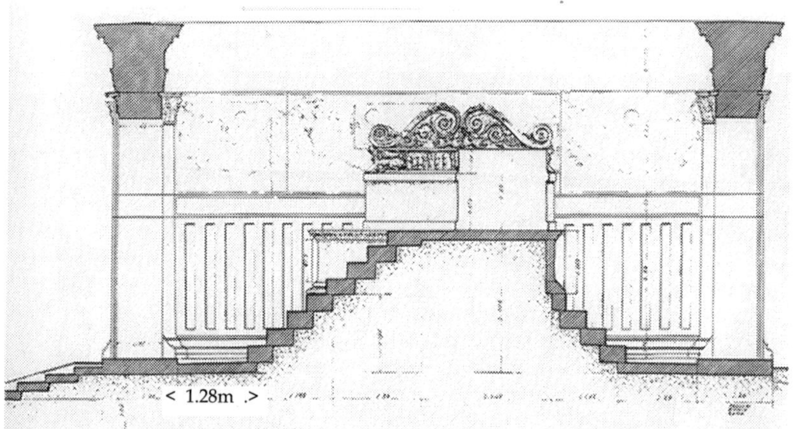

[8] Guiseppe Moretti's drawing. East-west section through the Ara Pacis reconstruction with dimensions in meters.

which historians of the monument depend. On returning to Paris and subjecting the modules and dimensions to simple computations, I came up with a remarkable discovery: the system of measure governing the reconstructed altar's major parts and proportions was metric! How could that be? No dimensions should come out exactly on the meter or one-half of a meter except accidentally. But several of them did. And I soon found that other dimensions in Moretti's reconstruction were metric but not indicated as such on his drawings, except for those of the hypothetical entablature that surmounts the walls, for which no original fragments were found.

What alerted me to this problem with the dimensions even before I'd made calculations was an abrupt disparity in step riser height. The altar's steps have four risers and three treads from the floor level to where the podium begins, then four risers and three treads rise to the standing platform, or *prothysis*, on which the officiating priests would have stood when performing their rites [9]. At the juncture between these two stair runs, which are continuous as one run, the fifth riser from the floor and fourth down from the platform floor measured 21.5 cm while the risers above it and those below it measured 24.4 to 26.0 cm.

Why was that one riser so noticeably less in height than the others? Surely Augustan building practices were as rigorously precise as those followed today within their respective limits of building technolo-

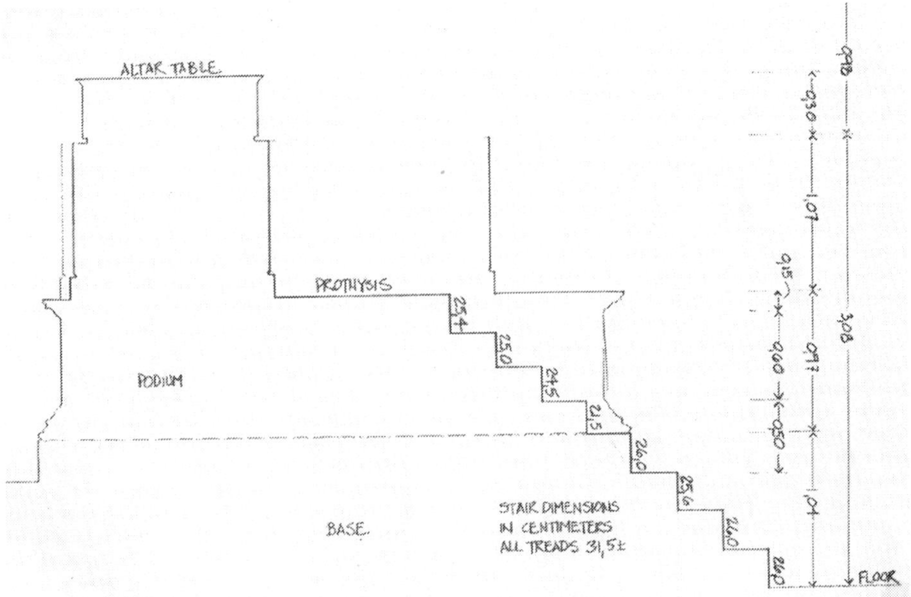

[9] Author's drawing. East-west section of the altar with dimensions.

gy. Surely codes were in place that specified riser heights, minimum tread widths, and a dimensional ratio of riser to tread for steps that alternate in sequence for the right and left foot when climbing. No architect in his right mind, ancient or modern, would change riser-heights at mid-course in a single stair run. If not uniform, users will stumble when going up or down quickly or absent-mindedly.

While references to building practices in Augustan Rome are few and not very informative, it is naïve to think that Roman buildings at any level of complexity would have been built without material and technical specifications. Romans did not build by instinct, not like beavers. Relevant in this case is the role of Hellenistic and Roman building commissions that hardy differed from how such commissions function today as design review boards, redevelopment authorities, and civic and corporate building committees. Records for one public-scale project, the ancient Temple of Asklepios at Epidauros, tell us that all major architectural projects had to be sanctioned by a decree of the highest governing council, with design and construction overseen by committee-like entities: a finance committee that reviewed contracts, controlled the budget, and authorized payments, and a building commission comprised of material suppliers, master craftsmen, stonemasons, and construction management experts. Alison Burford and Diane Conlin have contributed much to our understanding of contractual and building oversight practices in the ancient Mediterranean. Contracts when awarded were specific as to materials and methods: one contract summed up the building commission's requirements with the following command: "The contractor must not set anything permanent without our sanction."[9] A building commission overseeing construction of the Temple of Zeus Basileus in Boeotia made strict demands on the builders, as this clause in the contract testifies: "Make the undersurfaces of all stones, not less than two feet from the next joint with a close-toothed, sharp chisel."[10]

Nothing was arbitrary in Augustan civic architecture, especially for structures as important as the *ara Pacis Augustae*. Vitruvius' commentary on stair design, which I bring into play, was not his opinion but a recital of standard practice that would have been published in design and construction manuals:

> The steps are to be placed so they are always of an uneven number. For since the first step is ascended on the right foot, the right foot must also be set on the top of the temple steps. And the risers of the steps must be of such dimensions that they are neither deeper [higher] than ten inches [9.5 modern inches] nor shallower than nine [8.5 modern inches]. Then the ascent will not be difficult. But the treads of the steps, it seems, should be made not less than eighteen inches [17.1 modern inches] or more than two feet [22.8 modern inches].[11]

The dimensions Vitruvius gives are most likely for the stylobate of a temple, or of steps to a federal building, not for a stair run of the type one sees in the Ara Pacis, which would have had less depth for treads. Converted to Roman inches (1.0 inches = 0.95 Roman inches; one Roman foot = 29.59cm), the average dimensions of the Ara Pacis steps (excluding the odd one) are 9 Roman inches for the riser and 12 Roman inches for the tread, with the odd riser 1.75 Roman inches less than the average height of the others (The United States Uniform

Building Code allows a maximum of 3/8th inch variation in riser heights).

This inconsistent step-riser caused me to take a harder look at how the cut-in podium steps from the top level of the base to the platform level were made, for that riser occurs at the horizontal juncture of the base's top and the podium's bottom. One disturbing detail that no one seems to have noticed is that the saw-cut flanks of the returns on either side of the podium's steps lack moldings. Moretti's colleague in the reconstruction process, Antonio Gatti, who made a hypothetical rendering of the altar after its reconstruction was completed, must have con-

[10] Author's drawing showing saw-cut inset steps lacking moldings on the returns.

[11] Antonio Gatti's rendering of the reconstructed Ara Pacis

fronted this detail with disbelief, for in his drawing he adds moldings at both top and bottom edges, knowing they should have been there [11]. Moretti's drawing, which lacks those moldings, is true to the reconstruction [39, p. 48]. It seemed inconceivable to me that the *ara Pacis Augustae* could have been erected in Augustus' time—for that matter, at any time—with such a design fault. An altar of considerable importance, and the only one for which we have extensive remains—the so-called Altar of Domitian Ahenobarbus—supports what I am driving at [12]. The wonderfully preserved podium of sorts, perhaps the base for a colossal statue, is thought to have stood outside a temple dedicated to Neptune in the Campus Martius where the Ara Pacis was unearthed. The Ahenobarbus was not an altar, but one of its sides depicts in relief and in great detail the state sacrifice of a *suovetaurilia,* the bull, ram, and boar being led to an altar. Looking to have been about waist high, the altar has carved molding at its bottom and top edges, which is typical for all Roman altars, as for Hellenic altars of all types.[12]

The inset cutting caused the step-wide break in the moldings that had run along the front. The inset proves that the base had at least two lives, an existence before the steps were cut into its side, and another as a result of a reason to modify it. Other than that, there is nothing about the base that departs from the general shape of Greek and Roman altars, typically fashioned as a stepped base, a podium facing east, with barriers, usually in the form of scrolls at either side of the podium's top and sometimes at its back, the surface becoming a sort of table on which offerings are placed [14, p. 20].

The altar table of a so-called Pergamene altar recently assembled—ingeniously, yet hypothetically—by David Castriota, with only its two sidepieces as antique, would not change had Castriota

[12] Frieze on the so-called Altar of Ahenobarbus. Details below. Paris, Louvre.

set the table at floor level, on a platform, on a base with two to four steps, on a podium, or on a platform or stepped base [13]. The altar table is independent of its base or platform. It can be raised to any height and accessed by steps, which is true as well for the table surmounting the podium within the Ara Pacis enclosure.[13]

The disjunctive dimensions of the stair step risers, the dimensions in meters, and the missing moldings confirmed my suspicions that the Ara Pacis was not the ancient monument it is supposed to physically represent. I'll get around to detailing my reservations after offering a brief history of the altar's discovery and historical peregrinations.

[13] David Castriota's hypothetical construction of an altar using the Pergamene slabs as side-pieces. His reconstruction is based on the Ara Pacis as to the stepped base and the podium's cut-in steps. All altar tables can be placed atop bases of varying heights, which was the case for theAra Pacis.

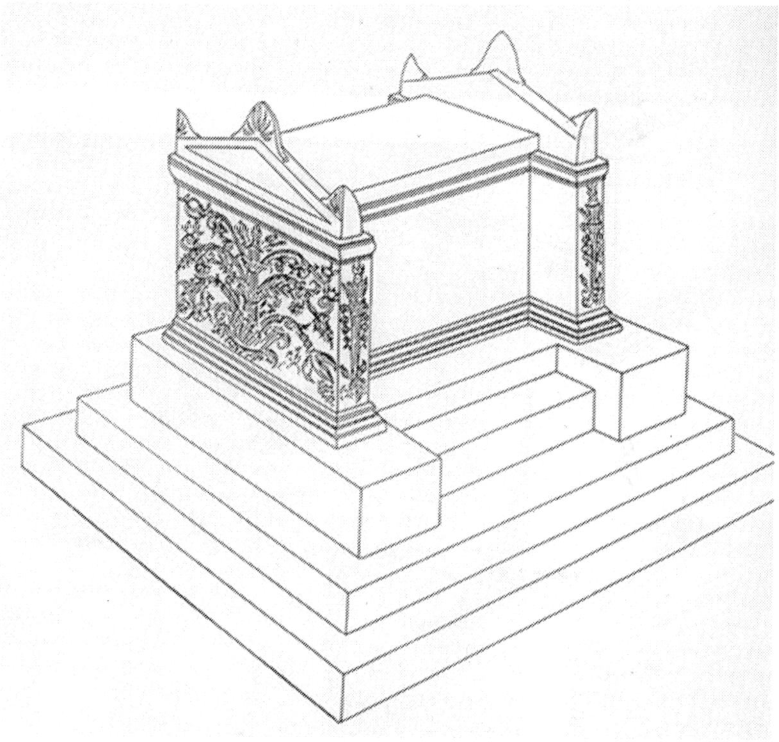

[14] Two altars from the street of tombs in front of the Herculaneum gate at Pompeii.. Two risers lead to the base of the plinth (podium), the top of which is the altar table with scroll barriers at either end.

3
THE DISCOVERY

Before his death in 14 BC, Augustus drew up a summary of what he'd accomplished over his tenure as *princeps* (principal, leading citizen, head man), the title by which he chose to be known rather than emperor.[14] Officially, the document was Augustus' *Res Gestae*, a description of the state of the nation as he altered it, reigned over, and left it. *Gestae* means "performance," or "what has been made to come about," as in "gestation." The word *res* may refer to one's own acts, but in political life the designation also applies to the State, the common weal, as expressed by *res publica*, meaning acts of state or civil affairs, or *res novae*, meaning changes the State had undergone during a period of reform and progress. The *Res Gestae* is an abstract of Augustus' deeds, ranging from military victories and closing of the Janus doors to lock in peace, to a summary of the many wild animals he'd provided for slaughter as public entertainment. The paragraph of the *Res Gestae* pertaining to the Ara Pacis reads:

> On my return from Spain and Gaul after successful operations restoring law and order in these provinces, the Senate voted, during the consulship of Tiberius Nero and Publius Quintilius, in honor of my return, that an altar to Peace be consecrated in the Campus Martius, and that on this altar the magistrates, priests, and Vestal virgins are to make annual sacrifices.[15]

For safekeeping, Augustus deposited his *Res Gestae* with the

Vestal Virgins, whose duties included holding and being vigilant over important documents of state, as they still did—symbolically, at such a late date in their history—over the communal fire. They were to safeguard Augustus' *Res Gestae* and give access to it only as he prescribed.[16]

In his testaments, Augustus ordered that after his death, which came about on August 19th, 14 AD at the age of seventy-six, the document was to be etched in bronze and installed at the entrance to his mausoleum. Tiberius Claudius, the adopted son of Augustus and succeeding emperor, no doubt carried out his wish—how soon after Augustus' death we cannot know. By the time Augustus' mausoleum became a subject for archeologists, the tablets were gone, most likely salvaged centuries ago, as was customary during wartime when bronze statues and ornaments are collected and melted down for recasting as weaponry.

Before explaining how Augustus' *Res Gestae* came to be found and transcribed, let me back up and tell how the *ara Pacis Augustae* came to be destroyed in the first place, its foundation covered over—why most of the decorative and figurative carved blocks were salvaged at some ancient time and set aside in the cellar of a nearby building. Perhaps after decades of weathering—Cararra marble, compared to granite, being very soft—the altar was destroyed during the Norman invasion of Rome at the end of the eleventh century, if not earlier.[17]

In the sixteenth century—1568, to be exact—a number of large, finely carved marble blocks were chanced upon in a cellar by contractors renovating a worn-out building in the Campus Martius, the Palazzo Fiano, which was built in the late thirteenth century for the cardinals of San Lorenzo in Lucina. Most likely ancient builders had admired the marbles and saved them from going into rubble that typically underlies foundations on such marshy lands as the Campus Martius, into which many streams drain before their remaining waters join the Tiber.

A year after this discovery, Cardinal Ricci di Montepulciano acquired eight of the blocks to present as a gift of appreciation to a church patron, Cosimo I, who would soon be the Grand Duke of Tuscany. Such gift-giving of antiquities and copies of famous paintings was common practice by then, having accelerated during the years of Lorenzo de' Medici as an aid to securing royal and church favors and to enhance business relationships. In a letter to Cosimo's secretary, the cardinal described these fragments as some fifteen to eighteen Greek marbles that over time had been broken, some having figures from triumphal scenes on one side, on the other side festoons. To allow the fronts and backs of the double-sided slabs to be more easily transported and viewed as separate panels, those blocks—very thick marble slabs—were sliced, thus separating the figurative and floral from the decorative faces.

By the end of the eighteenth century, the resulting fourteen panels and an unsawn eighth block had been moved to Florence and placed in the Uffizi Gallery. Sometime thereafter, two of the interior face panels disappeared; five others were removed from the gallery and said to have been placed in the Villa Medici on the Pincio. Two blocks that had not been acquired by Cardinal Ricci had also been sliced at some time or another. One pair made it to the Vatican Museum, the other pair to the Louvre. Again, both of the decorative-face slabs were to disappear—the Louvre's probably forever. The missing Vatican slab would eventually be found as a tombstone face in Rome's church of the Gesù.

At no time during the sixteenth century were these elaborately carved slabs—first thought to be Greek—identified with a specific Roman monument. Not until the latter part of the nineteenth century, after Augustus' *Res Gestae* had been transcribed, would all of the parts be fitted to the Ara Pacis, for it wasn't until the mid-nineteenth century that archeologists were alerted to the existence of an ancient altar by that name in the Campus Martius. Previously it was assumed that an *Ara Pacis Augustae* had existed. For in the Roman *Calendar of Feasts* for 9 BC, it is written that an altar of peace was dedicated to Augustus on January 30th that year (*feriae quod eo die ara Pacis Augustae constituta est*, meaning "day of feast, for on this day the altar of Pacis Augustae has been decreed"), but the entry gave no indication as to the altar's appearance or where it was located.[18]

The first inkling of the site's location came to mind when columns of engraved inscriptions were found on walls in the anteroom (*pronaos*) of the Temple of Rome and Augustus at Ancyra (modern Ankara), a major city in the Asia Minor district of Galatia (now part of Turkey)—a great distance from Rome, accessed at the time by an old Persian road that extended from Susa and ended near Sardis at the edge of Lydia. The

[15] Temple of Augustus at Antioch. Suggested restoration of the Propylaea by F. J. Woodbridge showing the triumphal entrance with the four podia on which were carved Augustus' *Res Gestae*. After David M. Robinson.

inscriptions, in both Greek and Latin, turned out to be Augustus' *Res Gestae,* which located the altar's site somewhere in the Campus Martius. Tiberius must have furnished the text to provincial cities where Augustus' reign was to remain indelibly exalted.

The Ancyra inscriptions are referred to as the *Monumentum Ancyranum*, the word *momentum* derived from *mõmen* or *moveo*, meaning movement or progress, a sequence of important moments bearing great social weight, in this case important moments-in-motion issuing from Ancyra. For the most part preserved, the Ancyra text can be paired with the 1914 discovery of another Latin version engraved on the front faces of four limestone plinths spaced equally on a very wide set of steps of what is believed to be a Temple of Augustus excavated at the city of Antioch in the Pisidia region close to modern Yalvaç [15]. This version, known as the *Monumentum Antiochenum*, has fewer missing letters and words than the Ancyra version, so what appears in the literature on the Ara Pacis is the Ancyra text with infill from the Antioch text. Another bilingual copy of the *Res Gestae* was unearthed at Pergamum, and also a Greek text at Apollonia, but these are too fragmented to add anything of value to the wording.

Here a problem arises that will not be resolved in this book—perhaps in no one's—but must be taken into account as a factor in the mystery of the Ara Pacis reconstruction. While the Ancyra and Antioch transcriptions have the same number of paragraphs and appendices, and differ only in accents and apecies, we do not have the initial text from which these and other copies were made. So how can we know how the original text read? How can anyone be sure that Tiberius, already fifty-six when he succeeded Augustus, did not edit the distributed text after Augustus' death, just as Augustus had edited Virgil's *Aeneid* after the poet's death?[19] Is it possible that he, or Augustus' widow Livia Drusilla, abstracted a longer text written on parchment for the purpose of reducing it to what could be modeled in wax and cast in bronze, or carved in bronze or stone, and read quickly by visitors to Augustus' mausoleum and at temples throughout the Empire?

As the distinguished scholar of ancient Greco-Roman political history, Paul Zanker, points out, public monuments as propaganda were essentially for local consumption, their political messages directed at residents of the capital with little meaning outside the city's borders.[20] When Rome came under Augustus' rule, the entire empire came into focus, and that exclusivity faded. The example Zanker offers is the distribution of bronze ship-prow replicas on Roman victory monuments that were copied in marble in other cities and elaborated with localized decoration. In turn, the élite in provincial urban centers commissioned copies of Rome's statuary and architectural details that would lessen the stigma of their not being at the core. This practice accelerated under Tiberius, who had everything to gain by perpetuating Augustus' fame with a populace that credited Augustus with having renewed the empire's glory and ushered in a new era of social and economic stability.

My suspicion is not unreasonable. Like any State of the Union address summarizing a leader's accomplishments during his tenure, the *Res Gestae* is neither as comprehensive nor as accurate an account of Augustus' reign as ancient historians recorded. I am referring to the historians Suetonius at mid-first-century AD, the late first-century AD Plutarch and Tacitus, and the third-century Cassius Dio, each having more information to go on than we have today. Dio was twice consul in Rome and governor of Africa and Dalmatia. His books 36-54, covering the years 68-10 BC, survive complete as a valuable resource for Roman history over the years of Julius Caesar and Augustus, even though his writing is subjective and colored by his having been trained in rhetoric. According to these historians, the *Res Gestae* is not so much dishonest as politically what one would expect—manipulated to put spin on Augustus' reign: negativities are absent, distorted, or played down, while positives are enhanced. Modern historians have long recognized the propagandistic purpose of the *Res Gestae* and its publication throughout the empire. Augustus wanted to be remembered as a great general and astute statesman, a generous benefactor of the people (responsible for transforming Rome from a city of bricks into one of marble, Suetonius tells us), and the recipient of senatorial honors. Tacitus, less impressed with the Julio-Claudian string of dictators, summarized what may have been the subsoil beneath the lofty canopy of Augustus' reign:

> He seduced the army with bonuses. His cheap food policy was successful bait for civilian applause. He attracted everybody's good will by the pleasurable gift of peace. Then he steadily pushed ahead and took over the functions of the Senate, the officials, and even the law. Opposition did not exist. War and judicial murder had disposed of all men of spirit. Upper-class survivors found that slavish obedience was the way to survive and succeed politically and financially. They had profited from the revolution, and enjoyed the security of the new arrangement better than the dangerous uncertainties of the old regime.[21]

Some scholars of the text say that Augustus wrote his *Res Gestae* at various times during his career, while others say at mid-career; still others opt for 2 BC with periodical updates. Augustus says he wrote the entire text in his seventy-sixth year, which would have been 13 AD. The text is short enough to have been dictated to a scribe in a single day with time left over for editing. In total, it adds up to about 2,250 words, the length of an academic paper read at a scholarly convention or a book review in the *New York Times* or *Times Literary Supplement*. I find it hard to believe that Augustus would chronicle his long and eventful career in such abbreviated fashion, but I have no trouble believing that his text was cut down and edited for public consumption. Can one count on the sequences in the text that have been found so useful? I'm referring to the fact that Augustus' mention of the Ara Pacis, as voted by the Senate in 13 BC, honoring his successful return from the northern provinces, appears right after his mentioning another altar, the *ara Fortuna Reducis* (Fortuna Redux), that was set up a few years earlier to celebrate his successful return from Syria, a southern province. It may be that these paragraphs were in that sequence when written by Augustus, but can we be absolutely sure of that?

The use to which I will put the foregoing will become evident later. Let us return to the story of how the *ara Pacis Augustae,* mentioned in the *Res Gestae,* was discovered, unearthed, and reassembled.

In the mid-nineteenth century, Napoleon III, who aspired to the status of Augustus and ardently supported Roman archeology, financed several excavations, especially in the Silesia area where Caesar had conquered Gaul. Like Mussolini, Louis-Napoleon dreamed of restoring national boundaries to where they'd been when France separated from the Roman Empire. His effort to regain the easterly border at the Danube and the Rhine led to the Franco-Prussian War of 1870-71, a disaster. Like Mussolini's ambitions, Louis-Napoleon's were crushed. His support of archeology was, nonetheless, a determinate factor in the Ara Pacis' discovery. Under his auspices, two French scholars, Georges Perrot and Edmond Guillaume, transcribed and translated the Monumentum Ancyranum text that located the Ara Pacis in the Campus Martius.[22]

Most likely aware that ancient foundation stone was not salvaged for re-use as building material, archeologists hoped to locate the foundation and additional parts of the structure buried among ruins in the Martian Field. When in 1859, debris of the Palazzo Fiano was sorted out to reveal its own footprint, some finely cut and polished marble pieces were found among rough-cut foundation stones. But not until twenty years later would anyone—in this case archaeologist Friedrich von Duhn—realize they were fragments of the marble walls that enclosed the *Ara Pacis Augustae,* and that previously found figurative and decorative slabs might be from the same structure.[23]

Another twenty years passed. By 1899, most of the uncovered

fragments had been deposited in the Museo Nazionale Romano within the Baths of Diocletian. Off and on, attempts to fit them together had been made. The curators could fashion a rough idea of what the structure might have looked like but could not establish a uniform scale to associate the pieces. They had no dimensions for the altar or its enclosure walls that only a foundation's footprint could provide. The Swedish archeologist Eugèn Petersen made the first sweeping attempt at restoration without a footprint guiding him. His plans were published in 1902, but his ordering of pieces did not result in a satisfactory structure to which all of the fragments could be fitted.[24]

The Tellus pane puzzled him most [7]. It differed significantly from other panels in its remarkable symmetry: the seated woman centered, flanked on one side by a nymph astride a seahorse of sorts, and on the other by a nymph riding a swan. This display of symmetry was so unexpected in Roman art that, on attempting reconstruction before the foundation plan was known, Petersen tried to locate the Tellus panel in the center of the east wall, figuring that its symmetry would have required an equally centered location.

[16] Plan of the altar within its shrine.

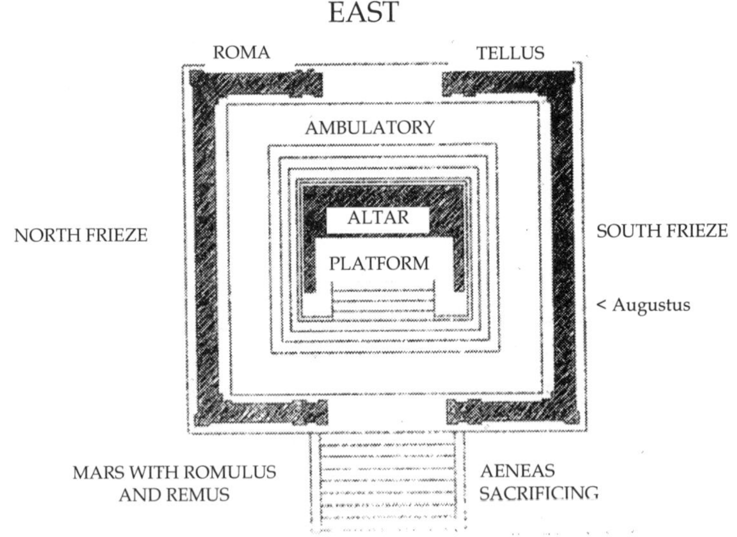

Although unsatisfactory, Petersen's reconstruction inspired him and others to dig around the old site of the Palazzo Fiano. He and his associate, Antonio Pasqui, found the foundation in 1903. Typically, it was fashioned of rough-cut tufa, a soft, dusty, plentiful stone formed when volcanic ash is wetted and put under great pressure by geological forces, the swamp stone hardening when dried. Only its dimensions were needed for the altar's reconstruction, so it still lies under the ruins of the Palazzo Fiano. It measured 11.625m by 10.655m (approximately 38 by 34.5 feet). Other measurements could then be calculated with reasonable accuracy and the floor plan plotted. The foundation revealed two entrances through the enclosure's walls, both dead center and very wide, so Petersen was forced to admit that, although symmetrical, the Tellus panel had been located asymmetrically. To account for this anomaly, he assumed that on some other monument there must have existed a similar relief, centered and flanked symmetrically by other panels. This hypothetical center panel on a hypothetical symmetrical edifice would have been the model for the Tellus panel. But no such model has been found, and no one today has reason to expect that one ever existed.

In the mid-1930s, Mussolini took an interest in the Ara Pacis. In 1937-38, he financed an extensive effort to dig again in search of the altar complex's foundation plan. The foundation was found. In 1937, plans got underway to create an exhibition hall with the Ara Pacis panels and major fragments displayed in an underground gallery within the newly constructed loggia on the southern edge of the Piazzale Augustae Imperatore. Mussolini's great interest in the monument caused him to overrule that plan. He ordered the altar's reconstruction at its present location between the Tiber and the Via di Ripetta [17].

[17]. The present location of the enshrined Ara Pacis.

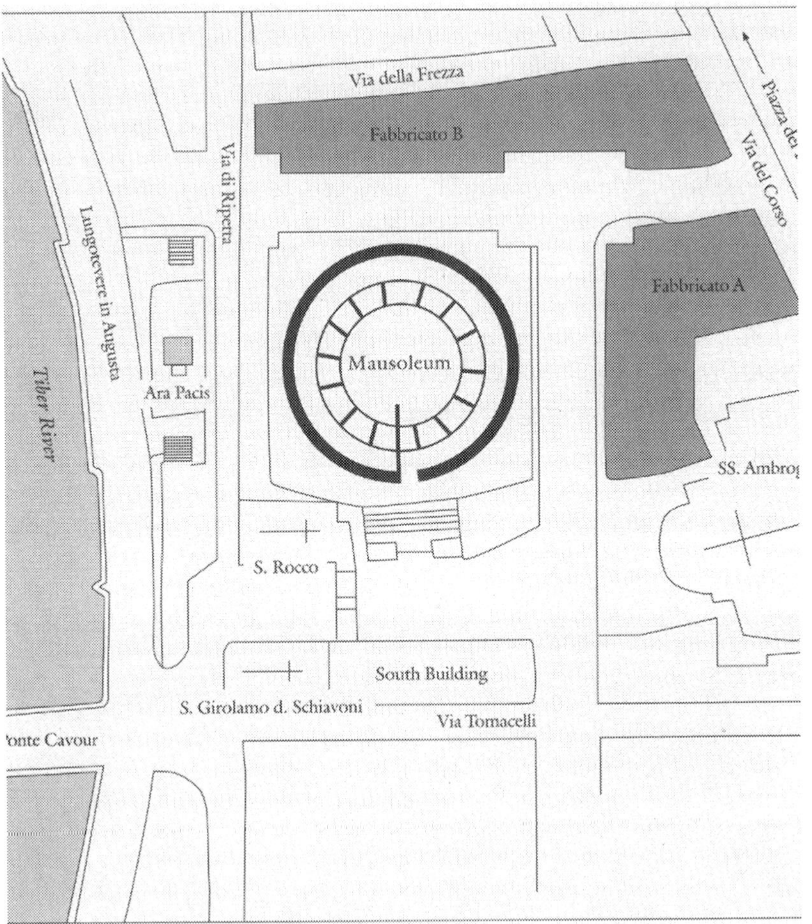

4

THE ALTAR DESCRIBED

In its original location in the Campus Martius—on the Via Lata that was renamed later the Via Flaminia and is called today the Via del Corso—the altar faced east, as the ancient architect and historian, Vitruvius, tells us is the rule for sacred edifices.[25]

Often it's said that the Senate's decision to locate the altar on the Via Flaminia was because it was the road of Augustus' 13 BC return from the northern provinces. I doubt if that was more than a circumstantial reason. The Flaminia was the major road from northern Italy heading south to Rome, so there was nothing special about Augustus' having returned on it. Later I will offer a more rational reason why it was located there, rather than in the city, or at the senatorial compound that was one of the locations given consideration by the Senate. Here I will mention that, before the Romans modernized it, the Via Flaminia was an old Etruscan road connecting Rome with the Adriatic. In 217 BC, under the consulship of Gaius Flaminius, it was rebuilt as a military road from Rome to the river Nar, where stood the Etruscan fortress Narnia. Augustus gave this worn down road first priority when he called upon the wealthy to finance repaving of aged consular roads. He offered to pay the costs out of his own pocket, a gesture most likely meant to prime others to match his funding. As incrementally financed, the Flaminia was resurfaced section by section. When the section most distant from Rome was complete, an arch in Augustus' honor was erected at Rimini.

On entering the enclosure up a run of steps and through the west entrance, which would be the altar's backside, one is confronted

[18] The Ara Pacis viewed through the west entranc into the shrine.

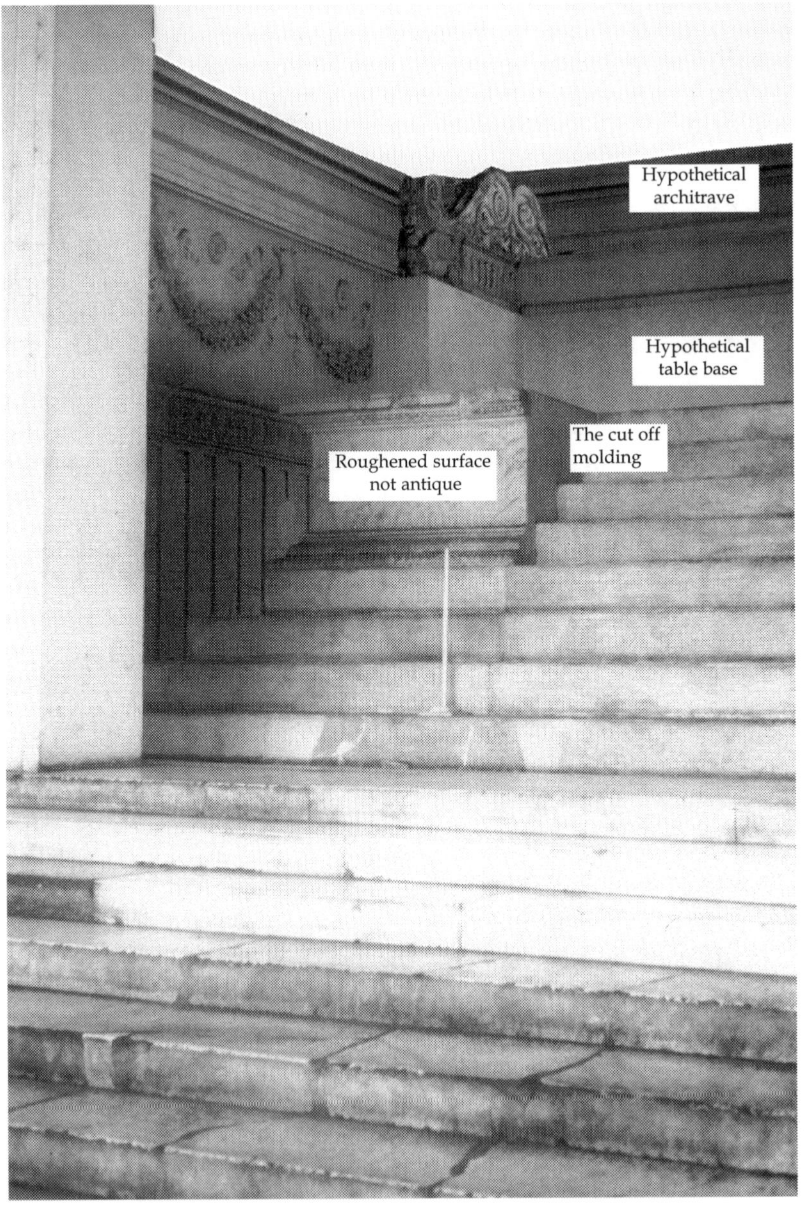

by steps mounting to the standing platform [18]. On entering from the east, one bluntly encounters the altar's front surface on the stepped base that acts as a stereobate with steps on all four sides, a convention found in Greek temple architecture when steps move up to a colonnade that surrounds the cella, but as well when the stepped base acts as a transition from the horizontal ground to the vertical wall [19].

As reconstructed, the altar's base is almost square—a bit wider on the east and west sides than deep, having the same proportions of width to depth as the enclosure walls because the ambulatory between the altar and the inner surface of the walls is uniformly one meter wide. The function of the steps all around the base is not for mounting, except at the west side to access the *prothesis*, which I am calling the platform on which priests stood when performing their rituals. Having steps at the back and sides that move up to a blank wall, topped by an altar table that cannot be accessed from the back and ends, even from the base's top step, may seems strange, but conventions often overrule function and common sense. Traditionally, in Greek and Roman architecture, the stepped portion of a base that supports a building, temple, or monument belongs to the ground level, to the street, a square, or a forum. On sloping ground, a stepped base carries the pedestrian paving upward, while also serving to isolate a private or sacred interior place from public space. When deployed for religious or sacred buildings, the stepped base along one or more sides, or all around, is secular, while that portion of the structure above the base, as is the case with this altar, is sacred, reserved for priests, like the altar of any church.

The foundation pad was a mix of tufa and travertine clad in marble on the south, north, and west sides (the east side at the Via Flaminia was at ground level; from there the grade sloped downward to the west side). The foot of the altar's enclosure walls is furnished with a sort of Attic-Ionic base molding, ornamented with interlacing and a Lesbian cyma. Inside the enclosure, atop the stepped base is the podium, its top surface the platform. The podium in this case is U-shaped to accommodate the inset steps, while its shape gives direction to the altar and allows ministrants to stand facing east. Only a few fragments of the podium were available to the restorers—just enough to suggest that carvings may have been on the outer surfaces—but no original fragments were incorporated in the reconstruction, their identity uncertain. The rusticat-

[19] Ara Pacis. Backside of the altar.

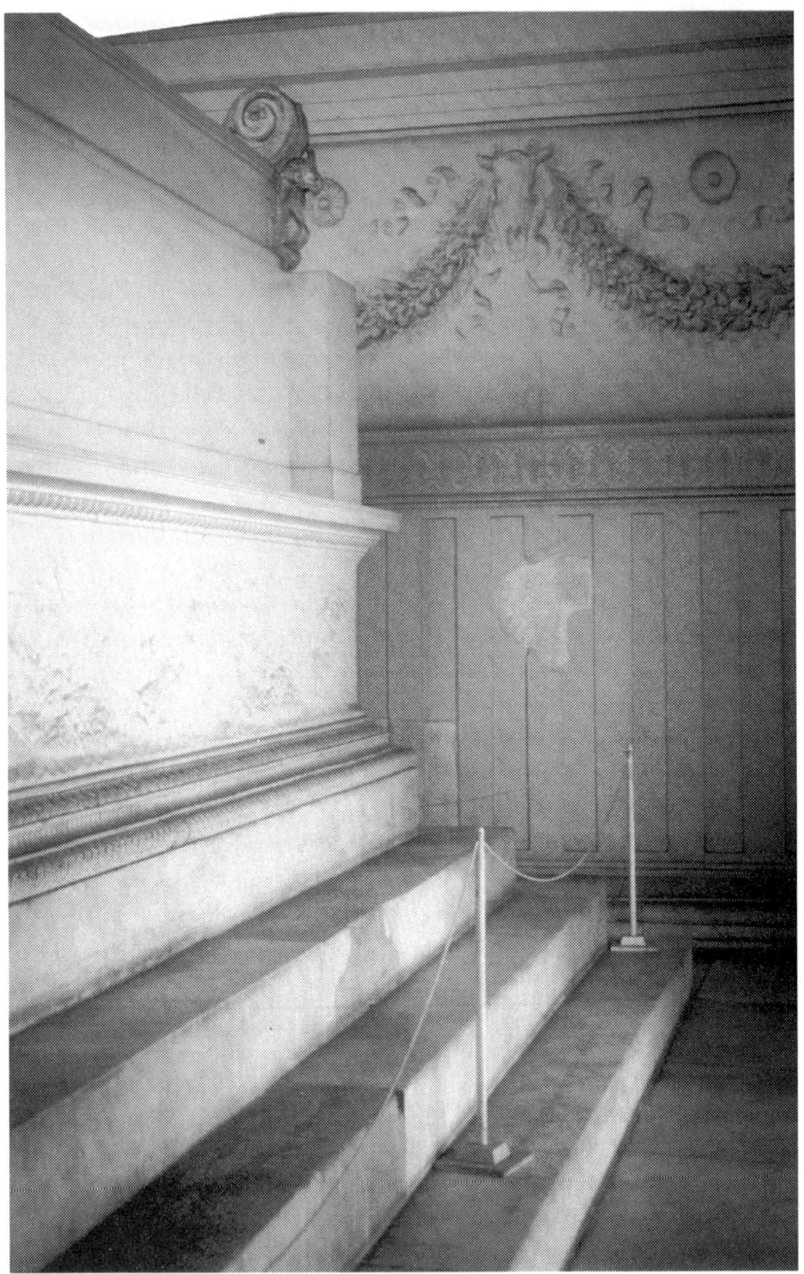

ed surfaces are meant to suggest that reliefs would have been located there. Enough pieces of moldings along the top and bottom edges of the podium were found to establish that they were fashioned as a combination of cable molding and Lesbian cyma on the lower part, with astragal (convex molding with long and short beads) and cymatium (egg and dart molding) on the upper. In both runs one sees interlacing and narrow tongues. These details combine as conventional ornament not confined to altars.

At the backside and both ends of the altar table is a horizontal marble parapet of sorts—barriers—elaborated by a collated set of figurative reliefs that are commonly referred to as the small frieze, or the small procession, in contrast to the large procession featured on the enclosure's south and north exterior walls (because the altar reliefs are independent of the reliefs on the enclosure, it doesn't make sense to say that one is small, the other large). Of the six horizontal zones, one runs along the east face of the barriers, one is on the west face, one runs on each of the north and south sides and on each of the returns. Above these zones, at each end of the table, is an elaborately carved, butted-scroll design of S-shaped volutes ornamented with leaves and resting on lion-griffons with distinctive crescent heads, ibex horns, and open maws.

The combined imagery of the altar friezes delineates an orderly list of personages by type and category suggesting a procession on the occasion of a sacrificial ritual. On the inner face of the north return, the six Vestal Virgins appear to be heading to a ceremony, each Vestal carrying one or another implement or vessel associated with sacrifice [23, 24]. They are flanked by lictors holding staffs (lictors were young men who preceded an important personage to clear the way; each Vestal was privileged to have one lictor at her service). On the outer zone of this return (its north face), a narrow frieze depicts a ram and two bullocks being led to sacrificial slaughter, pushed and pulled by attendants [22, 25]. On the east zone, at its extreme right, a fragment of a figure confirms that a carved frieze was on that zone, too. On the west return only one figure survived, and only partially, so one cannot say what was represented there, nor can one say what appeared on the inner face of this return, or on the west face of the altar table.

In addition to such standard architectural elements as ornamental pilasters and wainscoting with lotus-band trim, the inner surface of the enshrining walls are furnished with deeply carved bovine skulls, emblems in the shape of libation bowls (*paterae,* often used on walls in the sustained tradition of decorative plates) and festoons of woven fruit from vines and trees—features commonly found as well on funerary monuments [20].[26]

Friezes of personages that appear to be moving along in a procession appear on the outer face of the north and south walls of the enclosure. These remarkable reliefs surmount elaborately carved vegetal panels that occur as well on the east and west sides, ornamented redundantly with vining, flowering plants, and a variety of birds, animals, and insects.[27] The frieze on the south wall—only about two-thirds of which survived—depicts Augustus, his head half covered by his toga, suggest-

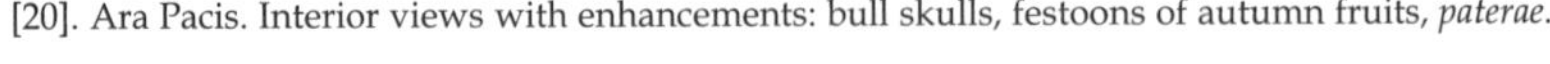

[20]. Ara Pacis. Interior views with enhancements: bull skulls, festoons of autumn fruits, *paterae.*

[21] Ara Pacis. North frieze of the shrine.

[22] Side barrier with frieze of preparation for a scarifice.

[23] Vestals arriving for the state sacrifice, with lictors. On inner face of the side barrier, with the procession of sacrificial animals on the exterior side.

[24] Detail of Vestals.

[25] Details of Fig. 23.

[26] The exterior south side of the Ara Pacis. Left half this page, right half facing page.

ing that he is acting as a priest [26, 28]. His features are seriously damaged, so one cannot be sure of what he is doing. He appears to be performing some aspect of a sacrifice, such as pouring a libation. At the left of his position are lictors that precede and clear the way for a privileged personage. Augustus having arrived, they wait for his next move. Grouped there as well are members of the chief priesthood, identified by their peaked hats; a ways down the right side of this frieze one sees

Marcus Agrippa, the admiral whose fleet decimated Antony and Cleopatra's in the Battle of Actium. He is depicted as the husband of Augustus' daughter Julia and with one of their two sons, Lucius Caesar. In the same group are Augustus' niece, Antonia, with her husband Drusus and their two-year-old son, Germanicus. Antonia and Drusus appear to be talking to each other. Behind them Augustus' sister, Octavia, appears with her hand to her mouth, the gesture taken by some scholars as an admonition for those around her to be silent. Other mem-

[27] North exterior wall of the Ara Pacis shrine.

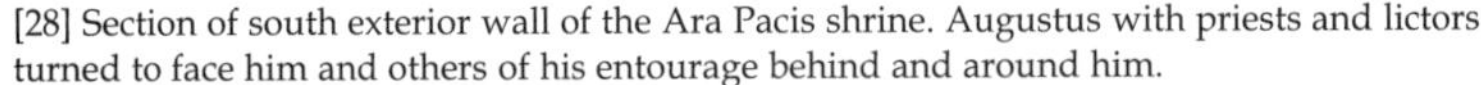

[28] Section of south exterior wall of the Ara Pacis shrine. Augustus with priests and lictors turned to face him and others of his entourage behind and around him.

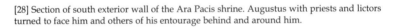

[29] Left:: Head of Agrippa. from the south frieze
[30] Right:: Head of Livia from the south frieze.

[31] Left.:Head of Augustus from the south frieze.
[32] Right: Head of Antonia Minor from the south frieze.

bers of the imperial family appear close by—Augustus' wife, Livia Drusilla, with her son Tiberius (by a previous marriage), Surely these personages are not lined up one after the other but form a group around Augustus, as do the priests on either side of him.

On the north side of the enclosure one sees more family members including Augustus' daughter Julia, and a girl who is perhaps Julia's daughter, also called Julia [27]. Certain others have been identified but not every figure may be specific—some not depicted in portraiture but with generalized features to signify an unspecified number of non-specific people.[28] As was customary for attendance at such official festivities, most of the attendees are laurel-wreathed and some carry laurel branches.

On the enclosure wall at the east entrance, which would be the front of the altar facing the Via Flaminia, two figurative panels flank the portal. The personification of Tellus as the Roman Mother Earth is on the left; on the right is Roma, a personification of the spirit of Rome, helmeted in military garb and seated on a heap of armor taken from conquered enemies [33, 35]. While the Tellus panel had been repaired and

[33] Fragments of what remains as the Roma panel on the east facade of the Ara Pacis shrine.

[34] The Tellus panel from the east facade of the Ara Pacis shrine.

[35] Hypothetical drawing as a reconstruction of Rima on the east facade of the Ara Pacis shrine.

[36] Mars and the Lupercal panel on the west facade of the Ara Pacis shrine.

[37] Aeneas Sacrificing panel on the west facade of the Ara Pacis shrine.

retooled in the sixteenth century and now appears intact, the Roma panel didn't offer the restorers much to go on, just one female thigh and fragments of military armor.

Flanking the west entrance—the backside of the altar—are two relief panels, the one on the left restored by hypothetical drawings leading to consensus among scholars that it depicted Mars standing there, looking at the infants Romulus and Remus suckling the wolf-nurse. Faustus the shepherd, who found and raised the abandoned twins, may be there, too. The context is the Lupercal, the cave on the Palatine hill where the twins were nurtured [36]. The panel on the right depicts Aeneas preparing to sacrifice a sow to the household revenants—the Penates as statuettes that he managed to bring with him when fleeing burning Troy [38], or more likely, if a white sow, to Juno Maxima, as Virgil tells us in the *Aeneid*. Aeneas pours a libation onto the altar while two boys (*camilli*, or altar boys) assist, one holding a food offering (perhaps) while the other controls the sow [37]. Aeneas' outer clothing—a toga without a tunic—marks him as Roman, no longer a Trojan, and like Augustus on the south frieze, he is *velatus*: his toga is partially drawn over his head (a departure from the Greek custom of bareheaded priests performing sacrifice). His son Julus (Ascanius, also spelled Iulus), who may be one of the boys, is said by Virgil to be out of Venus by Aeneas' father Anchises. Julus' birth established the *gens Julia*, the Julian line of descent that allowed Julius Caesar and his adopted son, Octavian, known later as Augustus, to claim a pedigree tracing back through Julus to the gods. More on that later.

[38] Aeneas fleeing Troy, with his father Anchises on his shoulder and his son Ascanius in hand. Altar of Gens Augusta, Carthage, ca. AD 50--70

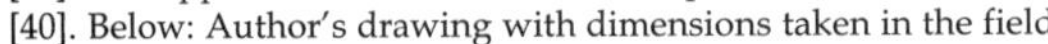

[39]. Guiseppe Moretti. The Ara Paris complex. Reconstruction drawing.
[40]. Below: Author's drawing with dimensions taken in the field.

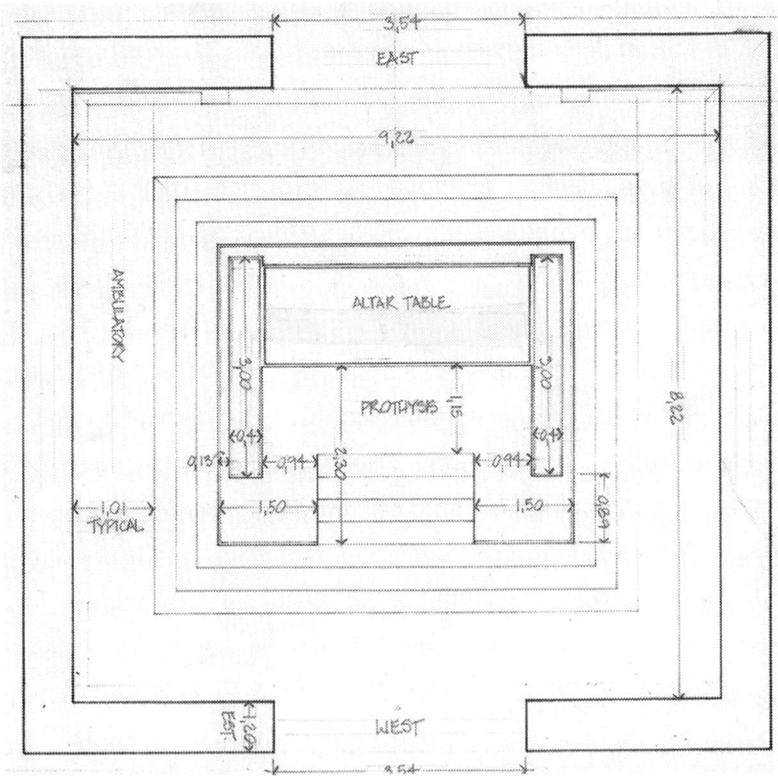

5

THE MYSTERIOUS DIMENSIONS

The area contained by the reconstruction's enclosure walls is usually referred to as the altar's precinct, or *templum* (sacred space), having been defined as such by priests sanctifying the ground when dedicating it to a deity. A *templum* is not itself a building but the sacred place of a temple or shrine that may extend beyond the perimeter of an enclosure (An altar out in front of a temple is still within the temple's precinct). And here I remind the reader that the Ara Pacis is not the shrine but the altar that's within it.

It is assumed that the Ara Pacis, as it stands today within its shrine, was decreed by the Roman Senate, and its precinct constituted as sacred space on July 4, 13 BC, the occasion of Augustus' return from the northern provinces. However that may be, I will not deploy the designation of the Ara Pacis enclosure as its 13 or 9 BC precinct, for I do not accept that the outer dimensions of the perimeter walls were determined before the altar was constructed. And I do not accept that the Senate decreed anything more than that an altar be built, and certainly not on July 4th that year. Let me explain why.

If the ground area occupied by the Ara Pacis' dimensions was the area defined as the *templum*, it would mean that the floor plan of the altar complex, as we see it today, would have already been drawn before the space was consecrated. That's impossible. The procedures through which the altar would have been put before becoming a plot plan would have taken months. And if the consecrated area were, in fact, laid out as the Ara Pacis precinct, the architect would have been required to design an altar to fit the ground space, like one designs a building's footprint to fit a city lot. That seems entirely unreasonable. I'm suggesting that the enclosure's dimensions were determined not by priestly ritual, but by the dimensions of the altar's base, which would be the case had the base been in place before the enshrining walls were designed—a fundamental assumption to support my redating the monument.

In architectural practice, whether ancient Roman or modern, one designs either from inside outward or from outside inward. When delimited by pre-set boundaries, such as plot size with prescribed setbacks (front, rear, and side yards they are called), easements and other restrictions that may pertain, and wanting to use for built-form as much of the site as possible, one must design from the site's outer edges inward. But when given a non-delimited space, as out on a prairie, or on the Campus Martius when much open space was still there, one may design from inside outward, which is why town houses are vertical and multi-storied while single-story ranch houses sprawl.

When the architect must enclose something, and when what's to be enclosed determines the amount of interior space needed, the perimeter of a building cannot be less than what it encloses; one cannot put an elephant within the dimensions of a birdhouse, but one can put an elephant in an enclosure that's a hundred feet square, or a mile square, or a thousand miles square. It's that simple. So, if the Ara Pacis were designed as it now appears, which apparently it was as to the dimensions of the base and the enclosure, the initial and critical dimensions would have begun with the size of the altar table—its width and length. Those dimensions are flexible but cannot be arbitrary. They would be determined like those of any table—by how many persons would sit around it or at one side of it. Leonardo da Vinci's table for *The Last Supper* had to be wide enough to accommodate Jesus and his twelve disciples; the room in which they dined had to be large enough to accommodate the table, the building large enough to include the dining room, and so on to a solar system large enough to include planet Earth.

So the number of officiating priests and attendants that would stand before the table, and the amount of sacrificial material that individuals would place on it, figured in the width of the table and platform. Then the platform's dimensions determined the height of the podium simply because the number of steps leading up to the platform and down to the ambulatory floor would establish, at the lowest level, the dimensions of the base [41]. Given the resulting dimensions of the base (the altar, not of the enclosure), the number of steps leading up to the standing platform could not be more than there are, for with each additional step the area of the platform and table top would be diminished; after two or three added steps, it would not be functional. It follows that the height of the reconstructed U-shaped podium is necessarily a function of the ratio of riser heights to tread depth, the four risers and three treads establishing the height of the podium's base. The height of the platform was thus predicated on the additional run of four risers and three treads (The eight riser set violates the rule recorded by Vitruvius that risers should be an unequal number so the right foot takes both the first and the last step).

[41] Author's drawing, with step riser dimensions taken in the field.

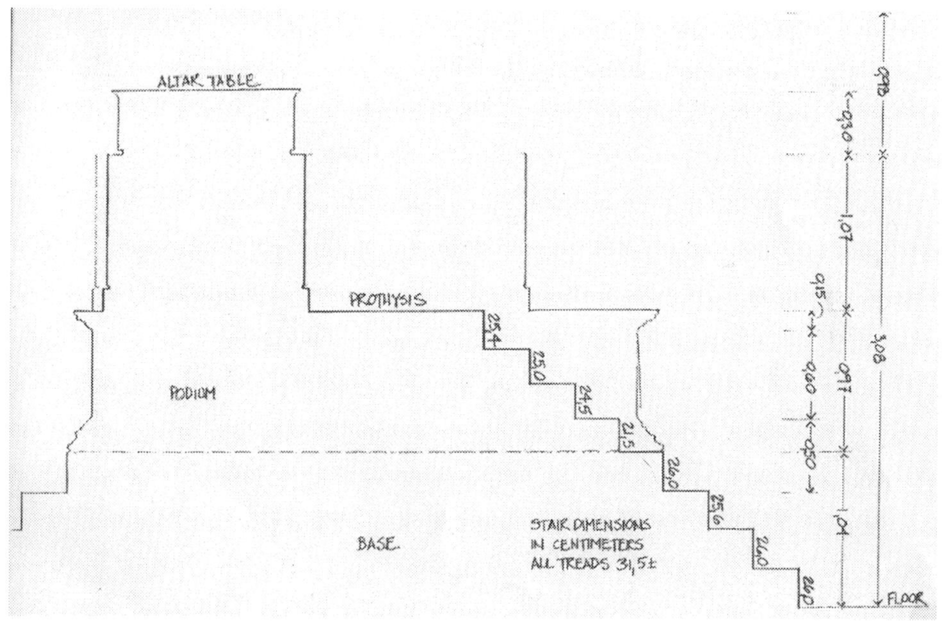

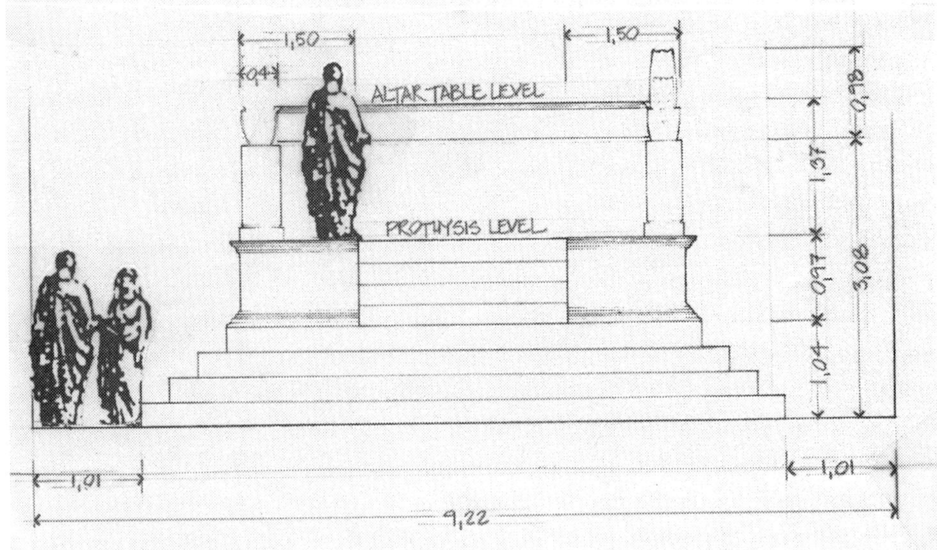

[42] Author's drawing. West elevation of the altar, with dimensions taken in the field, and human scale.

The dimensions I took when measuring the altar and its enclosure allow for joints, expansion, erosion, and foot traffic wear on floors and steps. I chose to allow 2% tolerance on either side of one meter. So any dimension between 98cm and 102cm would be equal to 1.0m, and any dimension between 49cm and 51cm would be equal to 50cm, one-half of a meter. Because the ancient Romans, and no architects or builders in Italy prior to the mid-nineteenth century, deployed the modern metric system, one should not expect to find on the reconstructed Ara Pacis any dimensions that are more than incidentally, such as once or twice, one meter or one-half meter, for that would signal use of the metric system just as the discovery of aluminum or plastic building parts found on an archeological dig would betray a non-ancient structure.

Referring to my diagrams [41-43], one dimension of the altar's base at floor level measured 6.05m (or 6.0m, the tolerance met). The height of the podium, from the top of the base to the platform level, measured 0.96m (or 1.0m, the tolerance almost met). The height from floor level to the top of the altar table is 3.08m (or 3.0m, the tolerance met). The altar table is 4.5m long by 1.6m wide—both 4.5m and 1.6m fit to the metric system. The stepped base of the altar expands these dimen-

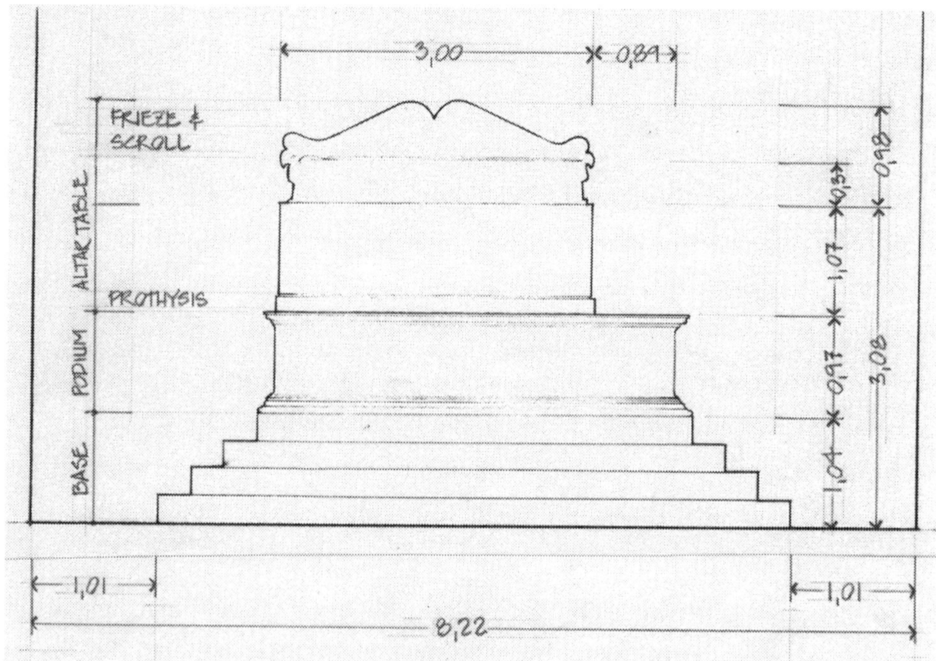

[43] Author's drawing. South elevation of the altar, with dimensions taken in the field.

sions downward to the floor where the rectangle defined by the lowest riser measures non-metrically 6.8m by the metric 6.05m. The length of the altar returns above the platform is exactly 3.0m. The height of the side barriers surmounted by scrolls is 0.98m (or 1.0m). The width of the platform at each return, from the stair cut to the inner side of the altar's podium return, is 0.94m (the tolerance not quite met). The width of each flank of the altar's base, where the steps are cut in, measured 1.47m (or 1.5m): the two total 3.0m (the tolerance met in each case). The difference between the width and the length of the precinct interior is exactly 1.0m, and the entrances are 3.54m wide (or 3.5m, the tolerance met).

To repeat and then be done with it, the length of Moretti's altar table returns is 3m, the overall height of the podium is 1m, the height from the floor to the top of the returns is 3m, the height of the scrolls from the top of the returns is 1m; the overall height of the altar from the floor is 4m. Therefore, the altar above the standing platform was fabricated entirely with use of the metric system. And the inset steps at the podium—with exact metric measurement of 1.5m at each side, and the sliced-through podium moldings—cannot be put back into antiquity unless one accepts, as I believe one should, that the podium was once a part of an earlier altar that had top and base moldings all around it.

The 1.0m vertical depth of the architrave is hypothetical, so the 5.0m height of the enclosure, from the interior floor level to the top edge of the architrave, would be hypothetical, too. Still, one might wonder why, when establishing his reconstruction of the wall-height and the architrave's dimensions (or, for that matter, the overall height of the altar), Moretti cast them metrically rather than in proportions he could have generated from proportional dimensions of the ancient parts.

It is no secret that Moretti and his team were under pressure from Mussolini to have the monument ready for the 1938 bi-millennial celebration. Three hundred or so fragments believed to have been part of the Ara Pacis were not used in the reconstruction. They remain stored in the Museo Nazionale Romano. When fitting pieces together, joints that did not match were joined with plaster infill. Some missing parts were fabricated in marble and artificially aged. The plinth and altar top were cast in artificial stone (ground marble mixed with calcined lime).

6

THE SUSPICIOUS CHRONOLOGY

We know for a fact that, at some point during the 13 BC summer, the Roman Senate voted that an altar celebrating Augustus' safe return after a successful sojourn be constructed in the Campus Martius. We know that an altar called the *ara Pacis Augustae* was dedicated on the thirtieth of January 9 BC. These dates, which span three-and-a-half years, are generated by two texts: the poet Ovid's *Fasti* (a record of feast days) and the Roman *Calendar of Feasts*. But neither text says that on either date a procession, as depicted on the north and south exterior walls of the altar, or a sacrifice, as decreed by the Senate, took place. Here I repeat the wording of the *Calendar of Feasts* for January 30th, 9 BC: *feriae quod eo die ara Pacis Augustae constituta est* (day of feast, for on this day the *ara Pacis Augustae* is decreed).[29] That is all it says.

Augustus had been away from Rome for three years. The court poet Horace summarized a national pining for his renewed presence:

> Sprung from the gods, first guardian of the race
> of Romulus, already your absence is too long:
> since you promised the sacred council
> of the Senate an early return, return.[30]

If the Senate announced its plan for the Ara Pacis on Augustus' return from the provinces in the 13 BC summer, then, for senators to have already proposed, debated, and voted on the altar, news of Augustus' success would have had to reach the Senate some time before he entered the city. Surely it did. Diplomatic couriers back then (*tabellarii*), relaying twenty-four hour days on light horses from one posting station (*mansione*) to the next, traveled on the average 80 km per day (with extreme urgency, as much as 200 km), many times faster than a royal cortege in team-drawn coaches and oxen-drawn wagons. The caravan depended on farrier, veterinarian, vehicle repair, diplomatic stopovers, and periods of rest. It was the fourth century BC Herodotus, not the United States pony express, who gave us the expression "Neither wind nor storm nor rain can halt these couriers in their appointed rounds." Miltary and naval runners made regular runs to and from home base, bringing back news and returning with orders. Mounted couriers would have raced to Rome at regular intervals, updating the Senate on Augustus' progress. To announce his climactic success and probable return date, they would have reached Rome weeks ahead of him. Under massive guard, Augustus did not travel at great speed.

Even this advance notice would not have afforded enough time for the Roman Senate to deliberate, vote, and decree an appropriate monument to honor Augustus for his successful mission, let alone commission an architectural and iconographic program for the altar, were it to be anything like the reconstructed Ara Pacis with its shrine. The Senate took time to debate alternatives, including the proposal for the altar to be built within the Senate chamber.[31] And certainly, the effort to select contractors, program the architecture, its decorations and extensive friezes—all those recognizable portraits—plus quarrying the stone, carving it, and constructing the monument, would have made utterly impossible any coincidence of Augustus' return with the celebration depicted on the reliefs as taking place during the summer of 13 BC at the Ara Pacis we see today

I am not denying that a ceremony took place then, or that almost every person represented in the reliefs was in attendance, or that a white bull was not sacrificed. I am only saying that none of this happened in or around the Ara Pacis that now stands in Rome. But the festivities may have happened around a portion of it—the four-stepped base and the podium that now has steps cut into it but didn't then. The altar would have been a simple but relatively large stone altar.

I propose that much of the Ara Pacis was in use before the altar table now above it was added, and long before the walls enshrining the altar were constructed. The podium's enhancements would have included the upper and lower edge moldings that were cut through when the provisional altar was modified later to serve as a base for a more elevated, more elaborate altar. This configuration would explain why no top or bottom moldings appear on the inset's sides in the reconstruction, even though they do in the drawing of the reconstruction by Antonio Gatti, who, as I mentioned earlier, probably couldn't believe they were not there in the first place. That the carved personages on the friezes came later is not precluded by their representation at certain ages. Long after the event, sculptors had access to their images. Archived drawings, paintings, wax effigies, and even death masks served then as photographs do today, which is why later portraits of Augustus could portray him as young and vigorous, and how Augustus could commission an array of portrait-statues for the sanctuary of Mars that included Marius, Pompey, and Drusus, who were deceased but their likenesses preserved. An important industry for sculptors was the production of portrait-heads of family members who had died: many homes contained shrines, or cabinets, in which such portraits were stored. Busts and portrait masks were typically carried in funeral parades and displayed in festivities, including triumphs [44]. In Augustus' funeral procession, persons carrying portraits of his deceased relatives followed behind a triumphal *quadriga* (four-horse wagon).[32]

[44] Roman with ancestor busts. Rome, Palazzo dei Conservatori.

If a feast occurred it would have been after an animal sacrifice had been enacted, if only because children, such as are depicted in the processional friezes, would not have been permitted to view the slaughters. Moreover, feasts featuring sacrificial slaughter were as much, if not more, for the sake of the feast than for the gods: the victim was consumed and thus made a part of the supplicants, as in the expression, "Our Lord within us," the ritual preserved in Catholic communion services and in the United States at Thanksgiving Day when turkeys are sacrificed by the millions.

The usual way to sacrifice a large animal was to pass the knife over its head and body while reciting sacred words and phrases, sprinkle its head with water, causing the beast to shake its head as a sign of vigor, and then stun it with a mallet before the blood-draining and disemboweling. The viscera and vital organs, alloted to the diety, were inspected to ensure their perfection, then burned, probably in bronze vessels, on the altar; the rest of the animal cooked and consumed by the banqueters if a feast were part of the ceremony.[33] Sacrificial animal flesh was not reduced to ashes. In fact, a steady side income for the priesthood came from selling post-sacrifice meat to butchers, with patrons having purchased the animals from farmers and donated them to the temple. The cost of large animal sacrifices must have been enormous. Aside from local needs for state sacrifices, some 2000 per year, each year thousands of sanctified bulls, bullocks, cows, sheep, and pigs were transported to military outposts throughout the empire for propitiating the gods, the meat becoming part of the outpost's food supply. That ritual is sustained today as the distribution of kosher meats.

A day of sacrifice did not always mean a day when a bull, boar, or ram was sacrificed to a male god, or a cow, sow, or ewe to a female god. Sacrifice meant giving up something of value—material goods of any type: coins, cereal grains, grapes, wine, with the donation of a perfect animal preeminent material for the *sacrificia*. On feast days it was customary for people of means to prepare meals for the homeless and the poor, sacrificing time and effort, and contributions to support a temple were also appropriate sacrifices. Offering dishes or baskets handed out during church services today are essentially the *paterae* of Greek and Roman times. All around the apse and off side aisles of Roman Catholic churches, one still sees altars with coffers to receive money, such offerings to saints and martyrs helping to support the Church, the saints having no need for money.

The walls enshrining the reconstructed Ara Pacis would not have defined the consecrated ground area—*templum* or precinct—in 13 BC. The area would have been much larger, sufficiently large to enclose within fencing a mass of attendees: the imperial family, the magistrates, vestals, senators (at least three hundred at the time), and other dignitaries with wives and children. Garden design and horticulture were important features of Roman life, so a wooden enclosure of the original precinct may have been decorated with festoons of harvest fruits draped between *bucrania* (bovine skulls) on posts, and with live flowering plants growing up trellis-like sides, surmounted by painted mythological scenes on panels or fabric. Perhaps at a later time the attendees were portrayed on panels or on canvas stretched between posts, giving us a material basis for understanding how, at some later date, the floral panels got to be where they are, with the pictorial panels above them.

Time and again it's said that the Ara Pacis enclosure in marble replicates wood construction. One scholar of the monument says it is an "imitation" of the original wood structure; another calls it a "faithful reproduction in marble" of an temporary wooden altar and its precinct walls.[34] While the interior wainscot of the walls does indeed resemble vertical wood boards in the manner of board-and-batting, and the corner posts and pilasters have wooden counterparts, all ancient building elements in stone resemble an original status in wood. Even fluted columns record their nativity as house-posts of bound reeds, or structural columns of bound saplings. Design features recording sameness in

[45]. Interior walls of the Ara Pacis shrine.

either wood, stucco, or stone are widespread in Roman architecture (even in eighteenth and nineteenth century buildings, such as the ornate lobby of Rome's Hotel Excelsior, where at this moment I'm writing). Temporary and some not-so-temporary structures fabricated in wood were as commonplace in ancient Italy as in Greece. This assumes, of course, that in 9 BC a state sacrifice with a grand feast happened, at which time the *ara Pacis* may have had an fence of some sort to define its precinct.

Few of the thousands of altars set up in ancient Roman times were enshrined. The earliest known is the Ara Pacis, so there must have been something special about it that greatly enhanced its function as an altar. The only reference I have found to such enshrining is the occasion in Judea when the Jews of the town destroyed an altar that the town's Greeks had set up in honor of the emperor Gaius (Caligula). This act prompted Gaius to decree that all places of worship, which would have included state altars, be converted into shrines of the imperial cult. At that time, altars of special significance to the state would have been enshrined. And if the Ara Pacis ever did have doors, as it and others like it are depicted on coins that will interest us later, the doors would have been installed to prevent vandalism, not to lock in Peace as is commonly believed. Were Peace locked up, on every occasion when the altar was used for sacrifice, Peace would have escaped out an open door.

Walls resembling those of the enshrined Ara Pacis would have taken no less effort to study, plan, and put through approval processes had they been of wood, and would have taken equal time and skill to execute. So it's wrong to think that wood walls would have been a time-saving remedy in anticipation of future marble. Cararra marble is soft and, when expertly blocked, easier to carve than oak (my having had considerable experience with both materials). Moreover, no elaborate woodcarving, such as the delicately carved horizontal rails and ornate pilasters would survive in summer heat without cracking, checking, and bleaching.

The 13 BC date for the Ara Pacis, as reconstructed, is out of the question for other reasons, were the iconography meant to be historically accurate. The presence of priests in a subordinate position to Augustus would imply he is acting the role of Pontifex Maximus, as his half-shrouded head also suggests. Were this the case, the event would not have occurred with official accuracy in 13 BC, for not until March the following year did he name himself chief of high priests, becoming then the *sacerdos maximus*, the top position in the religious order, just as the Catholic *pontiff* is chief of bishops. Until then the title belonged to Marcus Lepidus, who held it from 44 BC until his death in late 13 or early 12 BC, but had not functioned as such since his partially self-imposed exile in 36 BC. Augustus implies in his *Res Gestae* that he had not voided old Roman protocols. Because the *Pontifex Maximus* was appointed for life, he must have felt not justified taking over that supreme role from Lepidus, not wanting to set a precedent.[36] As a way around this chronological disjoint, scholars who date the Ara Pacis to 13 BC have had to assume that Augustus participated as Lepidus' proxy. But if the reliefs accurately portray a 13 BC or even a 9 BC ceremony, others depicted in the procession could not have been present at the event. In 13, Drusus and Agrippa were in the north on military campaigns, and by 9 BC Agrippa had died. Moreover, if there were a flamen *Dialis* (the flamen of Jupiter) on the south frieze, as some scholars of the monument have proposed, there would not have been one in 13 BC, for not until 10 BC was one appointed.

These obstacles have not deterred those who defend the 13 BC date by saying historical accuracy was not at stake, that the carvings would preserve for posterity not the actual participants but a record of those who would have attended had they been in Rome. One Romanist author, noticing that Gaius, the adopted son of Augustus, identified on the frieze, was age eleven in January 9 BC, uses the boy's appearance to justify that date as when the reliefs were carved. But they couldn't have been carved at that late date, considering it took, as most authors say, three and a half years to complete the project. Wanting to have both the depicted event and the carving of the processionals happen in 13 BC, another author comes up with a way to skirt the problem of the boy's apparent age, saying that the sculptors in 13 BC could have predicted how Gaius would look three years later and carved his height and features to look like that. Aside from the silliness of that assertion, how could anyone assume that the reliefs were carved in 13 BC but only put into the walls in 9 BC, considering the fact that the figurative panels are not applied but structural: they support the architrave and were keyed to the corners.[37] Anyway, how could anything—sacrifice, feast, procession—

have taken place at or around the Ara Pacis in 13 BC? The Ara Pacis, as reconstructed, did not exist.

Those that imagine it did, say that the corner stone would have been laid at the time of Augustus' return, but corner stones are not laid until a structure is programmed, plotted, and designed, not until contracts are let and construction is about to begin. So, with all matters considered—senatorial deliberations, choice of architect, reviews by building commissions, specifications drawn up, bids invited, contracts awarded and approved—it was more likely in 12 or 11 BC that a corner stone was laid, if one believes that the Ara Pacis and its enclosure now standing in Rome was what the Senate decreed and approved for construction at that time (it should be clear by now that I do not believe it was). On the other hand, if the procession took place three-and-a-half years later to celebrate the 9 BC *dedicatio*, as some historians claim, the Ara Pacis, as reconstructed, could not have been finished in 9 BC: the frieze depicting the event *could not have been executed until after the event took place*.

Alert to the implausibility of the carvings made after the event, the prominent Romanist historians, Paul Zanker and Karl Galinsky,

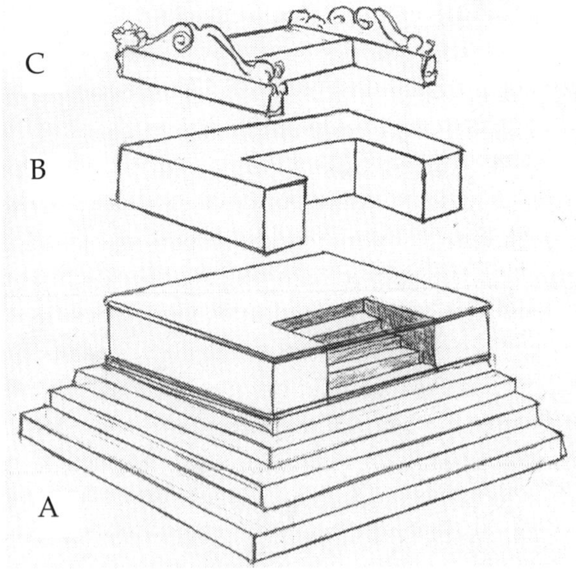

[46] Author's quick sketch made at the site.

A. The stepped base and podium would be the 13 BC altar, which was most likely furnished with barriers. The podium, which is the one on the Moretti reconstruction, had elaborate moldings on all four sides at top and bottom.

B. To serve as a base for a higher altar in 9 BC, the steps were cut through the moldings and into the podium. What was the altar table then became the prothesis, with an altar table placed atop it, which may have been similar to the table, with returns, as reconstructed by Moretti. But this part of Moretti's reconstruction is entirely hypothetical.

C. The altar's table top, which was (and still is) independent of its supporting base, was furnished with barriers. Those on the reconstruction could be from the 9 BC altar. Or they could have come from a demised altar that had special significance.

are reluctant to assign the ceremony to any date. Zanker says that the reliefs elevate the scene beyond the historical occasion into a timeless sphere.[38] Galinsky abandoned both dates, saying, "The exact ceremony in which Augustus, his family, and the Roman senators and priests are engaged on the reliefs ... cannot be limited to one specific historical occasion." His conclusion is that the ceremony pictured on the shrine's south and north walls is neither the one celebrated on the occasion of the senatorial decree or at the time of the altar's dedication. He is comfortable saying that the friezes represent a ceremony that *could have* taken place.[39]

Let's assume that there may have been two altars called the *Ara Pacis Augustae*, one from shortly *after* the consecration date and one dating *from* the dedication date, with the latter incorporating the earlier altar [46]. Let's assume that a third *Ara Pacis Augustae* , incorporating the earlier altars, was built later as a commemorative monument, a shrine, embodying the altar of the deified Augustus. The enshrining would acknowledge Augustus' elevation to godhood, as would the enhanced height of the altar. That would make sense to Vitruvius, who says that altars should be of different heights, each appropriate to its god. "For Jupiter [the high god of Rome] and all the celestials, let them be constructed as high as possible," he says. Augustus' "highness" came about during the reign of Tiberius, for which there is considerable evidence, including the Grand Camée de France in the Bibliothèque Nationale depicting Tiberius enthroned as the new Jupiter. Livia, the new Ceres, is at his side, and above them hovers the deified Augustus, like the Christian god over Jesus, the Jupiter of Michelangelo's *Last Judgment,* with the Virgin Mary, yet another Ceres, beside him.

Other than the reference to the Senate's order that animal sacrifices be made on this alter, we have no evidence of what sort of sacrifice took place other than what is given in one passage from Ovid's calendar entry for the date of the altar's dedication:

> Add incense priests to the flames burning on the altar of Peace. Let a white victim, with cloven brow, fall under the blow.And ask the gods, who lend a favoring ear to pious prayer, that the House of Augustus, the guarantor of peace, may last forever. [...tura, sacerdotes, pacalibus addite flammis, albaque per-

cussa victima fronte cadet, utque domis, quae praestat eam, cum pace perennet ad pia propensos rogate deos].[40]

Ovid does not say if the white victim were to be a bull or a sow, but "cloven brow" implies that it was a white bull, for bulls have a forehead with a forelock, while sows do not. A white sow would have been appropriate if associated with the sow found by Aeneas that augured the location for founding Lavinium—his augur was a female. A white animal can be sacrificed only to a female deity, not because it is white, but because female animals were sacrificed to female gods and male animals to male gods. Considering that Ovid was not in Rome but in exile at the time he wrote this entry, he wouldn't have known specifics, especially in advance. So his reference could be a sacrifice to Juno, except that swine of any gender were offered exclusively to divinities of the earth—*sus plena* sacrificed to Tellus, or a sow sacrificed to Ceres at the time of the *Cerialia* (April 19th, the time for harvesting) when Ceres separates from Tellus, in contrast to *bos*, or *porca praecidanea*, that is offered to both Tellus and Ceres before the harvest.[41] So, if the victim was a white sow rather than a white bull, and if the sacrifice was associated with Augustus' return, coming after April 19th, the offering would have been to Ceres. If the sacrifice was associated with January 30th, the offering would have been to Tellus. Either deity would have been appropriate as well for celebrating Livia's birthday.

January 30th was generally associated with peace, so without collaborating evidence that date cannot be associated with any sacrificial act. January was the last month of the old calendar, with January 30th the last day. Sacrificial events would have taken place at many locations through the land. January preceded the month of Janus the peacekeeper, whose month came before the first month of the new Roman New Year, which was March (*mars*). February (*februa*), Janis' month, was the month of cleansing in anticipation of the New Year, with cleansing having several implications, one of which was the cleaning of silos and granaries in anticipation of new harvest. Another was cleansing one's soul in advance of installing New Year resolutions.

Related to his role as god of gates and doors, Janus was the god of openings—understood as beginnings, such as are embedded in "opening the door on the new year," and "opening a new era" (One can understand from this role why Janus was so important to Augustus' political propaganda as his opening Rome to renewal). With January 30th came peace offerings to the dead so that mourning the dead would be put to rest and renewed life could be celebrated with joy. On that date, a state sacrifice to Janus would have been a ceremony to welcome and honor him on the opening of February, the cleansing month, just as today's Christians celebrate Christmas Eve, welcoming the birth of Jesus who offers a cleasing of the world of sin, and then celebrates New Year's Eve to welcome the New Year as birth a newborn and a rebirth. Celebration of the old year's passing might have been additional impetus for the Senate to select January 30th for dedicating an *ara Pacis Augustae* as a sign of Augustus' reign, having renewed the era of a stablized economy that, two millennia later, would be Mussolini's motivation as well.

Ovid's passage, quoted above, makes reference to *domus* (domicile) as "the House," meaning "the house of Augustus." It reflects the propaganda that Augustus created around his Palatine house, of which Livia was *mater domus* (lady of the house). Her birthday was January 30th. At every turn it seems that Livia's birthday compounds the problem of the date for the Ara Pacis' completion. The date may not have been January 30th but some time earlier, with the dedication held off to await a different event, such as her birthday. The dynastic policies of Augustus and his successors tend to make dedications of important monuments coincide with significant dates of the dynasty.[42] I would not risk swearing on a bible that Livia's birthday truly was January 30th. Persons of royal blood are prone to make up a birth date that coincides with some great event.

Tiberius dedicated an altar to *numen Augusti* on a seventeenth of January, the wedding date of Augustus and Livia. (In his will, Augustus renamed the entire month of September; it was to be called August to fix his name in eternity). As mentioned earlier, Livia linked the Julian and the Claudian families, the Julians tracing back to the conjugation of Venus and Anchises that produced Aeneas and thus provided the royal and divine blood that flowed to Caesar, then by adoption to Augustus, and again by adoption to Tiberius. Caesar's adoption of Augustus was sole justification for Augustus' place in the royal lineage. So Livia's birthday in 9 BC would qualify as a politically significant date for dedicating the *ara Pacis Augustae*, that date overriding the altar's completion date.

[47]. The thirteen altars at Lavinium. 6th to late 3rd century bc. The altars were not all in use at the same time. Photo courtesy Ross Holloway.

[48] Altar from a sanctuary of the *gens Augusta* erected by the freedman P. Perellius Hedulus, Carthage. A large altar with Aeneas fleeing Troy on one side and on one end Roma seated on a pile of weapons, like Roma on the Ara Pacis.

7

THE AUTHOR'S CASE

At one point in ancient Roman history, the Ara Pacis looked pretty much like it does now. But it is not the altar complex (altar + shrine) mentioned in the Roman *Calendar of Feasts*. Part of it—the stepped base surmounted by a low podium—might have served for a sacrifice in 13 BC (the time needed to fabricate it no greater than for the *ara Fortuna Augustae* , about which I will presently speak). I feel more confident saying that the altar as we now see it, but not the shrine and perhaps without the current table barriers, served for the *dedicatio* and was still in place until some point during the reign of Tiberius when the third stage, the enshrined *ara Pacis,* was constructed as one of several monuments erected in Augustus' honor. That monument, taking on the nature of a shrine for a deity (all gods needing a shrine), incorporated the 9 BC altar that had incorporated the 13 BC altar.

The simple form of Roman altar with inset and returns, giving directional orientation, has a long history. The so-called Thirteen Altars, excavated at Lavinium on the sandy coast of Latium south of the Tiber's mouth (the land of Virgil's *Aeneas*), record the shape [46]. Upon entering office, the chief Roman magistrates came to those altars to sacrifice to the Penates and to Vesta. Typically Latian, central Italian, the structure constituted a base pad upon which sat a podium-type U-shaped table. The earliest is thought to date to the sixth century BC with additional ones built over the next two centuries, and some re-built later.[44] The U-shaped altar was not common; it was typical for sacrificial rituals when a priest stands within the U, facing east.

Most of Rome's thousands of altars were table-like structures, usually placed at waysides where travelers made offerings to assure a safe journey and safe return. That function is implicit in the name of the other altar mentioned among the sacerdotal and religious honors listed in Augustus' *Res Gestae*—the *ara Fortunae Reducis* (Fortuna Redux—fortunate return). This altar was voted by the Senate on the twelfth of October, 19 BC, and, as Torelli informs us, dedicated a little less that two months later, on the fifteenth of December, to celebrate Augustus' return from Syria. It is mentioned just before the *Res Gestae* lines that speak of the *ara Pacis.* Its shape is known only from its appearance on a *denarius* (a small silver coin). From what that coin tells us, nothing about this altar is exceptional [49]. In keeping with Augustus' insistence on modesty and simplicity as to honors accorded him (that information given us by Suetonius and Dio), it was just an ornamented plinth on a slab footing, with barriers at either end of the table top. Its modest size classifies it with wayside altars as functional and not necessarily memorial, although in addition to the name of a deity an altar would at times also bear the name of a donor or a loved one memorialized. Wayside altars were placed at regular intervals so travelers could make entreaties for gods to grant them safe travel and safe return.[45] Farmers coming to town may sacrifice a token portion of their produce as an entreaty for getting a good price at the market. A herdsman driving livestock to market may sacrifice a lamb or piglet for the same purpose.

[49] Denarius of Q. Rustius. Believed to be an image of the *ara Fortuna Reducis* (Fortuna Redux).
(RIC Augustus 322, struck in the mint of Rome, 19 BC).

One cannot tell from our great distance, or from historical accounts in hand, whether Augustus' return from Gaul and Spain in 13 BC merited such an honor as the enshrined Ara Pacis we see today, for it makes no reference to travel. Efforts to make it into a substitute for a triumphal return by pointing to Roma in armor, seated or armor and weapons as trophies, doesn't make sense in the overall context of the reliefs on either the altar or its shrine. The elaborate argument for the altar having triumphal significance, as made by Torelli, comes with unanswered questions. To associate is with the *reditis* (the ceremony of a return), Torelli proposed that the location of the Fortuna Redux also intimates a triumphal return, considering its location "*ante aedes Honoris et Virtutis ad portam Capenam*," as Augustus says of it in his *Res Gestae*. At that location the people customarily greeted the "*profectio* to *provinciae*" and the "*reditus* from *provinciae* of proconsuls," and it was close to the temples of Honos and Virtus, which are, as Torelli says, were strongly connected with triumphs.[46]

Perhaps all of that is so, but perhaps also circumstantial. My explanation for Augustus' mention of the *ara Pacis* right after the *ara Fortuna* is simply that they recall each other, both having had the same function as altars acknowledging Augustus' safe return, and both to be classified as wayside altars, rather than triumphal monuments. That sort of *ara Pacis*, however, based on my assumptions, would have been just the 13 BC aspect of it, for the reliefs on the shrine that Totelli deploys to weave his intricate theory did not exist in 9 BC, and I feel no risk in saying that by then everyone may have forgotten about the single incident of Augustus' return from the western and northern provinces. He often traveled away from the capital. The Calendar of Feasts mentions an *ara pacis*, not an *ara reditis*. Augustus' trip was not a military campaign, and no greater state of peace prevailed on his return than when he left. Settling economic and governing disputes was not a grand accomplishment for the sake of peace, such that it would merit a triumph. It had been seventeen years since the Rome was engaged in a major war, the defeat of Antony and Cleopatra was the last battle of any homeland significance. And at the time when Augustus left for the provinces, Tiberius and Nero Drusus were conducting military campaigns north of the Alps in an effort to annex the territories of Raetians and Noricums, and extend Roman rule to the Danube. Drusus was campaigning, as well, even beyond the Rhine. Those campaigns were not wars. The battles had no effect on Rome. I'm sure that hardly anyone back home, other than senators, even knew they were going on in days before newscasting other than town criers and town-center chalk boards. Augustus' diplomatic trip to the northern provinces was a normal function of his office as governor of Spain and Gaul. Why would his return have been so significantly greater in meaning than his return from Syria a few years before that merited the modest Fortuna Redux? Suetonius tells us that Agustus traveled often to the provinces. "As far as I know," he says, "Augustus inspected every province of the Empire."[47]

The Augustan peace was not the absence of war but a successful reorganization of every branch of government from which a large majority of the Empire's inhabitants would benefit from uniform currency and flourishing international commerce. In spite of several setbacks, for the most part his measures to revive morality and family life, the Augustan peace was less measured as conquests over enemies as over outdated economics based on military exploits rather than sound governing principles.

My uncomplicated explanation for the location of the Fortuna Redux also draws upon Augustus' wholesale restoration of old sanctuaries that had been occupied at earlier times by enemies and were in need of having their sacred limits reconfirmed. In addition to the many new temples and restorations of old ones, he came down to the individual human scale by promoted reinstallations of such altars at entrance portals and crossroads. In that context, the Fortuna Redux takes on significance, as will the Ara Pacis in its initial state as a wayside altar. Every January 1st, Suetonius tells us, all classes of citizens offered Augustus their New Year's gift—always in cash. Augustus used this annual fund to purchase statues of gods (*pretiosissima deorum simulacra*) that he ordered mounted on old altars and set up at thoroughfare crossings, the altars rededicated. One of them bears the inscription:

> The Emperor Augustus, son of Caesar, has dedicated this altar to Vulcan in the year of the city 745 [9 BC] from money received as a New Year's gift while absent from Rome.[48]

And besides, what explains the Ara Pacis' "high altar" status in contrast to the waist-high Fortuna Redux? High altar status would have been entirely inconsistent with the political message that Augustus was delivering to the people at that time. Any association of the Ara Pacis we see today with Augustus' return from the northern provinces simply will not do.

One need also take into account that, on the minds of some, if not many, back in Rome was the thought that Augustus' three-year absence was motivated, at least in part, by his wish to stay away until unrest over his legislation of 18 BC settled down. His newly ennacted set of laws, the *Lex Iulia de maritandus ordinibus*, was designed to encourage reproductive matrimony and increase the population of the more valued classes, so out-populated were they by plebeians, immigrants, and freed slaves. This legislation laid down penalties for celibacy and childless marriages, with fines levied on young men who refused to marry and on couples that rejected parenthood. With marital conduct elevated to a crime, and guilty parties open to prosecution, including loss of property, outcries resounded throughout the populace. One scheme after another was devised to evade the law, such as older unmarried men becoming betrothed to pubescent girls, with wedding dates set years ahead. Tacitus declared that the new dogma contravened Roman tradition as an affront to the *clementia maiorum* (tolerance and moderation).

Augustus was aware that flamboyance as to wealth and power was a dangerous attitude for an emperor to assume. The memory of Julius Caesar's assassination over what many people remembered as an overestimation of personal power lingered, as well, in his mind. Surely he was aware that his ruthless treatment of enemies when he himself moved into power, including the massacre of some three hundred senators and the murder and mutilation of Cicero, had not been universally forgiven or forgotten. While Augustus' various victory monuments would find their place in the Forum, he made it a point to destroy his own cult-type imagery that, under the conditions of an uprising against him, would be melted down if in metal, or reduced to rubble and land fill if in marble. In his *Res Gestae* we find this passage:

> The statues of myself in the city, whether standing or on horseback or in a quadriga, numbering eighty in all, and all of silver, I had removed. And from this money [presumably the silver melted

> down], I dedicated gold offerings in the Temple of Apollo, in my own name and in the names of those who had honored me with having put up those statues.[49]

To sum up, I propose that the *ara Pacis Augustae* was at one time no more elaborate than the *Fortunae Reducis*. In 13 BC it would have been just a larger-than-usual wayside altar dedicated to Augustus and in use as such before the stair-cut podium in Moretti's reconstruction was fashioned, and years before the walls enshrining the altar were built. When confronted by the upper- and lower-edge moldings, so obviously cut through to fashion inset steps when the altar was modified to serve a more elevated purpose, one cannot evade my conclusion without offering a believable explanation for the saw cuts and cut off molding resulting in the lack of moldings on the returns. Such moldings appear on the *Fortunae Reducis* and every other altar, and as well on monumental sculpture bases and plinths flanking stairways. The supply of examples—whether altars, sculpture bases, or bases for flower urns or ash urns—is endless.[50]

In short, the fact that no moldings appear on the flanks of the podium's inset steps in Moretti's reconstruction, yet do appear on Gatti's, supports my assertion that the first use of the altar was when it was a plinth on a stepped base with the later altar fabricated when the inset steps were cut into the plinth and a table placed atop it. This sequence of adaptations would account for the disparity of stair-riser heights at the juncture of the stepped base and the podium, *for it occurs precisely at that point where the podium would have been removed and replaced after steps were cut into it.*

8

THE ARA PIETATIS MATTER

The Ara Pacis' table barriers—frieze zones, volutes, and scrolls—may have been taken from a different and earlier altar—an altar of special significance—that had been salvaged and stored for reuse, perhaps after the demolition of an altar in the path of new construction. The reliefs have the look of the indigenous Old Italian style with moderate Hellenizing, as one might characterize the reliefs on the Temple of Apollo built by C. Sosianus around 25 BC [49], and a mid-first century relief from the Cancelleria featuring a processions of the *vicomagistri* (freedmen who guarded the Lares, or household gods of a district), the procession associated with a sacrifice of bulls [50]. Even if found with the Ara Pacis shrine slabs and architectural parts, nothing says that the small frieze zones were remnants of the same altar as to their first use. Items of salvage and reuse abound in ancient architecture, and were often given significance for their reuse even if stylistically incompatible with their host.

Reliefs from the Claudian arch consecrated in AD 51 that spanned the Via Lata. were reused on the Diocletian Arcus Novus, and reliefs identified as from yet another altar associated with Augustus, the *ara Pietatis Augustae,* were found reused on a triumphal arch on the Via Flaminia that archeologists associate with the Arch of Diocletian dated AD 303-04. A number of reliefs, discovered in 1923 near Santa Maria in Via Lata along the old Via Flaminia, were recognized as having belonged to more than one monument, some from the late Republic, some from the early Empire, and at least one fragment from

[49] Detail of a stateacrifice depicted in reliefs on the Temple of Apollo built by C. Sosianus around 25 BC.

[50] Procession of the *vicomagistri*. Marble relief from the Cancelleria, Rome. Mid-first AD. Musei Vaticani, Rome.

the reign of Claudius. A group of reliefs found in the facade of the Villa Medici, known as the "Medici-Della Valle reliefs" [51-54], were for some time believed to be fragments of the *ara Pacis Augustae*. Archeologists now generally agree that they came from the *ara Pietatis*. Recent discoveries added a few pieces thought to be from the same altar. A few fragments that had been salvaged and reused were found near the Church of Santa Maria in via Lata along the old Via Flaminia. They had been reworked and upgraded in style to suit the later use (as were some of the *ara Pacis Augustae* reliefs). So any attempt to date the *ara Pietatis* fragments later than the *ara Pacis* reliefs on stylistic grounds would be futile. Even among fragments assigned by archeological concensus to the *ara Pietatis,* one finds inconsistencies that are not due to retooling (recalling what I've said about differences between the Ara Pacis reliefs on the exterior walls and those on the altar proper). Were one to risk professing a linear stylistic sequence, then the *ara Pietatis* relief of Vestals banqueting would date as early as the Ara Pacis altar reliefs, perhaps earlier [53].

Torelli's scheme for the chronology of the ara Pietatis is both original as to interpretation and a summary of known archeological data. The

Marble relief fragments attributed to the *ara Pietatis.*

[51] Fragment with a camillus (left) and the *flamen divi Augusti.*

[52] Portion of a procession associated with a state sacrifice.

[53] Banqueting Vestals

[54] Sacrifice of a bull, apparently in the Forum of Augustus.Plaster cast.

Senate voted the altar in AD 22. But due to a political crisis in 26, and to Tiberius' subsequent decision to play down the imperial cult by curtailing elaborate altars and other commemorative structures—in addition to his abdication in 27 by removing himself to Capri and leaving the government in the hands of the prefect of praetorians, Lucius Sejanus—the altar was not erected until 43, during the Claudian reign.

[55]. Altar to Providentia. Reverse side of a bronze As of Divus Augustus struck under Tiberus. (RIC Tiberius 81).

Torelli proposes that the *ara Pietatis* reliefs represent a ceremony that took place on the seventeenth of January 42, the day of Livia's deification. While agreeing that the reliefs are Claudian, Brilliant says they are "unequivocally based on the style and program of the *ara Pacis Augustae.*"[51] Torelli goes a bit further, saying that the *ara Pietatis* is an "imitation of the *ara Pacis.*"[52] He says the same for two other altars, the *ara numinus Augusti* and the *ara Providentia Augustae,* known only by its appearance on a coin [55]. While admitting that we do not know how close either of these altars were to the *ara Paci*s in physical appearance, considering that no remains have been discovered for either one, Torelli feels confident that, on an ideological plane, they were substantially the same.

As for the *ara Pietatis,* one has at least some archeological imagery in the form of the Medici-Della Valle reliefs to suggest what parts of it looked like, although it is not an absolute certainty that the reliefs are from the *ara Pietatis*. As I mentioned, they were once thought to be from the Augustan period, specifically from the *ara Pacis Augustae*. That assumption, taken to be credible for a while, should deter anyone from claiming I must be wrong by having assigned the *ara Pacis'* enclosure walls to Tiberius' reign.

Art history is not so linear that style alone can determine a sequence, such that the *ara Pacis Augustae* shrine simply had to be Augustan. From the late Republican to the Empire years, dozens, if not hundreds, of sculpture studios were established in Rome and provincial cities, staffed by artisans of several nationalities and uneven skills. So no linear art history can be imposed upon Roman art as uniformly progressive. The recent brouhaha over Beasley's chronology of Greek vase painting that, as undergraduates, we art historians memorized decade by decade, indicates how excessively-ordered data can be misleading.

Workshops vary in skill and style, having internal determinants—some progressive, most formulaic; some superb in craft, others mediocre. One needn't look beyond ancient Rome to see that style can be fickle when used to confine a work of art to a period, as if one style is the norm for all others. If, in a thousand years, one would dig up rubble of Paris' Arch de Triomphe, the hands of different sculptors would stretch its date over several decades, from the mid-eighteenth-century neo-classical style of the three conventional reliefs to the one by François Rude that could be dated to the mid-nineteenth-century. Yet all four reliefs were fashioned over the same one-year period.

Brilliant sees remarkably stylistic differences in the relief carvings of the Altar of Domitius Ahenobarbus: one of them as Roman as art could be in the Republican era [56], the other looking to be advanced Hellenistic [57]. He says of this juxtaposition:

Unfortunately for those who like their stylistic distinctions

[56] Above: Census and sacrifice, a relief on the so-called Altar of Ahenobarbus, late 1st. c. BC. Paris, Musée du Louvre.

[57] Below: Relief with marine creatures from the so-called Altar of Ahenobarbus. Munich, Glyptothek.

> wrapped in neat chronological or geographical packages, both reliefs [on the Ahenobarbus] were executed at the same time, in the late second or early first century BC [in] two totally different modes. The co-existence of two such distinct languages of form raises the qualifying spectre of incoherency within the artistic conception of the monument, as if the Romans were insensitive to the difference, unless such careful separation of parts is meaningful both historically and iconographically in the Altar of Ahenobarbus and in the evolution of Roman art.[53]

As I pointed out earlier—and this is important enough to bear repeating—of 600 fragments unearthed during the Ara Pacis excavations, only 300 or so were identified as belonging to the Ara Pacis. An equal number remain in storage, some of which may belong to the Ara Pacis, others to monuments demised at more or less the same time, hence found together but most likely from different hands and different times.

Augustus was made *divus* (divine) in AD 17, three years after his death, as yet another way to reinforce Tiberius' status and ruling power. This would have been an appropriate occasion to begin construction of the enshrined *ara Pacis* we see it today, in keeping with Livia and Tiberius' drive to spread a cult of Augustus throughout the empire. As I mentioned above, according to Torelli, the *ara numinis Augusti* (altar to the *numen,* or enhanced qualities of Augustus) was dedicated on a wedding anniversary of Livia and Augustus. The *ara Providentiae,* dedicated about AD 22-23, promoted the bond between Tiberius and Augustus while reinforcing lineage through Augustus' adoption of Tiberius. After Augustus' death, Livia was adopted into the Julian *gens* and given the honorific title, Julia Augusta. She would remain a powerful matriarch, loved by the populace and with considerable influence over the state. That status apparently brought her into conflict with Tiberius. Following her death in 29, he refused to allow her deification, leaving her celestial fate to her grandsons, who deified her when they succeeded as emperor.

If my reassignment of the date for the *ara Pacis* shrine were accepted, Torelli would have an answer to his questions as to why the *ara Pacis* is deprived of all signs that define the status of the *ara Fortuna Reducis*, why there is no mention of a solemn *ire obvium* pertaining to the *ara Pacis Augustae* like the one recorded for the *ara Fortuna Reducis*, and why it is so rare to find dedications, as portraits, to living members of Augustus' house "before the first decade of the first century, if not the early Tiberian period." So, rather than saying, "With the Tiberian altars we have an imitation of the Ara Pacis," as Torelli does, one might say instead that the enshrining walls of the Ara Pacis date to the Tiberian principate.[54] An exceptionally ornate shrine on which was recorded the personage, family, and court of Augustus in the context of Rome's exalted history would have been of great propaganda value to Tiberius, as it would be two thousand years later for Mussolini.[55]

9

THE PROBLEMATIC ENTRANCES

A rectangular building that's identical at either end is like a Janus with not just two faces but also two bodies, such that the wide-eyed gate sentinal can look in both directions without turning his head and also move in opposing directions without turning his body. Because the Ara Pacis, as we see it, is roofless and with wide entrances but without doors, its perfect symmetry, as to east and west and north to south is, in fact, as non-directional as if it were a sphere. It's the enclosed altar that establishes the cardinal points favoring east while determining a differential function for each mirrored entranceway.

The U-shaped altar has a front and a back, like a horse shoe. The shrine is subordinate to the altar, so it's enough to say that the shrine fronts on Via Flaminia, like a house fronting on a street. If located on the east side, it would have presented its backside to the road. This simple explanation should satisfy those who debate over which end is the front and which is the main entrance. Through one of the shrine's wide openings, the altar's front faces east, the gods and the sunrise, as Vitruvius said all altars must[56] (It should be clear by now that I believe the altar, or part of what we see today, was in that location before the enshrining walls were built). The altar's back is approached from the west, up steps and through the other opening [58].

From my point of view, there is no main entrance, such as street houses with front and back doors. The wide entrance through the east wall allows the altar to be visible from the Via Flaminia, and also to face the gods, while the wide entrance through the west wall supports the

[58] *Above*. Moretti's reconstrcution drawing. *Below*: Author's drawings of the plan, with dimensions.

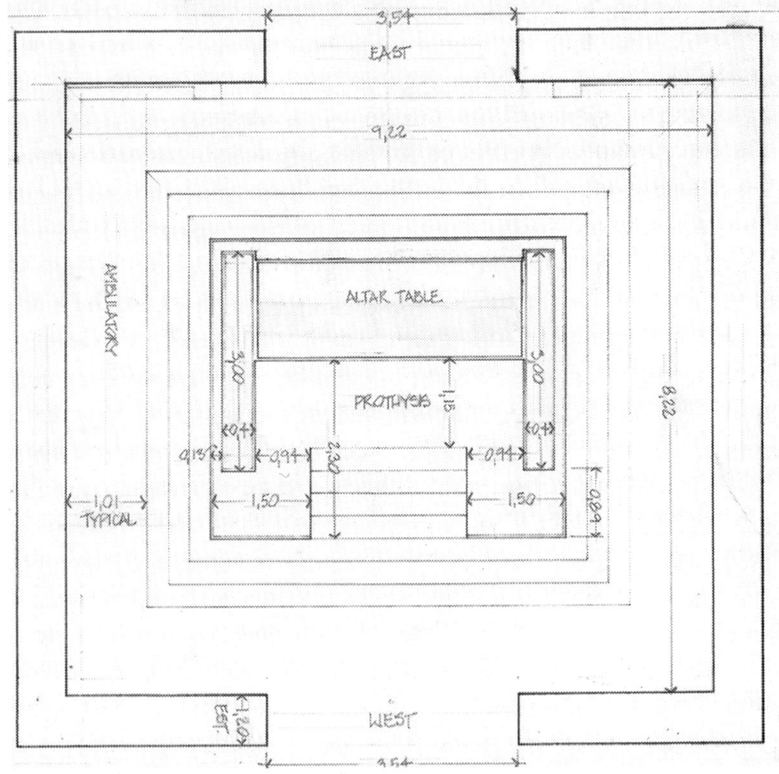

altar's use for state sacrifices. Because a major ceremony, such as prescribed by the Senate and recorded in Augustus' *Res Gestae,* would involve many participants—priests, attendants, senators, vestals, prelates and other notables, as well as chariots with horses and grooms, and a set-up for the feast—the staging area would not be on the road at the altar's east entrance, but rather behind the altar where the ground area was expansive enough to accommodate as many as one thousand people (the number of Senators at the time was at least three hundred). According to Moretti's notes and Gatti's rendering, the area at the back of the altar was leveled and paved. Whether that was so in either 13 or 9 BC may be an open question, but my answer would take into account that the paving the excavators found would be from when the shrine was built several years later.[57]

To account for the two entranceways, the Ara Pacis shrine is usually classified within the general category embracing sanctuaries. This seems odd, considering that sanctuaries would seem to have but one entrance. The Lupercal, in which the nurse-wolf cared for Romulus and Remus, was a cave, a prototypical sanctuary. An ancient myth says that Zeus was born in a cave (Hesiod locates it near Lyctus; others put it on Mt. Ida). The mid-first-century BC Sanctuary to Fortuna at Praeneste, which overlooked the plains of Latium, was one such shrine carved directly into bedrock to simulate a cave. Several caves in central Crete were sanctuaries housing deities, to whom food offerings were brought. But as a sanctuary—meaning a protective enclosure—the altar would not have needed that enhancement until Augustus was deified.

The two-entranceway notion comes from the *ara Pacis* associated with the shrine of Janus *Geminus* (Janus doubled, two-faced, double natured), but Janus' shrine was a passageway symbolizing a city gate, not a building. We have no floor plan of a shrine that some say once stood on the edge of the Roman forum, just an image of a shrine on two coins struck during the reign of Nero, whose short reign spanned the years AD 54-58. That puts us over fifty years later than the dedication of an *ara Pacis Augustae*. The coin reproduced here is the only visual record of a Janus shrine, so an exact description of it is critical to any promotion of its relationship to the *ara Pacis* [59].[58] The only other source of information as to a Janus shrine's appearance is given by the Byzantine Greek historian, Procopius, coming centuries later. He described it as a small

[59]. Bronze sestertius of Nero with the Janus shrine on the reverse. The rendering of the shrine shows both one side and one end on the same plane (RIC Nero 439). Drawing at the right, courtesy Marvin Tameanko.

bronze building housing a statue of two-faced Janus (Janus *bifrans*). It's generally assumed that the shrine to which Procopius was referring stood on the site of an ancient city gate, presumably the same structure mentioned in the *Aeneid* (Book VII) as a city gate of Romulan times. That would put it as far back in history as Procopius did. Procopius' years were roughly AD 500 to 560, while the Romulus era was so far in the remote past that Roman history had not yet begun. Still, if any late historian can be trusted, it might as well be Procopius, a major figure during the reign of Emperor Justinian and secretary to General Bellesarius, Justinian's favorite military leader and foreign diplomat. Procopius traveled with Bellesarius on his campaigns in Africa and Italy. He visited Rome, and had such a strong interest in architecture that, among his important books, he wrote one on the buildings and works of art in Contantinople and throughout the empire.

Torelli looks to the Janus shrine depicted on the Nero coin as a model for the the *ara Pacis* shrine. He shares Erica Simon's conjecture that the Ara Pacis is a replica of Janus Geminus, described by Simon as a new gate of the enlarged Augustan Rome resembling the gate of the Palatine Rome.[59] In turn, Simon calls the Ara Pacis a marble reproduction of the bronze Janus shrine in the Forum. Because no one knows what the bronze Janus shrine in the Forum looked like (if there even was a bronze Janus shrine in the Forum), Simon must be looking at the Nero coin and, like Torelli, comparing the Ara Pacis to it while assuming it is the Janus shrine in the Forum.

Torelli looks to the same shrine as a model for the two entrances into the Ara Pacis shrine by noting that the openings are also on the shorter side. But in fact they are on the longer sides (this error is made as well by others, difficult as it is for some scholars to visualize a building with a front wider than its depth). If the structural shape of the Janus shrine on the Nero coin is relatively accurate—the doorway side very narrow, just the width of the arched portal (which makes sense)—the doorway at the other end would be the same shape and width, the structure's meaning having been lifted off from referring to a city gate to become a symbolic, free-standing gateway, not unlike a free-standing triumphal arch, visualized as a deep arch or barrel vault, which is only symbolically an entranceway. Neither suggests architectural kinship with the Ara Pacis shrine.

By the Augustan era, the noun *janus* was spelled *ianum*, as it appears in Augustus' *Res Gestae* (par. 13, lines 1-5). The word's proper meaning is "archway" (In this passage, *Ianum Quirinus* is the syntaxical subject of *claudendum esse*).

> Ianum Quirinum, quem claussum esse maiores nostri voluerunt, cum per totum imperium populi Romani terra marique esset parta victoris pax, cum prius, quam nascerer, a condita urbe bis omnino clausum fuisse prodatur memoriae, ter me principe senatus claudendum esse censuit.[60]

As Procopius described it, the Janus shrine's arched doorway is higher than the sidewalls; above the walls is a grill that apparently was openwork, and above the grill an elaborate architrave. I fail to see any similarity to the Ara Pacis other than that the Janus shrine, with mirrored doorways, is like the Ara Pacis (which is not a building, either) only by it too having mirrored entranceways. In my opinion, this is not enough to establish a causal relationship.

Janus originated as a farm gate, farmyard, or farmhouse door, each having two faces: one facing the public, the other, as Ovid has Janus say, the household gods. Those gods would be the Penates of the house, if a door, and the Lares of the household's fields if a gate. Janus doors, or

Janus gates, were sometimes single, and so hinged at one side, and sometimes double, with each door hinged right and left and meeting at the center—not two separate doors at separate entrances. Even when placed within a city gate, which, like a tunnel, has two entrances/exits but usually only one gate, Janus sees comings and goings. In an ordinary city wall, an arched entrance would do, but if the wall was very thick, as a rampart wall would be, the entranceway would be a barrel vault. In any case, the doors, or gates, would be paired, hinged right and left and meeting at a centerline, thus two gates forming one gateway. That configuration does not altar two-faced Janus, or the two-face door. If "double door" is taken to mean a pair of doors within one frame and at one place, the pair would have four faces, unless the paired doors are understood as one door, an *ostium duplex* that, like a duplex apartment as one house, is one door made of two doors when the "one door" means "the doorway."

Ensconced within the passageway, Janus sees both outside the city and into it, taking note of comings and goings. Of course his closing the gates to keep in peace would certainly not be a closing of city gates. Janus says:

> My gate unbarred stands open wide so when people go to war the road for their return stays open too. I bar the doors in time of peace, lest peace depart. To not lose time by twisting my neck, I am free to look both ways without budging (Ovid, *Fasti* I)

Janus Quirinus did not actually originate as a two-faced door or gate. Quirinus was the local god of the ancient Sabines that had settled on what became called the Quirinal hill, the most northerly of the seven hills. After Rome was founded, Quirinus was incorporated into Roman religion and included with the state gods, Jupiter and Mars. Late Republican Romans identified him with Romulus, which explains how Janus Quirinus came to be associated with a Romulan gate.

Before becoming Janus Quirinus, Janus was a Greek king from Thessaly who founded a colony on the Tiber (the river named after his son, Tiberinus, who drowned in it). The colony occupied a small area of land in western Italy at the base of the Alban Mountain just a few miles south of what would become Rome. Appropriately, the colony was named Janiculum. The name survives as one of Rome's hills—but not one of the seven hills, but a hill on the west bank, opposite Rome. Atop this hill, King Janus built a citadel that functioned as a station from which sentinals could see in any direction. A flag flown atop the citadel, visible from the city, was the warning sign: when lowered it meant an enemy was approaching. Apparently, the citadel itself came to be called Janus; consequently, Janus became a sentry with eyes on the back of his head—for that matter, on all four sides; in earlier times, he was pictured citadel-like with four faces (Janus Quadrifons). He was reduced to having two faces (Janus Bifrons) when he became the god of openings, such as gates and doors, while retaining his role as god of beginnings, like "openings onto ..." The first month of the old Roman calendar was named after him because he was credited with opening a new year. His being associated with Romulus no doubt stemmed from Romulus as an opener, as bringing about the advent of Rome.

It may be that in the *Aeneid*, when Janus is mentioned, Virgil may have meant King Janus, who must have boasted that from his citadel he could see in all directions, thus being the primordial four-faced Janus.[62] Janus Bifrons is depicted on early Roman coins as a two-faced bust, perhaps associated with the ancient king or with Romulus. Virgil puts King Janus in the context of Aeneas and the Trojan forces about to assault a city on the Tiber where brave Latins once lived (a reference to Latium). Aeneas sends a hundred legates to offer the king gifts and to entreat a state of peace. King Latinus invites them in. Virgil describes the palace as it must have been like in the days when it was Picus' palace:

> The city fathers took their customary seats
> On benches, at long tables. Here also
> Were sculptures of their ancient forbears, ranked
> By generations, carved in ancient cedar:
> Italus and Sabinus, planter of vines,
> Holding a pruning hook, and Saturnus,
> Hoar with age, and the two-faced Janus...

Confident that the *ara Pacis Augustae* was a *templum* that "reproduced the shrine of Janus Quirinus," Torelli then says, "To achieve this, the precinct has the two doors on the shorter sides." But Torelli errs on that point, as had Simon, for the Ara Pacis' entranceways are on the longer sides. Torelli makes the same mistake when misreading the floor plan of what has been identified as an augural *templum* excavated in the Apulian town of Bantia [61]. He compares this temple to the *ara Pacis*, saying, "In the two monuments, the relationship between the size of the major and minor sides is identical, 11 by 10 meters in the *ara Pacis Augustae* and 9.20 and 8.50 meters in Bantia, and in both cases the long sides are the northern and southern ones."[60] But, as I just pointed out, the long sides of the Ara Pacis shrine are not the north and south, but the east and west. Moreover, nothing about the footprint of the Bantia shrine, if it was a shrine, suggests its having more than one doorway.

I am not convinced that the Bantia structure was a temple or a shrine. If a temple, what can explain why the entrance is on the west side? Were it an enshrined altar, or a housed god, for the altar, or the statue, to face east, they would face a blank wall. As for Torelli's assumption that the Bantia structure had two entrances, Simon says that it had only one, and that any assignment of the Bantia shrine to the company of the Ara Pacis is flawed by the fact that Ara Pacis has two doors. Lacking a

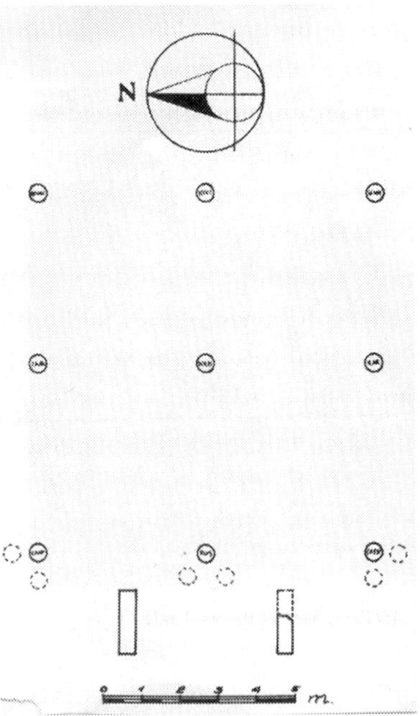

[61]. Plan of what is believed to be an augural temple. Bantia (after Torelli).

precise voice, her words need correcting: the Ara Pacis did not have doors—entranceways, not doorways. And Simon refers to the "two doors" in Latin as *ostium duplex*, making a grammatical error that I will take up in a moment.[65]

Torelli countered Simon's assertion that an inaugural temple of any sort had only one door. He turns to the second century AD lexicon compiled by Sextus Pompeius Festus saying that the *templum* "should not be open in more than one door," then explicates Festus' words: "Festus, in his text, wants to assert that during the performance of the *auspicum* the *templum* should have only one door open to allow communication between the auspicant, placed in the center of the *templum* and facing south, and the augur placed on the west side facing east, as all our sources on the *auspicia* attest." Taking the phrase "only one door" to mean there must have been more than one door, Torelli concludes that "the main entrance of the ara Pacis Augustae, facing toward the Campus Martius, corresponds precisely to such *ostium*."[66]

But does it? If the augur is placed on the west side facing east—facing the gods to whom he is looking for prophecies—he is facing a blank wall, for the plan of the Bantia excavation does not indicate an opening in the east wall [61]. And if the auspicant is placed facing south, he too is facing a blank wall. So, if Torelli's reading of Festus' account of the proper *auspicium* offers proof of two doorways equal to the two openings in the Ara Pacis shrine, it fails completely with the second door in the south wall (if there was a second door) and the main, or entrance, door in the west wall, when, were the building a *templum*, it would have had its entrance door through the east wall.

Simon uses the term *ostium duplex* when saying that the Bantia had two doors, mistaking this singular as a plural. Similarly, Torelli uses the term *ostium* when referring to two doors. But *ostium* is a singular noun, meaning a single door, and *ostium duplex* means a double door, not two doors in two places but a double door in a single frame, with one door hinged left, the other right, and meeting in the middle. The doorway on the Nero coin, picturing the Janus shrine, is an *ostium duplex*—a double door at one entranceway. Entrances to temples, shrines, churches, as well as most public buildings, back then as today, have one or more double doors. Shrines that shelter an altar, or a diety, as depicted on Roman coins, have but one *ostium duplex*. This confusion of singulars and plurals is just one aspect of a general muddle into which the Ara Pacis wallows. Torelli's summation of evidence he deploys to secure his connection of the Janus shrine to the *ara Pacis Augustae* here follows:

> This augural meaning of the precinct [the *ara*'s enclosure) brings us again to the *Res Gestae* and the Augustan conception of the altar. We have underlined that, in the Augustan document, the mention of the *ara Pacis Augustae* is preceded by mention of the *ara Fortunae Reducis* and followed by the record of the triple closing of Janus Quirinus. The sequence is not casual; the *ara Pacis Augustae* apparently constitutes a sort of *trait-d'union* between the other two references, It is in fact a monument *pro reduti* and as full of triumphal meaning as the *ara Fortunae Reducis*, and its structure.[61]

I find no triumphal meaning in the *ara Pacis Augustae*'s structure, location, orientation, or iconography.To lock in Peace, a Janus shrine would have to be closeable. So it could not have been just a passageway; gates or doors would be needed at both ends.

It may be that Augustus' reference to Janus was a figure of speech, such as the common phrases of our time: "Closing the door on this or that ...," and "Hold your peace!" and "Shut your mouth." To shut a door in someone's face, or to close a transaction, does not involve a real door, nor does a "war on poverty" mean that all the poor people will be slaughtered. While my examples may seem banal, I offer them as an antidote to thoughts that everything said by a Roman referred to an actual artifact. Augustus may have had in mind the generic Janus shrine. Some archeologists, whose thoughts now enter into this discussion, believe there was more than one Janus shrine, considering its ceremonial use at the opening of the New Year and the immense spread of a city in which commoners getting from one place to another on foot took time. Others, including myself, opt as well for another alternative to a singular full-scale bronze shrine—that being a miniature shrine in multiple copies.

Procopius described the Janus shrine as small. He didn't say how small. His words may have suffered in translation: he could have meant petite, or tiny, or miniature. A few archeologists, taking note that the shrine's walls represented on the Nero coin look to be stonework—

[62]. Altar of the Lares from the vicus Aesculeti. Probably the district president sacrificing. On the reverse side one of the twin Lares bearing a laurel branch

stones set with mortared joints—believe that the bronze shrine was portable, which makes good sense.[68] After all, the Penates—household gods—were miniatures kept in proportionally small houses, so miniature Janus shines, with a figurine of Janus inside, would not be exceptional. One recalls that, on escaping the burning Troy, Aeneas carried not only his father Anchises but also the Penates in the form of figurines.

As the god of beginnings, Janus was celebrated annually as the opener of the New Year. The celebrations took place in Rome's many districts and other Roman cities and hamlets, so a large number of Janus shrines would have been needed. A parallel example of such distribution is offered by Augustus' reorganization of metropolitan districts. To each he gave a shrine for the cult of its Lares (Lares being field-boundary gods that came to be boundary guards as well for urban districts). The shrine most likely housed an altar, or each district president would have seen to it that as altar was installed. The altar reproduced here is known as "the Lares of the Emperor," at which, perhaps annually, a pig was sacrificed to the Lares and a bull to the Genius of the Emperor [62]. The fact that each district had a shrine for the Lares supports my belief that each district could as well have had a shrine for Janus. According to Ovid, the city would have a thousand Lares distributed throughout the defined neighborhoods.[69] The city may also have had hundreds of Januses in shrines that could be taken out of storage at appropriate times and returned to storage after use for a celebration, like Christians set up a creche with figurines for celebrating Christmas (the birth of Jesus as equivalent to Janus as birth of a new year)—the creche reused year after year. Miniature Janus shrines could be moved about, carried in parades, and at appropriate times displayed in temples. As the model was improved, or altered, earlier versions could be melted down and new ones cast or forged—the same general appearance moving ahead in time. So it is possible that Procopius actually saw a Janus shrine—a small one, as he described it—made of bronze in the traditional shape of a barrel vault, with doors at each end and with a Janus figurine inside, visible through open lattice, or grillwork, for the gates would have been shut, as one sees on the Nero coin.

To such a shrine Procopius would have attached his thoughts about Janus' ancient history. Or he may have been looking at the same Nero coin that we have to go on as to the shrine's appearance. Coin collecting was underway as early as the Augustan age, with Augustus himself a collector. Suetonius says that Augustus gave gifts of special coins to his friends, which would of course be historical coins of some rarity. The Nero coin picturing an *ara Pacis* was restruck several times and was a collector's favorite. Some coins of historical interest or aesthetic value circulated for years; the best among them were often copied. The legendary denarii of Marc Antony, for example, were not only copied but found their way into royal collections and into mint archives for study by engravers when designing new coins.[62]

10

THE FOUR-SQUARE PLAN

The width of the Ara Pacis shrine's mirrored openings, as to the overall breadth of the east and west facades, references the intuitional logic of stability that rests most easily with the number three: the façade width divided by three, with entrances as the center one-third. The four-column, three-bay façade also suggests a fusion of the secular four with the theological three—the four corners of the earth and the four elements contrasted with the holy trinity, which is hierarchical: Jupiter as the "high" god, as he appears at the apex of the pediment of the Capitaline Temple of Jupiter—*Iuppiter Optimus Maximus* (Jupiter, best and greatest)—with state goddesses Juno and Minerva at his side. The association of the numbers three and four has made the number seven one of the most stable numbers (a seven-spot is the key roll in dice, one of the ancient Romans' favorite games—a winning throw called "a Venus"). Seven also images the most secure structure of a house: a square facade with a gable roof, whether human dwelling or temple for a god. The composition I'm speaking of is found in the architectural geometry of tetrastyle temples and in Etruscan and early Roman small-scale building facades, such as house tombs that tend to be square in plan and feature a tripartite composition even of the side walls.

Centering an entranceway is as typical of unsophisticated architecture as putting a centerpiece in the center of a table, or centering text on a page. One needn't explain why something is centered, such as one's nose, but would need to explain an off-centered condition. In architecture the explanation is typically given by function and site, such

[63] Sarcophagus of Lucius Cornelius Scipio Barbatus, from his tomb on the Via Appia near Rome. Musei Vaticani. Symmetry is associated with "rest in peace."

[64] Marble ash urn of P. Volumnius from Perugia.

as a building with multiple rooms but a very narrow front, requiring a door at one side or the other, while a building with a wide front allows for a central entrance into a centered hall with rooms off to both the right and the left—in the case of house tombs, with crypts on either side of a center hall (the current architectural term for this is "double loaded").

Symmetry is a state of silence, peace, and rest, while asymmetry is visually noisy, agitated, and active. Symmetry rules Roman funerary architecture, both the house tomb with a central entrance, and the *loge* tomb with a niche chamber behind four columns that form a porch. Thus altars and tombs share many traits and often the same symbols. "Peace

65] Model of the House tomb of Anni Regilla on the Via Appia, Rome.

[66] Model of the trastyle temple at Tebessa. Note the similarity to the house tomb of Annia Regilla.

offerings" and "rest in peace" are structurally commensurate. Sarcaphagi and ash urns often took the form of small temples or house tombs with architectural proportions and elements like those of the Ara Pacis [63, 64]. The marble ash urn of P. Volumnius from Perugia is a fine example [64]. Remove the roof and you have corner pilasters and an architrave like the one Moretti assigned to the Ara Pacis shrine. Bucrania, festoons with ribbons, and *paterae* ornament one side of the urn, recalling the shrine's interior walls with the same signs and symbols. And at the back side of the Volumnius urn one sees a garden, including birds at a fountain, inviting association with the Ara Pacis shrine's vegetative panels that include birds and ground creatures one finds in gardens.

The third to second century BC Capitolium on the Arx at Cosa is a good example of the old-fashioned Roman temple in tufa, terra cotta, and wood, fronted with four columns forming three equal spaces. From two or more centuries later, one finds essentially the same arrangement as the façade of a temple at Tebessa [66]. Consider as well the Tomb of Annia Regilla as to how it appeared when still furnished with a porch at the opposite end [65]. Remove the porch and the body of the structure is remarkably similar to the Ara Pacis as to footprint—almost square—and with lower and upper zones that, if not segmented by pilasters,

[67] Left: House tomb of Annia Regilla (ca. 160) on the Via Appia, Rome as it appears today.
[68] Right:: As modified by the author.

would coincide with the horizontal registers of reliefs on the north and south walls of the Ara Pacis shrine. The Regilla is higher and roofed, but the architecture is nonetheless similar, as I show in a drawing where I've removed the intermittent pilasters and sketched in figurative and vegetative reliefs [67, 68]. Now imagine the structure without the roof and it will take on the general appearance of the Ara Pacis shrine.

If one needs precedent for the architecture of the Ara Pacis' enclosure I suggest one look to this tradition of small temples and house tombs, with Etruscan and early Roman architecture as historical background. I am not proposing a causal relationship between the building types, as Simon and Torelli set up between the *ara Pacis* and the Janus shrine. The structures I'm holding up fit to a category circumscribed by shared traits but not dependent on each other for generating similarities.

The open top of the Ara Pacis enclosure has also been questioned. Did it at one time have a roof? It didn't. At the base of the walls are very wide drainage slits sufficient in number and distribution to drain off a downpour: four slits on the north and south sides and two on the east and west sides. They tell us that no roof surmounted the structure, for surely such generous drainage was for rainfall, not for draining a floor when being mopped. (It pains me to read texts saying that the

[68] Left: An As of Domitian (AD 81-96) depicting an ara Pacis. Drawing courtesy Marvin Tameanko. (RIC Domician 336).

[69] Right: A silver cistophoric tetradrachm struck in Ephesus for Domitian under Titus in ad 80-81, commeorating the deified Vespasian. Drawing courtesy Marvin Tameanko. (RIC Titus 75).

[70] An As minted in Lugdunum depicting Augustus, and on the reverse an altar dedicated to Augustus and Roma. On the face of the altar appear two shrines, two laurel trees, and in the center a *corona civica*.(RIC Augustus 230).

slits were there to drain off blood running down from the altar table, as if a bull could be led up those steps and asked to climb atop a table about the size of a single bed, bow to receive the axe man's blow, and lay there dying while the priests evicserate it!). Questioned too are the openings without doors, considering that enshrined altars that appear on coins have substantial doors. By responding to this question, I will expand on it by taking up the issue as to whether depictions of an *ara Pacis*-like shrine on a few ancient coins actually depict the *ara Pacis Augustae.*

Among the altars on coins that I illustrate are two taken to be the *ara Pacis Augustae.* One of them [p. 98, B] was minted in France (Lyon) during the reign of Nero (AD 54-68), the other [68] struck by Domitian (AD 81-96). So they are of no help in establishing a date for the imagery they portray, nor for that matter, can it be said with certainty that the peace altar they portray is the *ara Pacis Augustae.* Several enshrined altars were

[71] A. *Ara Providentia,* Bronze As of Divus Augustus struck under Tiberius(RIC Tberius 80).
[72] B. *Ara Pacis.* Bronze As of Nero (RIC Nero 456-61)..
[73] C. Shrine to Salus. Bronze As of Domitian (RIC Titus 105).
[74] D. Bronze As of Diva Faustina struck under Antoninus Pius (RIC Antoninus Pius 1191).

Coin drawings courtesy Marvin Tameanko.

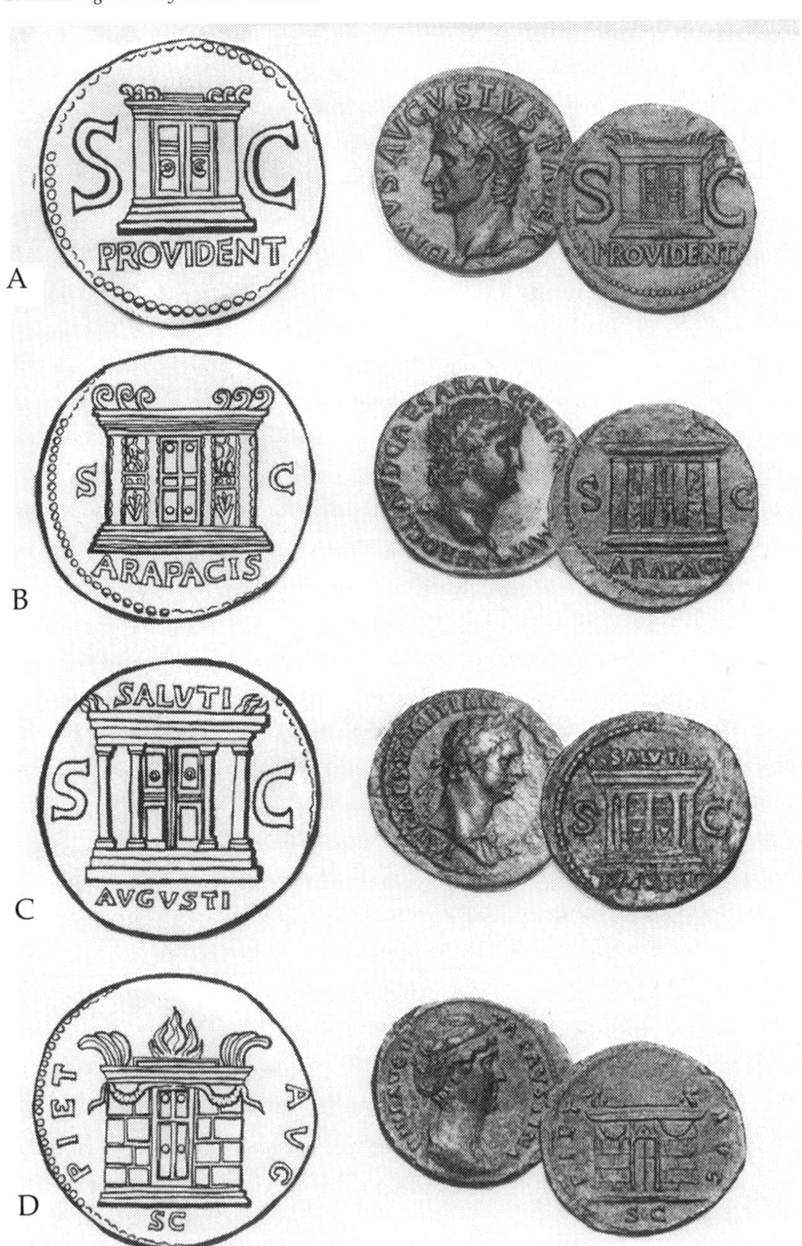

[75] The miracle of the palm tree altar at Tarraco, Spain.A coin struck under the reign of Tiberius (*Greek Imperial Coins* by D. R. Sear 234)

dedicated over the Julio-Claudian decades. The inscriptions "Pax" or "Ara Pacis" on coins need not refer to the *ara Pacis Augustae,* for that altar wasn't the only one dedicated to peace.

Claudius was the first to strike coins with the slogan *Pax Augusta,* while the earliest coin known that references Augustus depicts a waist high altar associated with "the miracle of the palm tree," the epigram based on a seedling having sprouted out of a crack in the altar's table top [75]. This altar was at the city of Tarraco in Spain. Quintillian, the Roman literary historian (b. ca. AD 35), tells us that the Tarracoan city council wrote to Augustus to tell him of the miracle and remind him that, because the palm tree was a symbol for victory, the aggressive seedling boded well for his reign. Augustus was amused. He wrote back jokingly, saying that the palm tree's sprouting from a crack in his altar only proved how infrequently the people of Tarraco burnt an offering to him. The story must have gained great popularity: Tiberius struck the coin depicting the oracular altar.

When looking at numismatic images of altars that resemble the Ara Pacis shrine, one must understand that one is looking not at an altar *per se* but at the façade of a structure housing an altar, which I've been calling a shrine, akin to shrines that house gods. We do not know what the actual altars pictured on those coins looked like, nor can anyone be sure that the depicted shrines had mirrored entranceways. While the two that are believed to represent the *ara Pacis Augustae* do, in fact, depict an *ara Pacis,* nothing about them—neither their appearance nor the date they were struck—says that the *ara* they show us is the one said to have been dedicated in 9 BC. The coin struck during the reign of Domitian shows figurative panels in both the lower and upper zones [68]. While the figures in the upper panels have the look of Tellus and Roma on the Ara Pacis, if the structure on that coin is indeed the *ara Pacis Augustae* – a Tiberian structure, as I maintain it was—those personifications are out of place. The coin pictures them on the west facade where one finds the run of steps rather than on the end facing the Via Flaminia. Might this mean that Moretti's reconstruction has the entranceway panels reversed? I suspect that had Moretti known this coin, he may have been inclined to reverse the position of the four panels, putting Tellus and Roma on the west wall.

As for the coin stuck during the reign of Nero, it could represent the *ara Pacis Augustae* furnished at some later time with doors (p. 98, B). Still, can one rule out that the shrine might be Nero's rather than Augustus'? Among other examples of such shrines on coins, we have the silver cistophoric tetradachm struck at Ephesus for Domitian, commemorating the deified Vespasian, depicting an altar enshrined, and also a sestertius struck by Antoninus Pius (AD 141) to commemorate his deceased wife, Faustina Senior (p. 98, D). The shrine on that coin may be a house tomb—the flames atop the structure refering symbolically to an altar, or perhaps to a sort of eternal flame representing eternal love.

So the coins depicting an enshrined altar span a hundred year period, while the only known coin from Augustus' reign that depicts an altar (but not enshrined) is a bronze As struck in provincial Lugdunum and restruck many times over the following decades [70, p. 97]. It depicts a waist-high altar dedicated to Rome and Augustus, remindful of Augustus' demand that, when depicted in the provinces, his image was to be coupled with Roma. It has been argued that the altar on this coin is a "large altar," that is, an altar within an enclosure like the Ara Pacis, and even that it is based on the Ara Pacis. Surely that cannot be the case. The depiction is not of a "large" or enshrined altar, but of an altar unto itself.

If the *ara Pacis Augustae* complex, as we see it today in more or less the form it took when installed as a memorial, rather than a simple altar like the *ara Fortuna Redcis*, and if it was copied in provincial centers, as was the custom for dispersing official monuments and declarations (such as the distribution of Augustus' *Res Gestae*), at one location a replica may have had doors, at another location no doors. At each geographical site, the form and iconography would have been adapted to local building practice, climatic conditions, and local deities. A marble relief found in Carthage, with imagery almost identical to that of the Tellus panel, is most likely from an altar built to emulate the *ara Pacis Augustae*, or a competition piece following the general specifications for that relief [75]. Rather than the aura on a swan, this panel substitutes Luna Celeste (Diana in her role as goddess of childbirth) above clouds, or over the

[75] Fragment relief found in Carthage that replicates the Tellus panel from the Ara Pacis shrine, with local adaptation of the imagery. Paris, Musée du Louvre.

horizon, holding a torch. Posidon and dolphins were added to sign for the sea [75]. The relief has all the aspects of a mediocre hand: it lacks transitions between figures; the sea's personification is crowded against the shore line, touching Tellus' feet; the babies are proportionally near to the small size of Egyptian cubits, such as one sees crowding around the Alexandrian sculpture of the Nile god, each cubit representing a meas-

[76]. Personification of the Nile. Paris, Musé du Louvre.

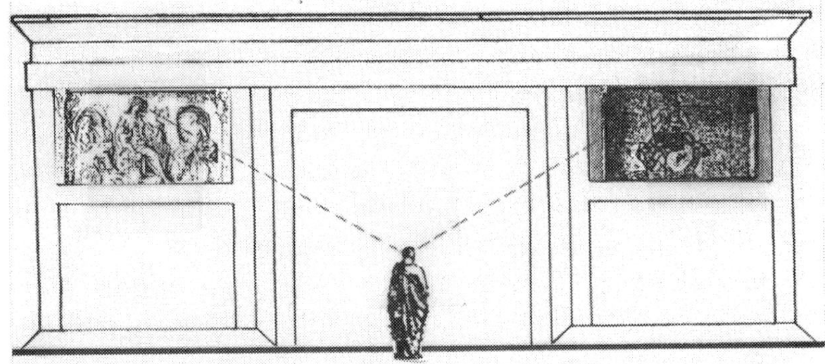

[77] Author's drawings demonstrating eye contact with the personifications and historic personages.

{78} Below: The author's position when making eye contact with the personages.

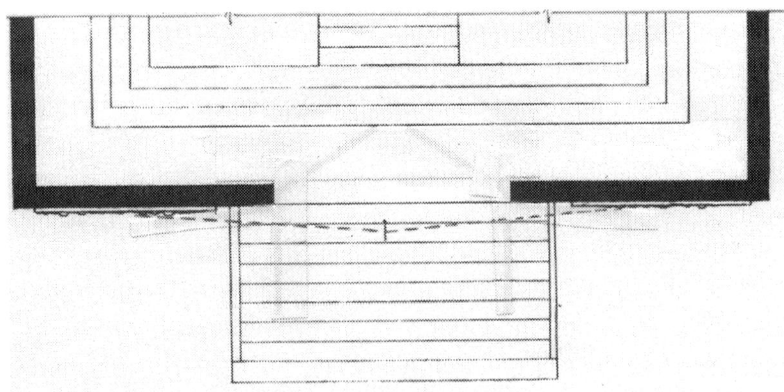

ure of the annual Nile flood that brings fresh and fertile soil to Egypt's long and narrow flood plain [76]. Take note too of the ash urn from Carthage (p. 94) that bears sufficient Ara Pacis traits to assure that the client and the urn-maker were familiar with the Ara Pacis shrine. But that familiarity could have come some time after Augustus' death—after the *ara Pacis Augustae* was enshrined.

[79]. Hypothetical reconstructionof the personification of Roma on the east facade of the Ara Pacis shrine..

If the reconstructed Ara Pacis had doors they could not open in. The interior space is too narrow to accommodate a door swing; the doors would hit against the altar's base. Doors hinged right and left could have opened outward, but they would have violated the integrity of each façade by obscuring a large portion of the reliefs that flank the entrances—each relief featuring major personages: Tellus, Roma, Mars, and Aeneas, their locations too specific and their imagery too important to be seen only when the doors were closed. The principal on each of the four reliefs faces one of the entranceways. Only

[81]. Below: Author's drawing showing the three improbable door swings.

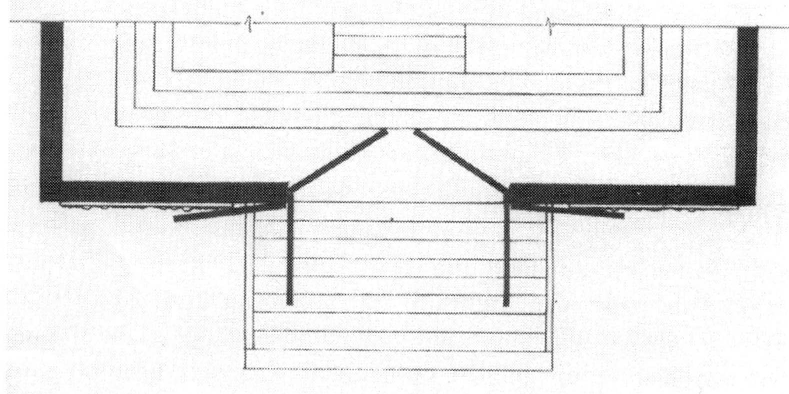

[81-82]. Supplicant's eye contact with Tellus.

Tellus and Aeneas are sufficiently preserved to see the down-turned angle of their heads and their eyes' line of sight.

To test my thought that the shrine did not have doors, I put myself in the place of a Roman supplicant approaching the altar from either direction. I positioned myself a ways out from each entrance, then moved forward until my eyes met those of Tellus on the east entrance wall. Then I moved around the shrine to approach the altar from the west, stopping when my eyes met Aeneas'. As recorded on my diagrams [77, 78, p.102], the designer who programmed these reliefs must have taken those viewer-positions and angles of viewing into account. If we had a complete head of Mars, surely the face would angle down to gaze at the same point as does Aeneas'. And that leads me to say that the hypothetical figure of Roma, drawn by a restorer on the entrance flank opposite Tellus, and looking excessively Greek, should not be gazing out perpendicular to her body [79]. Her head should be angled downward like Tellus' to confront the supplicant's eyes.

Accustomed as we are we to seeing Roman figurative sculpture out of its original setting and no longer painted, the angle of sight is not usually considered. Museum installations do not replicate an original placement. Even the usual photographs of the Ara Pacis are taken perpendicular to what is being photographed rather than at optical viewing angles. Were one to see Tellus as she appeared in her historical time—painted, her eyes bright and clear, her gaze intense, albeit the features may have been resurfaced in the sixteenth century—one would find her looking not as matronly as she appears from the straight-on view in photographs. And the faces of the *aurae* flanking her, looking rather flat-faced from erosion, appear more youthful and refined when seen from an angle [81, 82].

The personages and personifications on the exterior of the enclosure walls are high enough to satisfy Vitruvius by obliging the supplicant to look up. My proposal that this is so has conclusive support from Vitruvius' instructions for placing statues of gods in temples. In his chapter on altars he says that the gods should be placed so that persons undertaking vows, or who come to the altar to make offerings, are obliged to look upward to the divinity, and that the images should gaze upon those who make such vows and sacrifices.[63] Vitruvius might just as well have said that those who are about to sacrifice must look up at the divinity and be prompted to give plentifully. Surely that is why key personages in the four reliefs—Tellus, Roma, Aeneas, and most likely Mars—cast their look at an angle downward to engage the eyes of anyone about to enter.

11

THE UNKNOWN ARTISANS

We know the name of several ancient Roman architects, sculptors, and painters, but no name can be associated with a single work of art or architecture. It's not that artists and exceptional artisans were anonymous in their place and time, but just as actors do not write plays and singers don't write operas, artisans perform work according to plans, material specifications, design standards, workshop traditions, and building codes imposed by others.

Nothing about the design or iconography of the Ara Pacis complex says that the program for the reliefs on the altar proper was written by the same mind that programmed those on the enclosure's walls. Nor was the architect of the shrine the designer of the altar's base and plinth. The latter would have been accomplished by a stone-worker firm, of which there must have been several specializing in altars, tombs, and bases for statuary. Moreover, the reliefs on the altar barriers cannot be argued as integrated with those on the shrine's outer walls. Those scenes of a sacrificial ceremony—the arrival of the victims, of the Vestals—are ordinary as to both conception and style, entirely lacking in the sophisticated arragements and detailing of the figurative carvings on the shrine. The subject matter on the barriers is literal—simple narratives that only describe, like illustration without much art. Any standardized workshop could have produced them.

I wouldn't say the same of those relief panels on the shrine that combine personifications and real people, allegories and actual events, and symbols with natural attributes (a child is not the attribute of its mother, unless the mother is a personification of "mothering"). The north and south friezes picturing real-life personages would have required someone to have programmed the imagery as such. Protocol would have had something to say about who was represented and how the participants lined up according to status. Then chief artists or artisans would have participated in planning how to transform the programmed discourse into imagery accessible to the people. Most likely the reliefs were first rendered as terra cotta maquettes. The east and west panels may have involved competition submittals. The example of Florence's Baptistry door panels put out to competing artists—centuries later, of course—was a link in the continuity of ancient procedures followed still today. And nothing precludes my saying that the artists who designed the maquettes withdrew in favor of expert stone carvers to point up and translate the artists' imagery into marble.

The altar's scroll-barrier reliefs are less sophisticated in both spirit and execution than the shrine's friezes, the scrolls having an old fashioned look—that line-up of Vestals utterly pedestrian (pun intended), showing no advance over the Ahenobarbus or Sosianus reliefs. I conclude from this that the barriers were not conceived and executed within the same program that generated the shrine's friezes and panels. And I'm also of the opinion that a stronger motivation for the re-use of those earlier barriers overruled any concern about their stylistic appropriateness to a project that demonstrated in many ways an advance in absorption of Hellenistic art while still rendering all but the Tellus panel in what had become a definitively Roman style.

The south and north friezes give every indication of having been carved by a single workshop, with a unified style among its craftsmen enforced by a master. And it would seem from what fragments we have that the relief panels on the shrine's west end (Mars and Aeneas) are sufficiently unified in scale, depth of carving, and narrative presentation to be from one studio. As for the east wall's panels (Tellus and Roma), at least the Tellus panel would not have been carved by the same shop that fashioned those on the west end, and certainly not the same shop that carved the south and north reliefs. As for the floral panels, they could have been executed by yet another workshop, perhaps more than one, as decorative carving required only that the artisans follow the patterns (I suspect that, rather than finding profound symbolic meaning in the insects, birds, and snakes that one sees here and there amidst the foliage, one would come closer to facts by imagining the artisans adding them as pleasantries, like landscape painters-for-hire in large portrait studios adding owls and other creatures not necessarily called for by the studio master. That sort of playfulness led to the game, "Find the owls," that art patrons enjoyed when going through an exhibition of late Renaissance and Baroque northern landscape paintings).

Plutarch tells us that when cities invite bids for temples and other monuments, contractors compete with each other by submitting plans, models, and cost estimates; their plans and specifications subject to the magistrates' review.[64] As an example, we have Aulus Gellius mentioning plans for public projects exhibited in the open for public viewing:

> By Fronto's side stood several builders [*fabri*] who had been summoned to construct some new baths, and were exhibiting different plans [*pictas*] drawn on little pieces of parchment. When he had selected one plan and a specimen of their work [*formam specieque opereis*], he inquired what the expense would be for the entire project. And when the architect [*architectus*] said it would probably require about three hundred thousand sestertii, one of Fronto's friends said, 'and another fifty thousand, more or less'.[65]

That the stylistic and technical characteristics of the Ara Pacis complex—from panel to panel, panels to frieze, figurative to decorative—suggest different masters and workshops is easy enough to explain. During Augustus and Tiberius' reigns—considering efforts to respect Rome's provinces and bring them into the Empire—it would have been politically prudent to patronize distant realms and invite architects and sculptors from sensitive centers to present credentials and compete under fair rules (for the same reason why the Italian Bernini was engaged in the seventeenth century to design the Louvre in Paris, and, for that matter, why the American Richard Meier was engaged by the Italian government to redesign the Ara Pacis' area and the museum that will house it). One way to offset internecine fights among one's own architects over a major commission is to give it to a foreigner whom everyone can blame for a failure without risk of insulting a home-based colleague. Economics may be the driving force for building, but politics drives architecture's history as to what gets built.

Many architects, master builders, masons, sculptors, and stone carvers settled in Rome during Julius Caesar's reign to take advantage of lucrative commissions and the rapid implementation of projects the Roman purse promoted, and would continue promoting during the reigns of Augustus, Tiberius, and Claudius. Roman architects and artisans—their building technologies superior to the Greeks—also worked in Greece and geographically dispersed Hellenic cities in North Africa and Sicily. A fine example is the Augustan amphitheater at Syracuse that resulted, perhaps, in the first use of Roman concrete technology on the island. Another example is given by Vitruvius, who reports that a Roman architect constructed the temple of Zeus Olympios in Athens with Corinthian columns that Sulla later stole for rebuilding the temple of Jupiter Optimus Maximus on the Capitaline in Rome.

Throughout the late Republican era, Rome was obliged to import marble from the Eastern provinces. From Caryston came green-veined *cipollino*, from Chantou came yellow *giallo antico*, and from Phrygia came purple and white *pavonazzetto*. The expense and density of exotic stone restricted use in large pieces. Granite, imported from western Turkey, was not a suitable alternative for columns or elaborate carving. It was difficult to slice, wire saws at the time not up to the tensility of iron alloys yet to be developed. But rough-cut granite made excellent road surfacing and foundation material, replacing tufa, which had good strength under compression but was too soft to remain stable under iron-shod horses and wheel irons. After the marble quarries in northern Italy were discovered in the latter decades of the first-century BC, and large-scale processing had developed technologically, the marble trade that until then was almost entirely importation came into balance. Cararra marble was exportable and much in demand, for it was easier to work with than the harder, more veined, and multi-colored marbles from Greece and the Eastern provinces (Cararra marble's first notable use in Rome was the Temple of Apollo on the Aventine, for which the gleaming white marble was put in contrast with columns of exotic colored stone from Africa).

As Rome's reciprocating marble trade spread throughout the empire a proliferation of workshops offered opportunities for Greek and Roman artisans to find work in alternative cities. In turn, an industry developed at Italian quarries for designing, carving, and exporting standardized architectural components and features to overseas clients. Because it was cheaper to carve at the quarry than to cart huge blocks of stone to Rome, or ship them to foreign ports, Roman stoneworkers and sculptors were often employed at virgin stone yards to rough-cut and sometimes to finish marbles for export. Rome's merchant marine had a remarkable ability to deliver columns up to ten meters long and weighing fifty tons. As a result of this industry, many Roman-type building components and decorative pieces turn up in remote cities when ruins are unearthed.

The variety of architectural components and sculpture in Rome that displayed Eastern characteristics came largely from Roman and Eastern craftsmen who perpetuated the same art taken as spoils from Greek and North African cities. When displayed in urban contexts, and incorporated into architecture, artifacts of sacked cities transformed the way Romans envisioned large scale sculpture and architectural enhancement. The city must have appeared like an unsorted museum, the random collection of artifacts unsettling old Italian and early Roman traditions while affording opportunities for a wide choice of style, material, and techniques.[66] Major artifacts, stolen from Syracuse in 211 BC, were most likely still in the cityscape by the Augustan era. According to Plutarch, the triumphal parade of Aemilius Paullus in 167 went on for three days, with so many works of art looted from Macedonia—statues, paintings, armor, silver mixing bowls, gold utensils, and colossal images as well, carried along the parade route on 250 wagons drawn by oxen and mule teams—that the vanquished must have been left with naught but rubble. Plunder from the mainland of Greece and from Sicily mixed with that from Africa and Macedonia to create a medley of precious art equal to the racial mix of the empire.

Soberer minds eventually became concerned that Roman conquests and pillage were destroying what Rome most depended on: international trade and economic stability. Cicero reacted contemptuously to Gaius Verres' sack of the Temple of Minerva on Corinth—"sacked", writes Cicero, "not by an enemy who would still retain some sense of religion and the laws of propriety even in war, but by pirate robbers."[67] Just one of the many governors that plundered their assigned province, Verres had the temple's exotic marble columns and statuary shipped to Rome for his personal use. Livy ascribes to conservative, prototypical Roman, Cato, a somber speech lamenting the influx of Greek art and architecture, and the danger that sculpture from the sack of Syracuse, and ornaments from Athens and Corinth, that had been distributed throughout Rome were undermining traditional terra-cotta representations of Roman gods.

> You have often heard me complain about extravagances of women and just as often about those of men—not only of private citizens but magistrates—and about how the state suffers from two great vices, avarice and luxury, those pests that in the past have overturned all great empires. As the fortune of the Republic becomes greater and more pleasant every day, and as the empire grows abroad, I have come to fear these vices even more. Now we have moved into Greece and Asia, places of libidinous temptation, and are even putting our hands on royal treasuries that will make prisoners of us rather than we of them. They are dangerous, believe me, those statues brought into the city from Syracuse. I hear too many people praising them, and too many marveling at the ornaments of Corinth and Athens while laughing at the terra-cotta antefixes of Roman gods. I prefer our propitious gods, who will remain so, I hope, if we permit them their proper place.

To be modern during the Julio-Claudian era, one had to define what it meant to be Roman. The Greek's art and literary inheritance was refinement, while Old Italian art, architecture, and writing was more robust, energetic, and adventurous. The basis for the archaic human character was less the idealized hero of Greek art than the Italian rustic farmer as eulegized by Horace and in Virgil's *Georgics*. Roman history was, for the most part, artless and homespun, like Colonial American crafts contrasted with the parental British and French. I would liken Cato to the nineteenth-century American, Horatio Greenough, who applauded the colonial trotting wagon at the expense of the pompous British coach, and the American clipper ship when compared to the British Man-o-War, so overladen with ornament that it couldn't outrun a canoe.

To be rendered in poetry, Roman writers had to make out with a blend—avoiding the purely Greek while adopting its refinements. In fact, the emergence of Roman culture meant, to a great extent, repression of the Greek. Republicanism defined the prevailing principles of traditional Roman thought, leaving dispirited intellectuals to drift back to Classical ideals, to any old Golden Age that was free of capitalism and bourgeois values. Conservative Romans, such as Cato, opposed attempts to introduce Greek culture into Roman mores. On one occasion, as Plutarch tells us, three skilled Greek intellectuals, the orator Carneades, Critolaus the Aristotelian, and Diogenes of Babylon, came to Rome as ambassadors to negotiate relief from a fine that Rome had imposed on Athens. They found a ready audience of young Romans eager to hear lessons in Greek dialectics (thesis and antithesis). Cato and others looked upon the visitors as a corrupting influence; with the Senate's backing, had them expelled from Rome. The senate then passed a decree banishing visits by philosophy and rhetoric teachers. As a true Roman, promoting secularism and home values, Cato set an example of austerity and business acumen. He was a prolific writer, educator, moralist, and supporter of an industrial state. Even when an uncheckable wave of sentiment for cosmopolitan modernity wafted across Italy, the conservative attitude he represented was sustained as an undercurrent, especially in reverence for the domestic and the practical—a typical sentiment of the penisula's rural-based societies that resisted urbanization and the industrialization of agriculture that was rapidly modifying their lives as farmers, even as wiser minds, such as Cato's, were promoting it as a survival necessity. Such sentiments bear on the imagery of the Ara Pacis shrine's withdrawl from Hellenistic traditions to evoke reality fashioned not by gods but by human dedication to the ethics of hard work, social values, and love of country. Like the Protestant reformation coming centuries later, religion could be accommodated to secular life, industry, and and politics without diluting the sense of security that, in a not-yet scientific age, was given by the intuitional rationality of the mystical world, like modern religions to secular democracies with their enforced separation of church and state.

Aside from politics, protocols, and standard procedures for the building trade, the program for the Ara Pacis reliefs was controlled as well by traditions of art when integral to architecture. A tripartite mode of imaging art in architectural contexts developed in more than

[83] Above: Etruscan. Tomb of the Lioness. Tarquinii. The paintings take their format from the architecture. An expanded panel is surmounted by a symmetrical, pedimental zone

[84] The Dipylon Vase. Greek. Geometric period. New York, Metropolitan Museum. The pot shape allows a continuous frieze all around it. Where the handles intervene, the format changes to being a panel, as is the case with architectural settings where intermittent polasters and corners define places for pictorial placements.

[84]. Funeral procession. Relief on a Roman sarcophagus from L'Aquila. Compare with Fig. 84.

[85]. Pediment of the Temple of Mars Ultar in the Roman Forum.

one advanced ancient culture and was refined to the point of conceptual definition by fifth-century BC Greeks.

Architecture provided places for art. Three paradigmatic types of architectural space were available to Roman artists: framed panels on which iconic images and stills from narratives could be represented, such placements known to us mostly by pictorial panels on pots, grave steli, metopes, and wall paintings [83, 84]. As offered by architectural articulation, the isosoles triangle, the geometry of pediments that dictate bilateral symmetry [85], and the frieze, as a laterally extended panel that allows for linear progression and drawn-out narratives [86], were the most pronounced. Each format had much history behind it if only because architecture is an art of methods that involve technologies not controlled by architects, just as stone carving requires tools and the evolution of their design. Even when illusionist landscape developed at Alexandria and was carried out extensively at Rome, Herculaneum, and Pompeii, the imagery was illusionistic because the art was made on a real, materially flat surface, with placements and formats dictated by architecture.

The Ara Pacis makes use of two framed formats: for one, the panels for the east and west historical and personification reliefs; the other, the mono-directional frieze on the north wall of the shrine and the expanded panel composition on the south wall. With few exceptions, in the run from ancient to modern art, imagery on a panel, such as Aeneas sacrificing, or Mars at the Lupercal, represents something happening at a single moment of time, while the longitudinal expanse of the processional friezes allows for an event to be either in motion over time or a sequence of events taking place over time. Thus one finds on the shrine's friezes a directional line-up of personages in motion, and in the altar friezes, the arrival of vestals and sacrificial animals driven by handlers. If read as participants in the ceremony arriving one after the other—the vestals arriving one after another, the animals to be sacrificed driven one after the other to the altar—the prototypical frieze is self-portraying of directional motion within a span of time. One can thus read the combined spans on the shrine's north and south walls as evoking the time taken for the entire procession to reach where Augustus is standing.

An isolated moment of a narrative depends on the viewer knowing the whole story out of which that moment is extracted and represented. The imagery of the Aeneas and Mars panels are like stills from such a sequence: frozen moments when everything in the picture simultaneously happens, as, for example (to get away from Roman art for a moment), how a panel imaging the sacrifice of Isaac would depict the very moment when Abraham raises his knife to sacrifice his son, while at that very moment an angel stays his hand, and at the same moment a ram gets entangled by its horns in a thicket (my example, of course, is the competition panel for the Baptistry doors at Florence).

Real time, historical time, real space, and illusory space figure importantly in Roman representations. The populace was accustomed to seeing in one program such line-ups of real events along with portrayed allegories and symbols. Triumphal parades were just like that, at once real, historical, and symbolic—not just trophies and loot, victors and prisoners, but also paintings and moving pictorial stages (parade floats) depicting momentous events that happened along the way of the conquest and at the places conquered. The Ara Pacis' subjects, signs, and symbols would have been determined by thematic programmers experienced with such representations. The procession on the south and north walls, as a real time event, is fitted to historical events: the sacrifice of Aeneas and the circumstances that connected Mars to Romulus. In turn, those reliefs had to relate to the personifications of Tellus and Roma that are not implicated in time. In this fashion, real people, historical people, and allegorical people come together, comparable to a literary text that moves in time as one reads, or real-time events that stretch out in space-time, such as a presidential parade down Pennsylvania Avenue in the United States capital, with floats staging Washington crossing the Delaware and Lincoln emancipating the slaves, moving along with other staged spectacles fashioned as allegories of Liberty, God, Country, and Family, followed by real people, musicians and marchers with symbolic flags surmounted by an eagle—the assemblage embracing living people and events along with the historical and symbolic.

To locate the stationary focus of a procession, one distinguishes between two types of processional imagery: the representation of each component at the same moment of time, and an act that is stationary in time. Augustus is stationary—the lictors face rather than precede him, as lictors do when announcing a dignitary and clearing the way. The reversal fixes Augustus in place.

Were the Parthenon frieze the model for the Ara Pacis frieze, Augustus would appear on the east end, as does Athena on the Parthenon, directly above the east portal that leads into her sanctuary. But Augustus is not over the east entrance. Perhaps he would have been had the frieze also been above it. That would have required a higher architrave and a narrower frieze, such as the Parthenon's, or a taller structure. Here I will ask whether the architecture dictated the layout of the friezes—such that those on the south and north walls accommodating the structure—by putting Augustus on a sidewall? I am not satisfied with the usual explanation that he is on the side that faces the city, or placed where he would be "just around the corner" from Aeneas.

On the west end of the Parthenon, the rear of the temple, participants, mostly horsemen, are getting underway at an imprecise moment. On the Parthenon's north side, a large animal sacrifice is soon to happen: one sees bulls and rams being led to an altar, while the gods and dignitaries on the east zone of the frieze await. On both the north and south sides, the procession moves eastwardly *toward Athena*. Whether the procession is actually a double column, one on each side, or not even a procession but just people arriving from more than one direction, may be a toss up. On either side of Athena, other gods are seated on chairs; those on our right face south, those on our left face north, which is similar to Augustus' location on the south side of the Ara Pacis where lictors and others face him from one direction and others from the other direction.

That sort of composition is typical of the expanded panel format, such as most often seen, due to the artifact survival ratio, on the long sides of sarcophagi. What this "dislocation" of Augustus from a deity-like central spot on the east end—and not even centered on the south wall—tells me is that the south and north friezes are not integrated compositionally with the rigorously symmetrical architecture.

The general organization of the Ara Pacis frieze—the tight fit of the figures to the wall, and a tendency for isocephalism among adults, with most of the women's heights equal to men's—indeed follows the classic order of the Parthenon frieze, but directionality is less strictly followed. One sees much more turning and milling that reinforces the personages as individuals in real time and space. All along the frieze, people act and interact, the realism enhanced by having no personage look down to engage the external viewer's eyes, for that would displace the precise date of the event to the moment of the viewer's presence and involve the viewer as a spectator at that moment of time. This situation is entirely different from the Tellus and Roma personifications—and of Aeneas and most likely Mars as well—where, as I've demonstrated, direct eye contact is from deity to supplicant. But neither Tellus nor Roma is depicted at a moment in time, or even in place, for they are personifications of timeless abstractions. So only in general terms can the Ara Pacis procession be associated with the Parthenon frieze—perhaps to say no more than both happen to be processions depicted at the upper register of a religious structure, which isn't saying much. The location of Augustus, decentered and over neither entrance, marks a significant departure from the classical model. Efforts to use the Parthenon as a model for the ara Pacis frieze detract from seeing what is Roman as distinct from what is Greek.

On the south wall, Augustus is already performing some act or another. The personages on the north side would be those who are not yet witnessing what he's doing, simply because they have not yet arrived. But is that a fact? Is it possible that they are already there? Roman imagery does tend toward being teleological. Otherwise, the reliefs would be like a Last Supper, with Jesus' disciples arriving one by one but with Jesus already sipping wine and breaking bread. It may be, therefore, that the Ara Pacis friezes do not actually portray a procession at the moment when some have arrived and are in the presence of

Augustus. I prefer to believe that the representation is one of simultaneous arrival and presence.

It is said that when reading Republican Age reliefs, one reads from left to right—*ursus scribendi, usus legendi.* The principal personage or action is typically at the viewer's left, so one reads what is on the right moving toward it, hence left to right would be hierarchical and right to left directional. This holds true only on the Ara Pacis' south wall. The remaining procession comes towards Augustus' position from the right, moving leftward (from the viewer's point of view). So far, so good, but on the north wall, the procession is moving left to right. From the perspective of the viewer, it would seem more logical if the figures on the north side moved right to left. Then one could connect them directionally with the figures on the south side as walking along the north side and connecting across the east facade with those walking on the south wall. As they are, both alignments move towards the west, which seems rather strange, considering that the altar faces east. One recalls now that on the Parthenon frieze personages on the north and south sides move eastward, not as two processions, not even as two columns, but as one. The "two-column" arrangement fails completely on the Ara Pacis if read literally.

Historians of the monument who take this directional orientation literally say that the procession divided into two columns at the Via Flaminia end and skirted westerly around the sanctuary to reach "the main entrance," where the columns rejoined and the processionals mounted the exterior steps side by side, only to divide again, wind around the altar, and exit from the east door. How could such a procession have occurred? The Ara Pacis shrine, on which the reliefs are carved, did not exist. And even if, by Jupiter, it did, and if the architect followed the rule that an altar must face east, how could the "main door" be the one on the backside? Anyway, the procession is not moving toward either entrance. The head of the procession is near midway on the south side where Augustus is officiating. Nothing indicates that the procession passed through a structure, certainly not the Ara Pacis reconstructed as a shrine, for, to repeat, it did not exist in 13 BC, and, as I am relentlessly proposing, not in 9 BC either.

The author and the Tellus panel, at the east facade of the Ara Pacis shrine, 1992

12

THE TELLUS PANEL

The space/time organization of the Ara Pacis imagery to which I've been referring is structured by three concepts of time: 1) the frieze imagery as an event taking place in the present; 2) the panels depicting Aeneas sacrificing, and Mars with Romulus and Remus suckling the wolf-nurse, as specific events in Rome's history, however fictional they may be; and, 3), the panels representing Tellus and Roma as personified polar states of the Empire: its prehistory, or the earth before agriculture, represented by Tellus, and Rome's achieved status as the world's dominant empire by Roma.

The Tellus panel is the only controversial imagery on the monumen. A vast bibiliography debates who the woman personifies: Tellus, Ceres, Italia, Pax, Venus, or, in this era of polysemy, any combination of them, depending on how you interpret the imagery for your very own self. I attribute the polysemic confusion to an excess of faulty readings of the imagery that has moved through an excess of bibliography and dependence on poetry and on Greek, rather than Roman, source material.

Tellus' personification is seated on foliated rocks in a landscape setting with infants and fruit in her lap. Throughout the balance of my text I will maintain that she both personifies and symbolizes the pre-agricultural condition of the land, specifically agricultural soil, not forest floors, marshes, or wasteland. The setting for her in this relief is not farmland that would favor her identity as Ceres, but rocky grazing land bordered by a marsh and the sea. This place cannot represent the

[88] Detail. Center portion of the Tellus panel.

domain of Ceres, goddess of harvests, when decades before the Augustan era, Italian agricultural practice was highly developed as an industry. Yet time and again this panel is referred to as representing the fertility of the land, attested to by the fruits on Tellus' lap and the clump of plants to her left, not to mention the infants. But this panel cannot represent the bountiful plenitude of agrarian life under the reign of Ceres, or farming across the body of Italia, when there's not a sign of agriculture in it. Any farmer would die laughing should someone try to convince him that this bit of flinty land, a marsh, and a sea represents a return to lush and bountiful harvests under the reign of Augustus, as one after the other Romanist scholar, seduced by poetry, says it does.

The fruits and plants are pre-agricultural. Land gave those freely before Ceres taught men the techniques of seed management and crop farming. Moreover, not one plant species in the vegetative panels composing the lower register of decorative reliefs all around the shrine can possibly represent agriculture in such a way as to justify Horace's puff, "*tua, Caesar, aetas fruges et agros rettulit uberes*" (You, Caesar, brought back fruits and fertile fields). Other than grapes that neither Tellus nor Ceres provided mankind, but were a gift from the wine god, nothing portrayed in the relief is an agricultural crop. The grain heads are not of wheat but of barley, which is the primary, pre-agricultural genetic base of all cereal species that agriculture would develop as varieties of wheat and rye. Roman citizens ate bread made from wheat while people in poverty, prisoners, low-class slaves, and livestock ate barley. Soldiers who displayed cowardness, or committed misdemeanors, were put on barley rations—a humiliating diet, for barley was hog and chicken feed.

The Tellus relief setting calls to mind the sentiments of Virgil's herders Tityrus and Meliboeus. Tityrus says that only by the grace of god does his cattle browse, and he can play whatever tunes he likes on his country reed pipe. Meliboeus responds saying he won't begrudge him that pleasure, but he's amazed that, with such a flock of troubles worrying countrymen, he should feel at all content with his fare.

Meliboeus complains that his goats have no place to graze. "Look at this one", he says, "She can hardly move. In a hazel thicket she dropped her twin kids, the hope of my flock, but she had to birth them on bare flint." In turn, Tityrus laments that the city called Rome, which, in his ignorance he imagined as just the market town where shepherds herded their weanlings for sale, was in fact a rather awful place. "Rome carries her head above all other cities," he says. "Many a fatted beast I took there to sell to the temple. Many the rich cheeses I pressed for ungrateful townsfolk. Yet I never got home with much money in my pocket." He says he petitioned to the prince (Augustus) who granted him return of his land. At that, Meliboeus responds derisively (italics added):

> Fortunate old man!—so your acres will be yours still,
> They're broad enough for you. Never mind if it's *stony soil,*
> Or the *marsh films over your pasture land with mud and rushes.*
> At least no green vegetation will tempt your breeding ewes,
> And there's no risk of catching disease from a neighbor's flock.

This eclogue was written during Augustus' settlement of deactivated soldiers on confiscated farm and grazing land as part of his overall plan to resolve dissatisfaction among veterans, of which there were many thousands who had their land confiscated, mostly by senators, while they were away on battlefields. The displaced herder and small-plot farmer, with not enough acreage to farm profitably, was a popular literary motif and moral metaphor contrasting the lost virtues of old agrarian Italian life with the sordid state of urbanized Rome then teeming with the unemployed and uneducated, beggars, prostitutes, and internecine gangs. Because time and again the Tellus panel imagery is referred to as lush vegetation, attesting to Augustus' return of agricultural bountifulness, I will dwell for a few pages on the state of dirt farming and animal husbandry during the late Republican and early Empire decades.

Farming in Italy was not as highly developed as in several other countries to which Rome looked for imports. The peninsula had many swamps in the interior and in the Po Valley; numerous marshes were around Rome, including in the Campus Martius. One of Augustus' programs for rural redevelopment was in support of marsh drainage to add acres to Italy's dwindling top soil. Most of the peninsula's high land was rocky, with soil layers thinned over centuries of erosion and sheep grazing that followed deforestation. The soil in most areas north of

Campania was too poor in minerals to support field crops. Fertilization, widely and expertly used by the Gauls, came into practice almost too late in Italy. By the mid-second century BC, Italy had ceased being a self-sufficient grain-producing country. Wheat farming had become hardly profitable, causing marginal land to be set aside and grain fields converted to higher yielding cash crops, with oil-seed plantings, vineyards, horticulture, and market gardening the most profitable. Campania and Etruria were the only areas of the peninsula where grain farming continued on high-yielding acres of wheat, barley, spelt, and millet. By 70 BC, half the peninsular population depended on imported grain from Egypt, Sicily, and Sardinia, with most of Rome's wine coming from Greece.

Trade balancing was a perennial problem as Rome became increasingly industrialized. Lacking forests, ship builders looked to Turkey for pine masts and planking. From equally distant lands came materials for fabricating goods, implements, and machines. Cloth, carpets, and embroideries came from the east. From Egypt came linens, palm-wood, glassware, and papyrus. Spain was a source for metals, vegetable oils, and wool. Iron ore and massive drives of beef cattle came down the peninsula from the northern provinces. The lack of domestic wheat and uncertainty of sufficient importation from Sicily and Egypt was the catalyst for about every problem in the Roman economy.

Grain farming and livestock breeding were not admirable occupations. Both were labor intensive and of low yield per acre. Dirt farmers and herdsmen on marginal acres had been pushed down the scale to serfdom, however much eulogized for their proximity to nature. Among the rural bourgeois, crop hierarchy ranked a farm's status: the most prestigious were vineyards, market-gardens, osier beds, olive plantations, and citrus orchards. Less prestigious were cattle yards, sheep yards, and grain fields, while the meanest were oak tree plantations for acorns and hardwood on untillable land. Sheep and goat-grazing were for peasants on rugged, rocky terrain, such as one sees in the Tellus panel.

Impoverished farmers sold their land to the rich and sought work in urban centers, blending in with returning veterans, unemployed freedmen, and aged and abandoned slaves, all seeking social services and free grain. The metropolitan population was in the millions. To control this urban mass, dampen threats of uprisings, and deter thievery and looting of homes, shops, and warehouses, the Senate lowered grain prices year after year until grain was distributed free to the urban poor. So extensive was free grain distribution that Augustus restricted the number of people receiving it to two hundred thousand. One suspects that he would have solved part of Rome's overpopulation that was draining the state budget by letting them all starve, had prudence not warned him that opportunistic politicians would use the plight of the poor and unemployed to rally an insurgence.

Tellus is the land while Ceres is the cereal crop. The traditional separation of Ceres from Tellus occurs in April when the land has done its job and Ceres, who produces not plants but seeds, takes over when harvesting begins. In his calendar for the month of January, speaking of the festival that precedes sowing in early February, Ovid distinguishes Tellus from Ceres:

> Pray to Tellus and to Ceres, mother of grain. Tellus and Ceres discharge a common function. Ceres gives grain its vital force. Tellus gives grain its place to grow [*tellis, terra*]. They are partners in labor who reformed the days of old and replaced the acorns by food more rewarding.

As personified, Tellus is receptive to seed but cereal crops sprout and yield a rich harvest only when her body is properly seeded. Ceres taught men how to do that—an agricultural form of sex education. Ceres is the learning of agriculture, her gift the knowledge of agriculture. She had the power to refuse agricultural plants to grow, but no power whatsoever over pre-agricultural plants: grapes, poppies, wild flowers, thistles, oaks, willows, and other trees, or reeds and wild grasses, such as barley. When furious over Pluto's abduction of her daughter, Proserpina (the Roman Persephone), Ceres caused cereal crops to fail, but the natural plants of pre-agriculture continued growing and yielding their fruit. People were back to eating what Tellus before agriculture had provided freely. In a moment, I will tell in great detail how that situation came about.

The Roman Tellus and Ceres were modified extensions of the Greek Gaia and Demeter. Early Romans had adapted the rustic harvest goddess Demeter to fit their culture, blended with more ancient Italian agriculture gods. She was upgraded in 496 BC during a great drought when the sibylline books ordered the introduction of three deities: Ceres, Persephone (then named Libera), and Dionysus (then named Liber). This happened under the aegis of the farmers' grange, most likely as an economically driven political gesture to stimulate trade with Greece and its colonies. The ceremonial staging for Ceres' adoption was very Greek. Artisans from Greece built the first temple of Ceres. Itwas dedicated on a spur of the Aventine in 490 BC, with women of Greek extraction performing the dedication service in the Greek language. The temple had been planned and would be cared for by the plebeian aediles—sophisticated farmers, millers, traders, and overseers of the grain market.

Tellus was associated with Ceres as the two phases of cereal culture. On two consecutive market days, festivals were held in Tellus' honor at the end of the winter seeding period (usually in January). Simultaneously, the *paganalia*, a sowing festival, was celebrated in the countryside with a pregnant sow sacrificed to both Ceres and Tellus, whose combined functions generated the harvest. About this festival that marks Tellus retiring and Ceres taking over, Ovid wrote:

> Give rest to the earth with the sowing completed. Give rest to the men who tilled the earth. Let the district celebrate the festival, ritually purify the district, the farmers, and give the annual loaves to the hearths of the countryside. The mothers of crops, Tellus and Ceres [note the sequence], are pleased with their spelt [a primitive flour] and the innerts of a pregnant sow.

Long before the Augustan Age, agriculture in Italy, as in Sicily and much of Mesopotamia, had become highly developed. Learned farmers deployed double-plowing, crop rotation, seed hybridization, selective breeding of livestock, and castration of male animals and spaying of females to improve meat quality and produce oxen (this is as good a place as any to point out that the word "oxen" is misused by classicists. Oxen were, and still are, both male and female, but the males were castrated and most of the females were spayed. Oxen were not bulls, bullocks, or cows, but more like third-sex bovines put in harness for plowing and, along with mules, used for drayage. Oxen were bred to be exceeding large, heavy, big-boned, muscular, and very docile, hence the expression, "strong as a bull but dumb as an ox." Oxen were not substitutes for bulls or cows as proper sacrificial animals.The bovine in the Tellus relief is not an ox and not a cow; it's a bull).

The industrialization of crop farming, dairying, and meat production rendered the small farmer and herder as subsistence farmers rather than market producers. Cato's *De agricultura* promoted industrialized farming and modernization of animal husbandry as critical to a revitalization of Italy as an agricultural nation. Like Varro, who authored *Res rustica,* Cato was aware that it was economically essential to promote a national style of agriculture as noble work by human hands in order to dispel old Greek myths of agriculture as soft primitivism that reduced farmers to dependence on gods to do their farming. Crop farming and livestock management manuals had been provided since a century before when the senate ordered Punic manuals translated and distributed. Virgil's poetical treatise on agriculture, the *Georgics,* for all its sincerity over farming as a virtuous occupation for those who toil in the fields, as Hesiod had promoted centuries earlier, would have been of no value to farmers. As Seneca pointed out in *Epistula.* 86.15, Virgil wrote to please (*decentissime*), not to tell the truth (*uerissime*), to delight readers, not to teach farming. Real farmers would be nothing but amused over Virgil's recommendation of when to plant and when to harvest:

> This North Pole's always above us: the South appears beneath.
> The feet of darkling Styx, of the deep-down Shadow People.
> Here the great Snake glides out with weaving, elastic body
> Writhing river-like around and between the two Bears—
> The Bears afraid to get wet in the water of Ocean.
> At the South Pole, men say, either it's dead of night,
> Dead still, the shadows shrouded in night, blacked out forever;
> Or dawn returns from us thither, bringing the daylight back,
> And when sunrise salutes us with the breath of his panting horses,
> Down there eve's crimson star is lighting his lamp at last.
> Hence we foreknow the weather of the uncertain sky,
> The time to reap or sow.

Tellus reigned over the land and its natural plants, meaning the fruit of natural trees, shrubs and grasses. In the beginning, grazing animals—goats, sheep, cattle, horses, and deer—fed on natural pasturage, wild grasses, legumes, and shrub browse. Feral pigs fed on acorns, birds on seeds, beasts and fish on each other. Plants were Tellus' clothing. One could see and eat through vegetative layers to her nakedness. Her naked body is bare ground, vulnerable to sun-scorch and wind abrasion (one should not overlook that women's lingerie and dresses are often ornamented with floral designs, and that girls coming into sexual maturity are said to be flowering and destined to be deflowered). Still today, farmers speak of soil dressings and ground covers of mulch as undergarments for protecting Earth's body from hot summer suns and freezing winter air. Weeding prevents intrusion of bad seed, like fathers once weeded out unsuitable men courting their daughters.

In the pre-agriculture phase of ancient history, human populations were thin, scattered, and migratory. Vitruvius speaks of men in the old days as born like animals in forests, caves, and woods, passing their days without labor, feeding on natural foods of the land. He points out that agriculture could not happen until populations were organized to ward off raiding. Gods were needed: Janus, who could see the enemy coming, and Mars, who would defend the fields. Fortified hill towns would serve as both sentry stations and military outposts. That's when Cybele lent a hand as goddess of walled towns on hills. Most often worshiped on mountains—Mount Ida, Mount Siphlus—she was associated with caves overlooking fertile agricultural valleys.

The pre-agricultural state in Greek lore was fantasy. Humans and animals were motivated by impulse rather than intelligence. In the absence of science, nature was controlled by gods ("Acts of God" are stll today an insurance company's way of fending off claims of damage by earthquakes, tornados, and floods). In the olden days, man was not required to labor, but had only to gather nature's plenty and tend gentle herds and flocks. Hesiod was the first known writer to describe that primordial stage as the pre-iron age under Cronos, who was born of the union of Earth and Sky, who would be the father of Zeus, the Roman Jupiter. Life then was idyllic; natural forces were benevolent. But the Golden Age progressively deteriorated as inferior tribes mutated the naturalism of nature and lost virtue, the decline interrupted by a race of heroes, the great warriors who fought the Theban and Trojan wars. When revisited by the Augustan poets, Virgil, Horace, and Ovid,

Hesiod's theme underwent translation of the Greek word *genus* (race or generation) into the Latin *saeculum*, a fact of importance to my text, for while *saeculum* meant "a generation, an age, or a lifetime," it also meant "the spirit of the times," hence secular. The Greek *genus* was a stationary state, while the Roman *saeculum* was in motion. In the same sense, the Greek Golden Age was a fixed period of time, during which nothing changed, whereas the Roman equivalent was, like the seasons, a condition of periodic renewal following the general law of nature that everything degenerates unless rigorously maintained. That principle underscored Augustus' social policies, which were installed to restore the empire to a steady state of law and order, and maintain it as such.

Virgil's *Georgics* perfected the pre-labor state in pastoral form and condensed the expanse of the Golden Acres into a park-like Arcadia, even though Virgil subtely promoted a Stoic attitude defining human industry as relentless toil rewarded less by monetary gain than by pride and virtuous feelings. The *Aeneid* coincides with the achievements of Augustus that Horace eulogizes in his *Carmen saeculare*, celebrating the origins of the Roman Empire and its growth to world dominance under Augustus. Although based on Greek literary traditions, the *Aeneid*'s story line is thoroughly Roman as to motifs and morals, portraying Rome as a city built on destiny and greater Italy as a discreet nation of tribes gathered at Rome's feet. Virgil narrates this history along a continuous and glorious track, from Rome's founding to the promise of the Empire, to Augustus who brings the old age around to a new age of social order and prosperity, the *Pax Augusta*. The whole of Italy is consequential in the narrative: country set in contrast to city, rural compared with urban values, and the natural with the artful—what I will soon propose as the thematic play of Tellus against Roma, with the history of Rome represented by the Mars and Aeneas reliefs documenting the stretch of life that lay between them.

All myths are based on reality. Food gathering from vegetative nature and organized hunting were transitional to seed selection and crop management that define social group organization, just as selective human seed management (laws controlling marriage and child rearing) defines an aspect of civilization. When agricultural and civilized states regress and fall back into a pre-agricultural state, causalities are given over to acts of gods. But because the gods are fashioned by humans to replicate humans, as personifications of natural processes with whom humans can communicate, the behavior of deities can be influenced by thanksgiving sacrifices that originated in the act of returning seed to soil in order to be blessed with crops. Commensurately, among herding societies arose the practise of returning livestock as ritualized sharing.

Agricultural and social processes lent structure to the idea of progress but also to an awareness of potential regression, as when birds and locusts invade the fields and croplands go to weeds. When work becomes wearisome and social structures difficult to manage, one dreams of the pre-agricultural state of the earth, such as Horace's fantasy of abandoning Rome and sailing off to the Isles of Bliss, or when Virgil writes of the Arcadian condition, mentioning nymphs laden with baskets full of lilies, pale irises, poppies, narcissus, anise, cassia, marsh marigolds, blueberries, quince, chestnuts, waxy reed plumes—all pre-agriculture flora and fruits. In Arcadia, one is perpetually a youth; one loves but doesn't wed, tends flocks but doesn't labor. This sentiment is one of the many contradictions in Virgil's lines, as he struggles to maintain poetry while trying to be didactic and imbue the humdrum care of sheep and goats with dignity.

Here looms the distinction between nature and art, between poetry and prose, as between the religious and the secular. Early notions about art were summed up by the Aristotelian point of view that assigned art to any activity utilizing intelligence, reason, and skill—the natural as simplicity, the artistic as complexity. Cicero's *prima naturae* were basic impulses that developed into *ratio* through education and adherence to social moralities, with natural virtue furnishing the rudiments. The purpose of art was to move from those crude beginnings through progressive development until what the beginnings had projected is attained. One finds this scheme laid down beside the history of the Romans like a progressive yard stick: from rustic Italy to the high culture of the Augustan era, with achievements seeded in man's punitive state and nurtured in oracles and divinations, such that guided Aeneas during the early stages of Roman history, and would guide Augustus.

What I am saying here is simply what I've already said, and am likely to say again: Tellus is pre-art, while Ceres is the art of agriculture. Pre-art is a timeless and steady state, like Tellus on the Ara Pacis, while art is *ratio* in action, or motion. So it's a mistake to assign the Greek notion of a Golden Age to Republican and Early Empire Rome, just as it's unwise to substitute ancient Greeks gods, goddesses, and myths to fill in where knowledge of Early Roman and Republican information is lacking. Varro, Cato, Lucretius, Vitruvius, and Horace had a very different slant on primal mankind and the emergence of civilization than had Hesiod and Homer. To understand Roman history, the dynamics of secularization must come to the foreground, especially as to how the traditional religious beliefs and practises were respected at the same time when industry and politics supported secularization.

Here is Horace's theory of the origin of civilized behavior that substitutes a sense of reality for the old Grecian myths (*Satires* 120-142):

> When the first living creatures crawled forth upon the primal earth-dumb and unsightly beasts-they fought for their acorns and their lairs with finger-nails and fists, then with clubs, finally with weapons, until they discovered verbs and nouns by which they devoted themselves to ideas.

Now let us here a non-academic translation (Peter Levi) :

> When the first brutes crept on the first ground,
> Disgraceful herd without one meaningful sound,
> They fought with nail and fist for nut and bed,
> Then clubs and then with armaments instead.
> They then invented word and sound and sense,
> The town and law: so much for innocence.
> No more thieving and no adultery:
> Cunts had caused wars before Helen you see,
> But in those days they perished unrecorded
> In herds the big bull wholly overlorded,
> And law came from the fear of lawlessness:
> The ages of the world evolved like this,
> Nature knows not the unjust from the unfair
> Or how to deal out good, what to acquire
> Or what to flee, and reason is no use,
> With the same sin to steal young cabbages
> Or desecrate the gods of mysteries ...

On Tellus' lap are pomegranates, acorns, and grapes—all pre-agricultural, as are the plants clustered to her left: barley heads, Iris *germanica*, opium poppy flowers, pods, and leaves (*Papaver somniferum*), and a single flower head of arum (*Arum italicum*). The reeds to the left on the panel are Phragmites, or *Arundo donax*, the rampantly growing plant that still stifles the flow of Italian waterways. It's the great reed that is often seen in Mediterranean art and read about in classical literature—the tallest of the giant grasses, growing ten to twelve feet high in marshes and as high as twenty feet in sun-drenched shallows of slow streams. The bird at the left, supporting the nymph, or *hora*, is a swan. Beneath its flight line is a marsh. The overturned jug, on which a heron is perched, would represent a stream of fresh water issuing from the marshland.

The figures flanking Tellus are from the cast of minor deities visualized as nubile girls generally divided into nymphs of land, air, and water. Those of the sea are usually called Nereids, daughters of the old sea-god Nereus, while nymphs are associated with phenomena on land—the effects of air and water, like breezes and mist. Homeric hymns refer to Demeter as the bringer of *horae*, even though the sun would have called them forth and taken control of them, for without sun, vegetation will not grow and water from streams underground won't flow into daylight. One fragment of text by Euripides describes Helios as having hitched to his chariot of many fruits the harmony of the *horae* in their four shapes—the aura of seasons, not the seasons themselves. The Egyptian three-season cycle, which fit precisely to Egypt's climate, had some time ago given way in Italy to include winter, but the agricultural seasons remained as three: spring planting, summer tending, autumn harvesting.

The plants at Tellus' left form an unlikely bouquet—not a cornucopia, for the cornucopia, like the festoon, typically contains harvested fruits and seed [89]. In cases where the infant twins, Romulus and Remis, appear at the mouth of a cornucopia, the symbolism is not of their birth, as if the cornucopia were their mother's womb, but as their role as having seeded the Roman race. The male essence is the seed of plants, while the flesh of fruit is female. Acorns, figs, and nuts are male. Acorns, the fruit of the oak tree, resemble an infant boy's penis that will grow and harden (from little acorns, mighty oaks will grow). The oak tree, represented great and virile strength, was the tree of Jupiter.

Pomegranates, acorns, and grapes should not be associated with agriculture but with the natural fecundity of the earth. That holds as well for grapes: the grape vine was a gift of the wine-god, not of Tellus or Ceres. Acorns had no place in agriculture as other than pig-food, and were thought to have been the main diet of primitive people at the time when Aeneas founded Lavinium. In Virgil's *Eclogue X*, the exquisite Adonis of Arcadian bliss, while grazing sheep on tender grass beside a stream, was obliged to witness the vulgarity of swineherds soaking acorns in the water to prepare them as winter mash for their pigs. When Philostratus mocked the affectations of Arcadian yearnings, he dismissed the Arcadian poets as acorn-eating swine. Ovid casts back to Rome's origin in 753 BC to bring up Ceres as the first to offer food more tasty and nourishing than acorns.

> The sustenance of the first mortals was green plants that the earth [*tellus*] yielded without cultivation. They plucked grass blades from the turf and tender leaves from tree-tops. After that, the land [*tellus*] produced the acorn. Ceres was the one who invited man to better sustenance when acorns were exchanged for more useful food.

The child on Tellus' knee holds a pomegranate up to its mother. While apples are associated with seduction and sex, the pomegranate is associated with the breast and womb. It has a nipple-like protuberance rather than a recessed calyx, like the apple's. Its color is reddish; the redness deepens with maturity until the fruit splits open and discharges its seeds. Until discharged, each each seed is suspended in a jell-like red pulp, like one might envision premenstrual seed in a womb. The pomegranate had a biblical name, in Hebrew *rimmon* from *rim*, meaning "to give birth." It is the fruit of the African and Asian berry tree, *punica granatum*, its common name combining *pomme* with *grenate*, meaning "seedy fruit." Its shape may suggest to some the woman's breast, its juice her blood, or her womb as a sign for fecundity and caring love, explaining why this fruit was eaten by souls in the Greek and Latin underworld to hasten their rebirth. Persephone was induced by wily Pluto to taste of it, knowing that goddesses must not eat it. A natural food, it is appropriate only for mortals, its many seeds suggesting mortality, for what is seeded must have previously died. Eurydice, too, was detained in the

[89] Detail of the Tellus relief.

Underworld for having tasted a pomegranate. At Capaccio Vecchio near Paestum, Hera was worshiped as Our Lady with the Pomegranate. As queen of marriage—not herself a mother goddess—Hera sat enthroned with a child cradled by one arm and a pomegranate in her hand. Though historically late (still worshiped today at Paestum), the persistence of the theme proves its efficacy in earlier times when swollen poppy pods and pomegranate carpels could recall from deep history the belly of Tellus in her first form as Gaia. The seedy pomegranate and the seedy poppy were appropriate symbols of her well seeded womb.

The plants in the Tellus panel are not just a random assortment. The four species coincide with the three seasons of plant growth and maturity. The iris is represented with one flower stalk still partially sheathed, and another coming into full flower. This common variety of lily grew copiously in the the valleys and plains of northern Italy, and in the province of Gaul (becoming, in time, the French *fleur-de-lis*). A dry soil plant, this oldest cultivated iris flowers from May to June; its foliage wilts in mid-summer and disappears amidst grasses growing about it.

Irises and lilies of all varieties call to mind virginity and spring passion—beliefs that are well founded, since the iris root and the lily bulb send up new shoots spring after spring without need of being re-seeded; in that sense, they are perpetually virgin. Some Gallo-Roman texts refer to the virgin mother as Lily-Maid, like the Virgin Mary—her attribute a lily—who was held to be eternally a virgin. In one of Ovid's poems, Juno conceived her son Mars with the aid of a magic lily given her by Flora (perhaps acting out of annoyance at the birth of Athena without a father). Virgil writes of the long-stemmed lily as if it were a leggy girl. Juno's temple on the Capitaline was called Juno Moneta (the word for money derives from *moneta*), and the building adjoining Juno's temple was the government mint, where capital seed was made to inseminate Rome's economy. The Roman women's festival, the Matronalia, celebrated exclusively by women on New Year's Day, was called the Festival of Juno. Prayers were offered to her and her son Mars, after whom the first month of the New Year was named. Although the field guardian, Mars was also, by some traditions, the protector of women when in the woods or any wild place.

The opium poppy in the clump originated in Asia Minor and spread to Greece and Italy through trade. It blooms in full summer sun and goes to seed when the air and soil take on late-summer dryness. This strain of poppy was associated with peace of mind. Ovid writes of an impoverished woman who, strolling by her humble dwelling, picked a poppy that grew on the waste ground, tasted it forgetfully, and found that it stayed her hunger. The fourth plant, the Arum *italicum*, native to Italy, flowers in April and early May. It is related to the amaryllis and often confused with the mandrake. It grows in shaded and very rich, moist soil of the kind where Persephone was playing when Pluto abducted her. The Arum's flower stalk emerges hesitantly in early spring after wintering in the underworld, so the plant is easily associated with death. Its bloom resembles a milkweed pod split at the seam, like a parting vulva. Without fully opening, the flower dies, and nothing seems left to the plant until autumn when the leaves sprout but without a flowering stem and only for a short time. The separation of the flower from its parent calls to mind the separation of Persephone from her mother, Ceres. During that separation no useful plants grew but wild ones did, for they were the produce of Tellus, not of agriculture, just as wild girls are not morally fruitful (I might as well add here than historians of the Ara Pacis fail to distinquish between botany and horticulture, which are distinctly different professions. Botanists study natural plants, the plants of Tellus' primal state. Horticulturists are attuned to Ceres, for horticulture is concerned with non-natural propagation: hybridization, grafting, espaliering, and the development of new and improved varieties. Agriculture is not associated with botany but with the cereal and other field crop farming categories of horticulture. Plantsmen of all ages are horticulturists in that sense).

The marsh plants at the left in the panel would perhaps not have had symbolic value, but only to picture a marsh. New shoots of the reed appear at the lower left; a mature cane rises and bends in the breeze. Phragmites is associated with both the marshy sources of streams and aged rivers like the Arno. Its foliage hides danger. Predators lie in wait in the reeds to threaten those walking along stream banks; it harbors satyrs that prey on carefree nymphs and maidens coming to fill water jugs. In Roman art one sees the giant reed as cover and brood-dens for wild pigs. I've illustrated a marvelous Imperial relief from a fountain in Praeneste depicting a brood-sow sheltered among reeds [90]. There one also sees the stalks' terminal plumes that confirm my identification of the plant in the Tellus panel. It can be associated with the marshes of the Field of Mars itself that fed the largest of the streams flowing from the Quirinal to become the pool and baths of Agrippa. Plumes of these reeds were often affixed to warriors' helmets as symbols, perhaps, of the Martian field, and as camouflage when lying in ambush.

On the same fountain appear two other reliefs, one depicting a lioness with cubs in a rocky shelter, the other sets up a contrast between natural animals and those raised under animal husbandry [91, 92]. Representing the latter is a ewe with her lamb in a walled sheep yard, the stone wall nicely laid up in contrast to the arbitrary rockiness of the lion's den. The yard is furnished with a sheep shed, the door open, offering shelter, and with fresh spring water, symbolized by the overturned jug. While contrasted, the reliefs join in dispensing a message that the care a feral animal gives its young must be observed as well when caring for domesticated stock.

The swan on the Tellus panel has been a problem in interpretation. So determined that the bird was a goose, one early art historian suggested orthopedic modification of its neck to reduce the length. But even if we allowed the artist license to elongate a goose's neck to that extreme length, we would have to admit that no other element of the panel's imagery is exaggerated. The undulating neck might just as charitably be taken as the artist's effort to make sure it is seen as a swan, for in flight the swan's neck is fully extended, straight out. It's flight over a marsh recalls and perhaps can be explained by Lucretius, who writes of the waters of the marshes, of the tripartite composition of the world, as in the Tellus panel: "Look at the sea, the earth, the sky, their triple nature and their three structures." When he says "sky" he does not mean air. Air could not be seen; it had to be represented as what is between earth and sky. Lucretius offers a secular explanation for non-perceptible air that supports the flight of birds. Mist rising from marshes turns into air, he says. A bird flies by opening its wings, flapping to gain forward speed, then being lifted by the updraft of new air. This explanation was no doubt taken as plausible, for it also explained soaring birds that need not flap wings except to accelerate. It explained how moisture from the marshes passes as air over the land and falls out of evaporation as rain—the rain water going down into the earth, or entering rivers that replenish the sea, only to rise again as swamp water becoming mist.

Swans were to the ancient Romans what the vulture was to the Egyptians, what spy and weather satellites are to us now. Like the vulture and the hawk, the swan could foresee the future. High-flying when migrating to its summer breeding grounds in the distant North, it could see vast distances. The swan was sacred to Apollo, the far-seeing god—Augustus' personal deity. Apollo was introduced into Roman religion as a god of healing, for like the swan, he could foresee death and thus help prevent it. This oracular power promoted him to the rank of a god of prophecy. In Virgil's texts, he figures as the god of oracles—credibly so, for Roman history was the fulfillment of prophecy. Apollo's use to Augustus was as a god of economic health, of a healthy empire, but also as a seer, an advisor god. Augustus transferred the Sibylline Books of prophecy from the custody of Jupiter on the Capital to the Temple of Apollo that he'd erected in the Forum after declaring that the source of Sibyl's foreknowledge was Apollo.

Reliefs from a fountain at Praeneste. Early Imperial.

[90] *Left:* Ferel sow with litter. Palestrina, Museo Barberianano

[91] *Below left:*Lioness with cubs. Ewe with lamb. Vienna, Kunsthistorische Musem.

92] *Below right*: Ewe with lamb. .Vienna, Kunsthistorische Musem.

Nothing of the foregoing submits that the swan in the Tellus panel represents Apollo, or says that the swans high up in the decorative panels on the exterior lower register of the Ara Pacis walls are symbols of him or of Augustus' reign. Those swans most likely mean "air" in the Lucretian sense. Because air cannot be seen, it must be visualized by some representation suggesting it. Just as fish imply water, swans suggest air. Egyptian painters differentiated the waters of the Nile from that of the delta and the sea by putting crocodiles in the water. Waterfowl among reeds identify the delta. The swan in the Tellus panel may represent the retreat of winds from the land; the sea dragon, a retreating sea.

Tellus on the Ara Pacis shrine is not merely auxiliary to a narrative, as she appears in the *Gemma Augustea* or on the breastplate of the *Augustus from Prima Porta* [93]. In those examples, she is represented as Virgil describes her in *Georgics II* – her body open to receive fruitful showers (seeding, insemination). She lies prostrate, or propped on an elbow; although she's with children, she is not mothering. Her sole function is to be furrowed and seeded, and to grow seed within her body. She cannot rebel with earthquakes, floods, or droughts: those powers belong to the male power gods. Even Gaia could not push off Uranus. Her plight over being overseeded was assuaged by the act of her son, Chronos, whom she called upon to castrate her husband. By contrast, the

[93] The breastplate of the Augustus from Prima Porta. Tellus at lower center.

[94] Raphael, *The Alba Madonna*. National Gallery of Art, Washington D.C.

Tellus of the Ara Pacis is upright and attentive to her babies—a secular mother. Here is a Lucretian version of the ever-compliant Tellus:

> In spring, Earth yearns and cries for the life-giving seed. Then the lord omnipotent of Sky descends in fruitful showers into the lap of his laughing consort and mingles with her mighty body, nourishing her fruits. Bountiful hand breaks into birth. The fields unbosom to wavering breezes of the West. Eerywhere delicate moisture overflows, and the grasses dare trust themselves to spring suns.

The Augustan image of Tellus enhances her status by an aura of actual motherhood. The infant, holding up to her a pomegranate, will reappear in Renaissance art under similar social conditions, with the infant holding up an apple to his mother, the apple to redeem Eve and the original sin. The Virgin Mary's Byzantine status as Queen of Heaven is brought down to earth as a Madonna of Humility, as portrayed in Leonardo da Vinci's *Madonna of the Rocks* and Raphael's *Alba Madonna* [94]. Caritas, the nurturing mother, is the goddess that most likely governed how the Tellus panel was interpreted when discovered in the sixteenth century. A century later, the Roman sculptor, Bernini, fashioned Tellus as Caritas on the tomb of Urban VIII in Saint Peter's (Bernini was a true successor to the sculptor of Tellus, with consideration given to the fact that the panel was somewhat reworked in the late sixteenth century. We do not know to what extent it was altered, if at all. Bernini

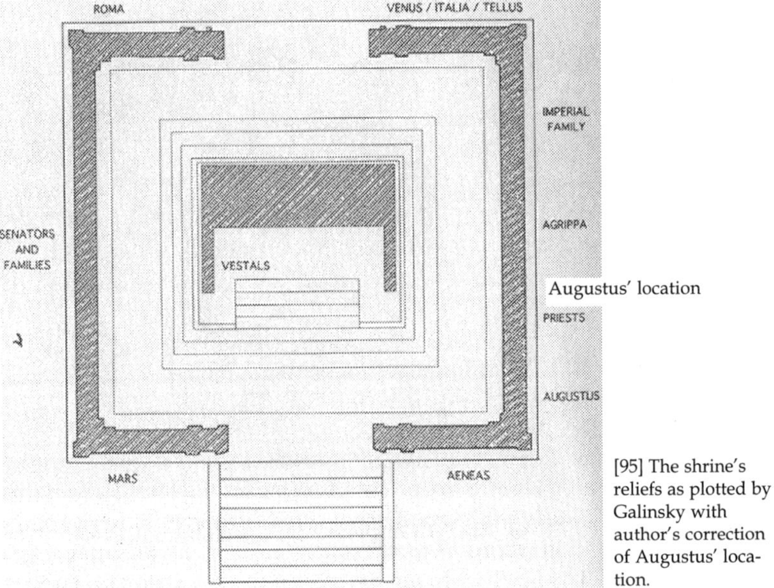

[95] The shrine's reliefs as plotted by Galinsky with author's correction of Augustus' location.

brought Renaissance sculpture to a fresh beginning with his first masterpiece, *Aeneas and Anchises*, then *The Rape of Proserpina* and *Apollo and Daphne*).

Like the *Alba Madonna* and Bernini's *Caritas*, no literary explanation is required for Tellus as we see her, as one must bring to the Lupercal and Aeneas panels. To read them one needs to know the story in order for the imagery to make sense. The Tellus imagery differs. Tellus fuses the human situation with divine significance into one visionary entity that is indivisable by any logic of narrative. Tellus does not communicate to her beholders, and what she sees in the infant's eyes is herself. She is a self-representation, within her own sphere, not given over to a narrational episode.

The Aeneas panel is often taken as the most important of the four endwall reliefs because it's to Aeneas that Augustus traced his royal lineage. Torelli and Galinsky pledge their interpretation of the Ara Pacis's iconography on the Agustus's image being "right around the corner" from Aeneas. But Augustus' location is not even close to the corner, and between him and Aeneas are lictors that have turned to face him, indicating that Augustus had arrived at the point where he is standing and is not about to continue in the same direction when concluding whatever he is doing. Reading around the corner doesn't make sense. And it doesn't help scholarship to ease Augustus closer to that corner than he is. Galinsky diagramed Augustus' position as 1/8th of the south frieze's length from the corner, when his actual position is 1/3rd of the way.[63] Here I reproduce his diagram with my correction [95], and later I will make a point of saying that the processional friezes bear no relation, as to their placement, to the east and west panels, not even to the entranceways.

Still, I will not ignore that the mythical Aeneas was to Julius Caesar what Caesar would be to Augustus. Both traced their royal lineage to Virgil's gift of creating history by devising believable myths. Aeneas was the creation of Virgil as set forth in the *Aeneid*. The story behind the Aeneas panel is the prophesy that, on fleeing Troy and making his way to the Italian peninsula, Aeneas would know the right place to found Lavinia when coming upon thirty piglets under an oak tree. Romulus' founding of Rome came earlier than Aeneas establishing Lavinium and the Roman race, so the left panel on the west side precedes in historical time the right panel. In the *Aeneid* one reads the prophecy of Apollo:

> I give you signs: hold them fast in your mind.
> For in your search, when you find
> beside the waters of a secret stream,
> along the banks beneath ilex branches,
> a huge white sow stretched out upon the ground
> together with a newly delivered litter
> of thirty suckling white pigs at her teats,
> that place will be the site for your city;
> that place will bring rest from all your toils.

As the story went, Virgil's origin of Rome as a fusion of god and country was having Mars seduce Rhea Silva, the daughter of the king of Alba Longa (the chief city of the Latin League). Virgil must have made up the girl's name. Rhea Silva combines Rhea, who was the wife of Cronos, the couple that gave birth to the Titans, and *silva* meaning a dense wood or forest, the density implying abundance, or plenty, which seems appropriate, as from Silva's womb will come the entire Roman race. When Amulius, the last of the early Roman kings, ousted his brother, Numitor, he forced Silva, who was Numitor's only child, to become a Vestal so she would remain a virgin and not produce an heir to the throne. But Silva was already pregnant (certainly not by Mars). I would imagine that, to cover up and not expose the father, she claimed she had been seduced by Mars, which in ancient times, and not so ancient times, was a common excuse for an otherwise unexplainable pregnancy (one need only think of Leda and the swan, the rape of Europa, and so on).

Silva gave birth to the twins Romulus and Remus. Her *post partum* reward was King Amulius' throwing her into prison and the babies into the Tiber. Silva must have survived, for some time later she was known as Ilia, meaning from Illium (Troy). Some accounts say she was also thrown in the river, where she comingled with the river god, Tiber, becoming his wife, hence *uxorius*. The twins, on washing ashore, were discovered by a she-wolf that carried them to her den (the Lupercal) where she nursed them. At some point during this nursing phase, the royal hunter Faustulus discovered them, and with his wife, Acca Larentia, raised them to maturity. When ready for revenge, the twins led an army against Amulius, decimated him and his forces, then restored Numitor to the throne of Alba Longa. With that deed accomplished, they set out to create a new settlement at the place where they'd washed ashore. At some point in the eighth century BC, that place, situated on the Palatine hill, became Roma, named after Romulus, who had killed his brother, thus getting the story back to a single originator (all start-ups are from a number one).

Because Rhea Silva was from the Trojan family of Aeneas, Aeneas could be fixed as well to Augustus' family tree. Mars, the father of Romulus, would then be a divine ancestor. Venus enters the picture as Mars' love for her. As the reputed mother of Aeneas, her identity as Venus Genetrix (literally, "she who brings forth") was added to her basic qualities. Julius Caesar devised that role in 46 BC on the occasion of his dedicating a temple to Venus in the Forum Iluium. Venus then became honored as the mother of the Julian family, the universal mother of the Roman race. Her inducements for women to forsake virginity, and Mars' valor in consummating marriage, were the basic Love and War aspects of marriage. Virgil needed a way to introduce divine blood into the lineage that would lead to Augustus. Since the blood line started with Anchises at the time of the Trojan War, the geneology had to start with him. What more suitable diety to pair with him than the ultimate seductress but forever virgin, Venus. To consummate that connection of Venus with Anchises, Venus had to transform herself into an earthly woman, for gods were forbidden to have sexual relations with humans. As I mentioned earlier, Venus' divine virginity would not be lost if the child was born of a human surrogate. Apparently, Anchises was led to think he was making out with the divine Venus (a reasonable assumption), for he bragged about it later, causing Zeus to strike his leg and render him crippled (Freud would explain that leg disabling in quite a different fashion).

Augustus needed a Venus Genetrix to unify his sovereignty with Roman history. He had no obligations to Zeus' rules against gods seducing earthlings, considering Zeus' own proclivities. Augustus' successor, Tiberius, would need a Venus Genetrix as well. This myth of divine descent was fragile, however, for it was a Republican pedigree-myth. In time it would run out with Hadrian and Antoninus Pius for the simple reason that by then the Republican families had entirely died off.

13

THE PERILS OF POLYSEMY

For all that denies it being so, the personification I'm calling Tellus is time and again referred to as Venus, and even more often as Ceres. In the German translation from Latin that is widely used for an English translation of Horace's passage from the centennial hymn (the *Carmen Saeculare*), *tellus* is named Tellus. Here I will repeat that triad:

Fertilis frugum pecorisque tellus
Spicea donet Cererum corona;
Nutriant fetus et aquae salubres
Et Iovis aurae.

Let Tellus, rich in crops and cattle,
deck Ceres with a cereal crown.
May Jove's wholesome breezes and rains
give nutriant to the newborn.

But in English translations from Latin, *tellus* is usually translated simply as "earth." That is correct, but only if taken to mean soil, not the planet. When tellus is not translated as Tellus, Ceres stands out in the passage and Tellus is suppressed. Yet Horace does not fuse the names: his Ceres is not Tellus. Here I will repeat that Ceres provides only the cereal crown, the grain heads, as the harvestable crop. She is the goddess of cereals, not of the soil in which vegetation grows, for soil is Tellus' body as both *terris*, meaning the territory (Italy), and *tellus*, meaning the land as an agricultural surface.

The title of Horace's centennial hymn is *Phoebe silvaumque*. Here again one encounters Silva, as *silva*, meaning, literally, a dense wood. Phoebe is Diana of the woods and the sister of Phoebus (Apollo the Bright, the Seer). In another of Horace's odes (Book IV.15), this one to Phoebus alone, peace and plenty are joined. The poem is titled *Phoebus volentem* (Apollo of good tidings). The first stanza is given to agriculture:

> *Tua, Caesar, aetas. Fuges et agris rettulit uberes* (Your age, Augustus, has brough a return of rich harvests and fertile fields).

The "plenty" to which Horace refers is only metaphorically the wealth of agricultural harvests. The gold crown as golden grain (*corona spicia*) is exalted both as headband and coinage, acknowledging wheat as both cereal and money. Surely the wheaten crown that Horace asks to be placed on Ceres' head—while a metaphor for the fruitfulness of agriculture—is an overdetermined symbol for wealth-in-plenty, grain having been for centuries a reliable stock-in- trade. Wheat and barley were currency in many ancient cultures and, at least symbolically, in the most sophisticated places today. (The honorarium for an article published in the British art journal, *The Burlington Magazine*, is an amount equivalent to the market value of two bushels of wheat. And the tuition for a course in Harvard University's Extention School, by the order of its endower, is based on the current price of wheat. Over the years of my publishing in the *Burlington*, I earned eight bushels, and the attendance in my several 1960s extension classes at Harvard added several wagon loads of grain to the university's budget). Still today, money is referred to as bread; the wages of the husband and father are to put bread on the table; the wife's womb is her breadbasket. Horace's poem should not be taken literally, as if Augustus' reign was destined to restore the agricultural lands of Italy to abundant wheat production. No amount of fertilizing showers could do that. Jupiter would be wasting his semen. The "Over amber-waves of grain," line in *America the Beautiful*, sung a million times in 2001 after the World Trade Tower atrocity, had nothing to do with wheat.

The Tellus panel tells more about itself than one can gain from the poets, for poetry does not subsist on the banalities of truth, nor did Greek art, with few late exceptions, mostly pornographic. Whether serving propagandists or enjoying the freedom of release from the restraints of Hellenic classicism, Roman artists and the truly Roman writers seized upon physical and material presence to represent an art more accessible than poetic play with words. The deep tradition underlying Roman art was illustration rather than an aesthetic based on the perfect human body as representative of beauty. Roman art expressed ideas by being literate, more explanatory than poetry and much less governed by ideals. As a nineteenth-century art historian, I cannot help but associate the likes of Courbet, Daumier, and Daubigny, in the context of academic classicism, with the cutting edge artists of Republican and Imperial Rome. And one must not ignore that the artists were dealing with prolem of art, not with the politics of their commissioners.

Artists' imagery had to be presented as seen all at once, even if segregated by sequential panels, as on the Ara Pacis shrine, while poetry flows word by word, thought by thought, with visualization up to the reader. The artisan-illustrator's work comes pre-visualized, from which condition the viewer can extract poetry through the recognition of similes, symbols, and allegories. As an entry into the Tellus panel's imagery, the beholder would see a woman with children, fruit on the woman's lap, and plants and pastured animals nearby, one standing for herds, the other for flocks. The picturing could be left at that, just as Raphael's *Alba Madonna*, or Leonardo's *Madonna of the Rocks*, can be grasped simply as a devoted mother to two youngsters in an idyllic landscape. To get at the first level of meaning, one needn't know that the woman gave virgin birth to a boy who would one day be crucified on the cross held in his hand, which is structurally the same as the infant on Tellus' lap holding out a pomegranate, acknowledging its mother's womb that signs for promise, and thus auguring well for Rome.

Through customary viewing of art around them in their daily lives, other beholders of the Tellus panel would recognize the woman and the *horae* as personifications, and would know that dragons with equine heads and webbed wings inhabit the sea and swans the air, with as much credibility as Christians today accept angels with wings. Some viewers might connect up the tripartite world—earth, air and water—and expand the woman into Terra Mater or Ceres and the two children into representations of human progeny. And they might reflect on the fruit, plants, bull, and lamb, as rural. The imagery could have variable meanings with interpretation open to variable receptions. But this does not imply that the program for the imagery was polysemic to the extent of sprouting every sort of seed planted in the same field.

How does one perceive an intention that was intended not to be intentional? To claim that the programmers of the Ara Pacis shrine intentionally imbued this panel with multiple meanings is no further from promoting absolutes than saying they intended for the imagery to have but one meaning. Confusion must not be given rational status by saying the multiplicity of meaning was intentional; layering one meaning after another onto something for which a meaning is not known results in nothing more than an obligation to confess no knowledge whatsoever of its meaning. And to believe that a work of art, in this case the Tellus relief, finds its meaning only through the eyes of the beholder is to regress from an adult way of relating oneself to the world to a child's way of relating the world to itself.

When description falls short, there is no defense against faulty interpretation. Say that the woman herein called Tellus is "surrounded by children, animals, and lavish vergetation" and one can associate her with the renewed prosperity of Augustus' reign. Call the round fruits on the woman's' lap apples when they are pomegranates, call the swan a goose, and the iconography opens up to an array of interpretations centered on Venus. Call the woman Pax and the door opens wider by introducing Eirene. Then Peace as peace of mind, peaceful sleep, and "sleep in peace," get entangled with peace as a nation not at war. Call the woman Ceres and the distinction between Ceres and Tellus collapse onto each other.

To my knowledge no one has asked why it is that only the Tellus panel offers the sort of polysemy that is boasted for the altar's iconography. Were I to call Aeneas anyone but Aeneas, or Mars anyone but Mars, every Romanist would be up in arms. As for the personages in the processional friezes, they are not going to a masquerade ball. If Aeneas can be no one other than Aeneas, and Mars no one other than Mars, why does Tellus have to be every mother figure that one can think of?

Mother images were specific: Ceres was the mother of Proserpina, Venus the reputed mother of Aeneas (her motherhood created by Julius Caesar, not by sexual intercourse with Anchises), while Tellus was the mother of herself, for earth is the *prima forma*; an origin can only be sungular. The difference of course is that, as one moves from the identity of a physical individual to a personification, materiality yields to spirituality. Spirits are functional: every god is the god of a function, whether Janus as sentinal, Apollo as all-seeing, Venus as love-inducer, or Vulcan as arms maker. When functions are confused, the gods are confused, as when seeding and harvesting are taken to be one and the same thing, or when sexuality is confused with fecundity.

I am not arguing that proper names are in every case rigid designators, only that the search for identity of an image through accurate description must allow the image to controll the search, with description constituting the identifiable sense of the proper name. One needs a sufficiency of properties to support belief that the proper name signs for an individual identity. But in the case of the Tellus panel, the image is usually layered with information coming not from the elements as pictured in the relief but from beholder-suppositions based on imagery that's outside the relief. And because those suppositions vary from one beholder to another, it is unwittingly assumed that the imagery was intended to be imprecise, as if God created the elephant so its anatomy would fit to any one of the blind men's description and interpretation of an elephant—an elephant like a tree (its legs), like a giant snake (its trunk), like a rope (its tail). To say that an elephant is like all those things isn't saying much of use to zoological taxonomy: elephants are not rooted in soil; an elephant doesn't slither and can't be made into a noose. While attributive descriptions of the elephant may be partially true as to similes and metaphors, the referential conclusion as to reality is not.

A fundamental problem with the polysemic approach to the "truth" is that the quality of any interpretation depends on the accuracy and extent of description; "accuracy" is not of the work but of the interpreter. Accuracy of description (*ekphrasis*) was a characteristic of Hellenistic landscape painting that found favor with sophisticated Romans. Houses and villas were decorated with detailed descriptions of nature. The thrust of the Roman education system was to render perceivable things as specific things. The Roman school system, with reading and writing taught to children seven years and up, was to prepare them for real, rather than religious, life. An industrialized society depended on a literate work force and a literate clientele. To be effective within a variegated population, education had to be secular; to be consistent as to knowledge about things as physical within the operation of physical systems (*de rerum natura*), education had to be kept separate from religion. Then varieties of religious belief could continue as belief systems within a heterogeneous society, as in the Western world today when a school system must embrace students from all religions and not promulgate a single one.

Urbanites with romantic feelings about rural and seaside life (not having grown up in such environments, not having come to know things by cultural osmosis) needed specifics—true to life forms identified, and proper names for real things, like guidebooks to birds, plants, and mushrooms. The panels making up the lower zone of the Ara Pacis shrine abound in identifiable plants and creatures—birds, lizards, scorpions, snakes, grasshoppers, snails—that Cartriota carefully and exhaustively identified and photographed, while offering examples in other media and at different times, especially on silverware and grave stones. In wall paintings from Pompeii and Herculaneum, one sees identifiable details. Doves can be distinguished from wood pigeons; differentiated are the song thrush, titmouse, and golden oriole; plants are specific as to roses, oleander, lemon blossoms, viburnum, myrtle, cherry blossoms, daisies.[64] To search for didactive symbolism in every aspect of this kind of imagery, as in the Ara Pacis' floral panels, works against the grain of Roman art that, in line with real economics and social planning, increasingly embraced the real world. As Otto Brendel wrote when addressing this subject, "One must distinguish between narratives with veiled allegorical intent and simple decoration."[65] This means, of course, that overinterpretation risks being as serious a misrepresentation of meaning as does arbitrariousness.

This raises the issue as to how much interpretation can be read into the vegetative panels on the Ara's shrine. John Elsner has taken a hard look at what he calls David Castriota's "single-minded devotion to the altar's abundant floral decorations," to what Castriota calls "the single most widespread mode of ancient decorative art" justifying his claim that "to the ancient spectator, familiar with the accepted lore and tradition of divine symbols and attributes, it was the various plants and other emblems that disclosed the sense and nuance of the monument." In other words, the Ara Pacis "is only fully intelligible in terms of its Classical and Hellenistic prescedents."[66] In my opinion, Castriota gives infinitely more credit to the ancient spectator and not enough to himself for having catalogued the symbols and attributes he claims the public would recognize and understand. He assumes that the massive amount of antecedents available to the research historian was in the eye of those who, in their own time, beheld the Ara Pacis. But no one back then had at hand the 627 bibliographic endnotes that Castriota amassed in his book. The altar's beholders did not see as art historians; that is, their eyes did not trace the hundreds of Hellenistic roots that Castriota finds nourishing the decorations, any more than my ancient grandmother could recite the history of wallpaper cabbage-roses that ornamented her parlor, however much they gave her a pleasurable sense of abundance. The question that begs an answer when confronted by such historical excursion into intelligibility is: Intelligible to whom? Surely, the historian's intelligibility, like an eagle's optical scan of an entire valley, cannot say that the rabbit far below sees as much. Art historians can never say truthfully what anything meant at the time of its meaning. Those who are willing to admit that art history is itself an autonomous mass of evolving data that undergoes its own history will never claim that they write the absolute truth about the past.

The current fashion of believing that all texts (words, images) are polysemic—open to anyone's sense of their meaning (or interpretation of meaning)—runs counter to the flow of language studies in ancient Rome. Varro's twenty-five volumes on the Latin language, completed about 43 BC, were dedicated to the precision of words. He was concerned above all with whether linguistics was governed by analogy or anomaly, whether there are immutable regularities and rules for the formation and inflection of words. To know the name of an image is to know what it is, he wrote. To communicate with a god, one needed to know the god's correct name. Augustus, himself, was concerned with the correctness of words as to signification. He engaged the ex-slave Verrius Flaccus, author of *On the Significance of Words*, to oversee his grandson's education. Inspired by Varro, Flaccus was the first to create a dictionary listing words alphabetically rather than by topic, and so giving each word independence from a class of subject matter; a diamond could be a diamond rather than another sort of rock. Roman realism is extricable from this dictionary sense: each word looking and meaning what it represents. The fourth-century BC Xenophon was so concerned about appropriate words that in his *Art of Hunting* he listed almost fifty names just for hunting dogs. Varro expressed the same care for accuracy, saying, for example, that an angus lamb is so named because it is *agnatus*, born as an addition to a flock. That proper identification allowed one to talk about a lamb as a lamb, which is neither ewe nor ram, and about a bovine that is a bull, not an ox.

Roman prayers were precise and formal. To be effective the deity had to be properly identified, as were personages when represented in portraiture. To be the person, you had to look like that person; to be called upon as a god, you had to look like that god.To impose polysemy on Roman imagery is to force the Roman artists back to Plato, regressing them to belief that the world is one word and everything in the world just different names, such as many gods as aspects of the one god. Cicero was aggressively, if only humorously, opposed to the notion that the entire earth was god. In his *On the Nature of the Gods*, published in 45 BC, he wrote:

> Then again the earth, as it is part of the universe, would also be part of this god. But we see vast expanses of the earth that are uninhabitable deserts. Some of these parts are scorched by the all too near approach of the sun, while others, remote from the sun, are frozen solid. So if the world is one god, and the deserts and cold places are parts of the world, it must follow that god is roasted in one part and frozen in another.

Of course a visual text that's appropriate at one time to one population can shift to what works as meaningfulness in favor of another. But changes in meaning that a work of art's subject undergoes over time does not change the work of art or the history of its conception. So the professional art historian must ask: What sort of history is being made today? Are we dedicated to understanding the past or only to investigate and analyze various ways of understanding it, like the joy of sex and the Kama Sutra having nothing to do with procreation, but only with variations of erotic pleasure.

I am obliged to bring in an example of where polysemy leads when carried to its ultimate and disastrous effect on education, in this case about the Ara Pacis. Art historian Minott Kerr proposes that two radically different contextual interpretations of the monument's iconography can be equally valid because "interpretation depends more on who is doing the interpreting than on what is being interpreted." Two essays are cited: one by Natalie Kampen, the other by Peter Holliday. Neither one, this historian says, "is marred by factual or logical errors, so one cannot say that one is bad, the other good."[67] Unfortunately for Kerr's argument, her own essay is racked with assumptions taken as facts and errors in reading the architecture, so it wouldn't make much difference whether Kampen or Holliday's essays were good or bad. And it doesn't help Kerr's defense of just any willy-nilly interpretation being valid when she takes Aeneas to task for "getting it all wrong" when he examines and interprets the temple of Juno in Carthage. A good rule to follow when confroted with equally valid interpretations is to recocognize that, if equally correct, they are equally incorrect.

It doesn't take much creativity to recognize real objects in a real place and time, or in a sequence, grid, or lattice, when one has a text or time line to follow, as in art history surveys. The Aeneas panel's imagery is easy to decipher because it illustrates a specific event in a story. The character cannot be extracted and replaced by an alternate personage who might generate an alternative interpretation. The Tellus panel imagery differs: its subject matter is given as an allegory built around a personification rather than a narrative into which the imagery precisely fits. The most identifiable aspects of it lend structure to the whole while suppressing alternative readings that might corrupt the allegorical matrix. The fact that the imagery is allegorical prevents identification of its elements from imposing absolute meanings should one fail to understand the reality base for the allegorical contents. It is incumbent on the art historian to search for that reality base as to its identifying ingredients, just as to know how to fit the *ara Pacis Augustae* pieces together, one had to excavate the foundation.

Before taking up in greater detail the reality-based determinates that favor Tellus and preclude Venus and Pax as the personification that I'm calling Tellus, I will explore the second quality, or aspect, of *tellus*, namely the word *terris*, from which is derived the English word "territory." The *terris* I'm referring to is, of course, the Italian peninsula.

The Tellus panel has impressed some scholars to think that the topography it pictures would identify the woman as Italia positioned symmetrically with Roma.[68] To grasp this topography, one reads from the inland marsh across grazing lands to the sea, which would correspond to Italy's interior marshlands from which rivers flow seaward. The *hora* on the swan flies toward the interior mountains, where fierce winds are stored in caves, while the *hora* on the seahorse heads offshore, both leaving the land in peace. This topographical landscape mode is familiar from Egyptian and Alexandrian art, particularly the Nilotic landscape.[67] The Nile lent itself to that form of narrative because, like a story line, it is linear. Events happen along its banks, which explains why the Nile is still a favorite cruise, for cruises are narratives, whether cruising dating bars or the Internet. The fifth-century BC Greek historian, Herodotus, was delighted to report a discovery that the Nile originated in Ethiopia. The Nile could then be visualized as a single river with an origin, ending, and distinct cross-section, making it a geological narrative. Its exceptionally fertile riverbed is flanked symmetrically by rising hills, and beyond them desert. One side is the East, where the sun rises and the gods dwell; the other side, the West, is where the sun dies each night and where Death resides.

The ease with which a natural-looking setting combines objects as attributes of a landscape—crane, jug, sea-horse, the reed bending in the breeze—favors an Alexandrian hand for the Tellus relief. In the Carthage version of the relief, a frog serves to identify a swamp, and Posidon and dolphins assure that the body of water is the sea. The *Nile* in the Louvre [76, p. 101] combines the river's personification with carvings around its base: a bird on a crocodile's tail, a bull and a hippo ornamented with water plants. Herodotus tells a story of an Egyptian artist wanting to depict a naval battle between the Egyptians and Persians at the Nile's delta. Finding that painted river water looks just like seawater—unable to accomplish the difference "by his art," Herodotus says—the painter confirmed that the setting for his picture was Nilotic by painting a donkey on the bank and a crocodile in the water, lying in wait (there were no crocodiles in the sea, as everyone knew).

The tradition for such symbols to support a setting extends throughout art history. In 1863, Èdouard Manet painted peaceful streamside personifications: his *Déjeuner sur l'herbe* includes fruit, an

[96] Êdouard Manet.. *Le Déjeuner sur l'herbe,* 1863. Musée d'rsay, Paris. The frog is in the lower left corner; the finch is midwaym high up.

[97] Below: Marcantonio Raimondi. Engraving after Raphael's *Judgment of Paris.*

overturned water vessel, a frog, and a finch in flight. His model for the grouping and poses was the Nilotic-type detail of Raphael's *Judgment of Paris,* where one sees minor earth gods among reeds. One of them holds a symbolic oar, and the nymph with them is portrayed with a crock from which virgin water flows [96, 97, p. 155]. Raphael's picture depends in turn on a Judgment of Paris scene on an ancient Roman sarcophagus.[70]

Even if the landscape of the Tellus panel were topographical from inland marsh to the sea, it cannot represent Italy as meaningful propaganda, as a land of bountiful agriculture. As I've pointed out, a third of the landscape is given over to a marsh, a third to a rocky place, and a third to the sea. Lucretius lists the marsh and sea as two of the three most defective components of nature, proving that nature's scheme of things could not have been framed by divine power (the third defect is the existence of wild beasts).

Harsh seas, storm winds, and scorching sunrays repeatedly violate Tellus. The sea pounds on her flanks; earthquakes rupture her; harsh winds erode her body; the North Wind chills her; the sun in full heat takes vengeance for the castrated sky god Uranus by drying Tellus' foliage and transforming her blossomed maidenheads into dry seeds. After exhaustion in autumn and a cold winter's sleep, the spring sun warms her up, getting her ready for spring plowing that opens her, furrows her. She is made to take seed back into herself. Her ordeal of motherhood endlessly repeats as the seasons come round, as Sky revolves around her, lording over her, raining semen down on her (warm rains were at that time semeniferous).

The Tellus panel can be read as a swift retreat of the sea on one flank and retreating wind on the other, moving across the marshes. This would explain the *horae* moving away from Tellus, both looking with sweetness back at her. So important was this concept to Virgil that he made Aeneas' founding of Italy dependent on a merciful act of the sea, its becalming, and a withdrawal of the winds back to the central hills where they dwell in caverns. Lucretius says, "Look at the sea, earth, and sky, their triple nature and three structures—the three forms so unlike, their three so wondrous textures that will one day give over to destruction." This ultimate end of the world—earthquakes and slow destruction of *terra firma* by the action of harsh elements—was supported by everyday observation, and probably as widely believed in antiquity as today.

The most disastrous state of the universe would be a return to the original chaos when land, sea and sky were comingled. In many of Lucretius' passages where this forecast is given, wind and sea are destructive forces, but Lucretius acknowledges both as necessary to fertilize the earth's body. Rain showers are a loving and gentle, fertilizing gift of the Lord Omnipotent of Sky, as, in so many words, Lucretius calls him. Virgil, too, was clear on the distinction between showers and rainstorms, breezes and winds. The hard rains are the passionate attacks of water washing the yielding land into rivers that carry onward to mix with seawater—the land raped and wasted. Virgil speaks of the wintry blasts from the east and north causing Earth to grow cold and resist the plow—a frigid woman. Yet Favonius, the favorable Latin wind from the West, sends wavering breezes to dance gaily across fields and meadows and play among treetops, exciting the leaves. From this activity are derived the aromatic nymphs and teasing zephyrs. This is, of course, poetry, but as well the conditions under which the farmer suffered gains and losses, bountifulness and famine. They, too, based on reality.

The poetic concept of withdrawal and return are found throughout the literature of this period as reflections of popular beliefs as the only way the people could make sense of how the world operated. Only to this extent can I accept the Tellus panel as topographic, but not in the sense of a allegorical map. In any case, the personification would not be Italia, who represents the *terris* of Italy—its territory, not its soil. And besides, we have no exemplar that would tell us what Italia would have looked like.

Those who identify "Tellus" as Pax (goddess of Peace) run up against the simple fact that we have no image of Pax—in my opinion, at least, we don't. And Pax was not made a goddess until the reign of Hadrian. Before then she was the spirit of a times, most likley because war is physical and representable, while peace, like a calm sea, is without substance. Representations labeled as Pax are actually of Eirene, a spirit of good health, who would hardly be sitting on a rock holding babies, with a bull and lamb at her feet, and harvested fruit in her lap, even if allowing for peacefullness as a condition of well being.

The very idea of peace—the Augustan peace—has been debated for some years. Quite a long time ago, the historian Harold Fuchs, prompted by the Tellus relief's imagery, wrote that the Ara Pacis' representation of peace was thoroughly Greek, the notion of a contented Mother Earth.[71] But Professor Fuchs was thinking Greek, not Roman, as was the tendency in his day. Others, including Arnoldo Momigliano and Eugène Strong, picked up on Roman differences from teleological Classical art and noticed that the fuguration of Tellus had aspects of a wholly new concept, not a passive Greek Gaia (world-mother with thighs spread and breasts full) in just another format.[72] Countering Fuchs' proposition, Momigliano proposed that the ideal of peace expressed by this panel was strictly Roman, more complex than the ideal of peace that dominated the Greek mind. The true Roman ideal he found in the processional reliefs on the enclosure walls: serene men piously following a leader within the frame of a past that is present, because divine, and a future that is certain and therefore again present; no fleeting truce, but security. He concluded that the Ara Pacis entirely ignores the Greek symbols for peace, which are found nonetheless on certain Augustan coins, such as his reading of personified Pax (Peace) holding the caduceus of Eirene [99]. Resisting that everything Roman was Greek, Momigliano intrepidly transformed the Greek Eirene on the coins into the Roman Pax.

[98] Top: Ceres with wheat stalks, poppies, and caduseus. Aureus of the Civil War (RIC Civil War 115).

[99] Bottom: Ceres with wheat stalks, poppies, and caduceus. As of Galba (RIC Galba 291).

Nancy De Grummond is the most recent art historian to go wholly out to identify the personification on the Tellus panel as Pax, specifically *Pax Augustae*, though many others have agreed that the meaning of the panel's imagery only associates peaceful Tellus with Pax.[73] In my opinion, those who do confuse Tellus with Ceres. De Grummond's arguments to support her claim entails going all the way back to Hesiod, in whose writings she finds peacefulness represented by Eirene, one of the three very ancient Greek *horae*, with Dike (Justice) and Euromia (Good Order). De Grummond then says that only in the Hellenistic period did the *horae* at times turn into goddesses of the four seasons: Spring, Summer, Fall, Winter. She goes on to say it is easy to believe that Augustus and his advisors could have found it appropriate to bring to Rome the Hesiodic political idea of the seasons and the original role of the goddess of Peace, and relate them to the Pax Augusta.

But a great difference lies between an aspect of seasons and a goddess personified, as in Christianity where saints and angels are aspects of divinity but not themselves gods. When designated as nymphs of the seasons, *horae* were not the seasons any more than signs of spring are spring, or heralding angels are gods. De Grummond is yet another student of the Ara Pacis who points to the mother in the Ara Pacis relief as surrounded by children, animals and lavish vegetation, but as I've been arguing, the woman is not surrounded by children or animals and the marsh reeds and scanty clump of plants should hardly call to mind lavish vegetation that renewed era of prosperity would bring about.

Having concluded that the woman personifies peace, De Grummond says it is but a small step further to say she actually is Peace, which I take as equivalent to saying that, because a mirage looks just like water, it's but a small step to say that it actually is water. This misreckoning leads De Grummond to propose that Augustus' concept of peace was personified as a deity. If that were true, a statue of Pax in some form or other would have suited the program, which is what De Grummond calls for. But no one back then knew what Pax looked like, for the simple reason that Pax did not exist as a likeness. Not a single image of Pax has ever been found in Roman art. That the word PAX appears on coins depicting Eirene does not mean that Eirene is Pax, anymore than does the likeness of Thomas Jefferson on a United States nickel, on which is written, "In God We Trust," imply that Jefferson is God. Yet De Grummond claims that a likeness of Eirene is identical to a likeness of Pax. As evidence, she offers a Roman copy of the Greek sculpture known as the *Eirene of Kephisodotos,* but I am not at all convinced that the representation is Eirene, and even if it were, nothing says it is also Pax. That mother with child is entirely unlike the representation in the Tellus panel. Nor should the carved gem that De Grummond also offers as evidence, saying it is a copy of the *Eirene of Kephisodotos,* tell us anything about Pax as the personification I'm calling Tellus. There is no resemblance between them: the woman on the gem is posed differently, and the "infant being cradled in her right arm," as seen by De Grummond, is not even an infant but a hovering winged figure offering the woman a piece of fruit—most likely it's Cupid, with the woman personifying Venus. This gem may have been designed as a man's gift to a woman—the woman handed a golden apple, as Venus was by Paris.

That Roma and Peace & Plenty (wheat heads and a caduceus) appear on the opposite faces of a 68 AD coin from the reign of Galba does not validate the flanking reliefs on the Ara Pacis as Pax and Roma.

Deploying the same Galba coin as vidence, Barbette Spaeth identifies the woman not as Roma but, as the inscription on the coin says, as Ceres Augusta holding wheat heads in her right, and a caduceus in her left, hand [99].[74] Spaeth calls the caduceus a symbol of Pax in order to validate that "Pax, like Ceres, tends the fields, supervises the plowing, and nourishes the crops." But even if stated that way in poetry, it's not Pax, not even Ceres, who does those things: farmers do the plowing and tend the fields, while at most Pax would be a farm at peace with weather and family, cows grazing peacefully, like Borden Milk Company's "contented cows," the phrase applicable as well to the "contented wife." Farmers follow through with Ceres' gift of knowledge as to how to farm. Eirene may indeed play a role in the state of peace, not as Ceres or Pax, but as the healthfulness of life under peaceful conditions—the health of crops that are subject to many diseases: rust, black spot, viral rot, and of livestock: milk fever, bovine tuberculosis, and hog cholera. The caduceus is not the symbol of Pax, as Spaeth says, but of Eirene.

Eirene had a modest origin as one of Aphrodite's three *horae*. The caduceus entwines a serpent, whose death-dealing infections are controlled by Eirene (As a symbol of health through medicine, the caduceus is still widely used on hospital facades and the letterheads of physicians). Fear of the serpent's venomous bite was widespread when serpent and phallus, venom and semen, were subliminally equated, as in Genesis. In any era before bacteria and viruses were could be visualized, when penises were snake-like and spermatozoa were not seen, infectious diseases could only be understood as mysteries. So Eirene's command over the serpent was also taken as sexual peace. Mount Athos monks, and priests of the Temple of Eirene on the acropolis of Constantinople, castrated themselves to calm the turmoil of sexual temptation, which was one way to remove the venom from the phallic serpent writhing on the caduceus.

By Augustus' era, among sophisticated people anyway, such notions were remote, eccentric, and culturally impractical. Disease among metropolitans was not as mysterious as in earlier times, for the Romans had advanced medical practices, prompted by the need to treat soldiers and sailors when wounded. And peace as the path to economic prosperity when economics was shifting from pillage to import and export marketing, had become definably Roman. Eirene could be associated with health as a peaceful state, as she is today when speaking of healthy economies and healthy governments.

Galinsky countered De Grummond's notions with a substantial argument that the entire program of the Ara Pacis is *Pax Augustae*, not just the one relief, and that it would not be possible anyway to represent Peace by a one-dimensional image. "Pax is not represented on the Ara Pacis," Galinsky concluded, meaning not personified by a single image.[75] Yet several other students of Roman art are caught up in the search for Pax, driven by the logic of symmetrical expectancy. So determined that Pax must be personified somewhere on the altar, Weinstock concluded that her absence signifies that the altar simply cannot be the Ara Pacis![76] Hanel identified some fragments from the south frieze of the Ara Pacis as possibly remnants of Pax—there where Augustus' lictors stand in place, but in the context of Roma on the east facade, any sort of representation of a spirit amonst all those real life people seems far-fetched to the extreme.[77] Finding that an image of Pax does not appear on the altar or its enclosure, Simon proposed that a statue of Pax would have stood outside the precinct walls, her argument based solely on fragments of a colossal statue of Apollo found in the vicinity of the Ara Pacis. Simon's conclusion is simply this: because Apollo was represented by a statue, Pax must also have been. But it is not certain that the fragments of statuary she has in mind are of Apollo, or that being found in the vicinity of the Ara Pacis is evidence that, if of Apollo, the statue was there at the time the Ara Pacis was built. Pliny mentions statues of Apollo in Rome during Augustus' reign, but for each example he pairs Apollo with Diana.

To repeat, Pax was a quality, not a goddess, not a corporeal personification. In these lines by Horace, Pax is listed with other qualities of character: Faith, Honor, Modesty, and Manhood.

> ...iam Fides et Pax et Honos Pudorque
> priscus et neflecta redire Virtus
> audet, apparentque beata pleno
> Copia cornu.[105]

Had the representation of Roma across from Tellus not been tagged the goddess of War, the Tellus representation may have escaped being called Pax, the goddess of Peace. Did the programmers of the Ara Pacis mean to contrast War and Peace? I think not.

Recently, the head of Honos (honor), from where Moretti had placed it into the Aeneas relief on the west wall, was moved to the Roma panel. If this head does indeed belongs to the Roma panel, then it is possible to believe that Roma was flanked by the figures Honos and Virtus (virtue). But the tautology of putting Honos there, then saying, because Honos is now there, we can assume Virtus was also there, should not be overlooked. The love of Rome, evoking honor and virtue, easily fits the politics of the Augustan Age. but if Honor and Virtue were on that relief, the panel across from it, the Tellus panel, would surely not be a representation of Venus!

Symmetry engenders mechanical binaries, such as up and down, right and left. When only one of a binary is identified, it is logical to hypothesize the opposite: there can't be an up without a down. So if Roma is interpreted as a personification of the State, not of War, the Tellus figure becomes expectedly the only possible contrast, the Country. That requires distinguishing *tellus* from *terris*, land from country, as when Seneca writes in *Mede'a*:

> venient annis
> saecula rerum laxet, et ingens
> pateat tellus Tethysque novos.
> detegat orbes, nec sit terris
> ultima Thule.
> [A new age will come when Ocean will relax its hold over the world and a vast land (*tellus*) will open to view, and Tethys will reveal a new world (*terris*)].

Roma personifies Rome as the physical body, the lap, the seat of power—the personification of the tellurian mother. If from such fragmentary evidence the personification is indeed wearing a warrior's helmet and seated on a pile of weapons from defeated armies, does she sit there as the goddess of War, paired with Pax as goddess of Peace? The standard Roman representation of a defeated nation, like the one on the Early Imperial relief in the Naples Museum, is a woman seated on the ground, usually bereft of adornments. Does that representation make her a goddess of Defeat?

Let us conclude that neither Roma nor Pax were goddesses, that Roma was a personification of the Empire, and that no personification of Pax is known, other than by an aspect of peace, represented at times by Eirene.

Ovid wrote, "May the world near and far dread the sons of Aeneas, and if there be any land that hasn't feared Rome, may it love Rome instead!" The many Temples of Roma that Augustus promoted in the provinces were to promote devotion to Rome as the locus of the empire embodied. In cases of sculptural representations, where Augustus is represented side-by-side with Roma, as on the *Gemma Augustea,* it is not that Roma is a goddess but that Augustus is identified with Rome and Rome with him. The altar of Augustus and Roma at the junction of the Rhône and Saône near Lyons, erected in 12 BC, and the one at Cologne just a bit later, were votive altars for sacrifice to Government and Nation, not to gods but under gods.

Sacrifices to Augustus and Roma were manifest acknowledgments of their pairing. On the occasion that Octavian was honored with the name Augustus, that night the Tiber swelled and overflowed, flooding the lowland of the city. For that sign, Dio tells us, soothsayers predicted that Augustus would attain great power and hold the whole city under his sway. This may have been taken as a sign that Augustus and Roma were partnered. A certain senator, in a bold act of ingratiation, proclaimed himself dedicated to the emperor and ordered everyone to offer sacrifice because of the portent. By "sacrifice," this senator did not mean that everyone should axe a bull, cow, sow, or lamb, but should make some sacrifice, give up something of themselves. He himself offered a financial sacrifice, to make Augustus an heir equal to his own son.

Just as paleontologists look for missing links, and physicists for elements known by their absence, historians enter into and become part of the procedures and apparatus of art history, like the telescope's participation in astronomy. I submit that a "goddess" with the name Pax is a phantom of the kind historians tend to create out of expectancy. When one projects a phantom image onto a historical gap, one fills out the features by looking back to when images were more clearly defined, as in Greek art and legends. Early in this text, I mentioned that, when Petersen found the symmetry of the Tellus relief unimaginable if located asymmetrically to the architecture, his level of expectancy emerged from Greek architecture. He fashioned for his mind's eye a phantom structure, an unknown monument where a relief looking like the Tellus relief would be located dead center. Here I will mention as well that, because Tellus lacks a cornucopia, Schäfer concluded in 1959 that the bunch of plants and the fruit on Tellus' lap surely implied a cornucopia hidden behind the rocks. Schäfer needed this phantom to bring Tellus up to his expectations. Torelli fantasized a cornucopia at the side of Roma, held by an Amazonian or helmeted Virtus, but Virtus is not there and may never have been there. De Grummond needed a caduceus to be held by Tellus to nail her argument that Tellus is Pax. She said, "We cannot be absolutely sure that the caduceus was never there, for the proper right hand of the goddess is completely restored." The historian of antiquities, Benndorf, couldn't believe that any female riding a swan could be other than Aphrodite. Galinsky couldn't accept that Tellus would be sitting upright, clasping her children, simply because she hadn't done that before. She had to be someone else, he concluded, not allowing for anything to happen for the first time, even when the examples of Roman art we have in hand are but an infinitesimal portion of what was produced over the centuries.

Art historian expectancy is generated by a need for sameness and continuity: sameness in order to classify, and continuity to sustain historical linearity—a fusion of etymology and evolution, of stable matter and repeatable cause and effect. The thrust of art history by methodologies motored by sources and influences is to make art imagery dependable. Because the Greek goddess of health, Eirene, was represented as a personification, the Romans must have a personification of Peace named Pax. Because the Greeks made physical representations of Eirene, the Romans must have made representations of Pax. Continuities thus become imperatives. Such anxiety over a missing member is deeply rooted in human psychology, having its survival function in missing children from the mother's side, members of a family or tribe who don't return—missing persons. Expectancy, the function of accounting for anything missing, gave rise to tribal names, family names, sequential numbers, accounting, inventories, and anxiety over the missing at the base of augury when what is predicted to happen is expected to happen.

The oracle predicts that the son born to King Laius and Queen Jocasta will grow up to kill his father. Oedipus grows up and kills his father. The oracle predicts that where Aeneas comes upon a white sow with litter he will found Lavinium. He comes upon the sow; Lavinium is founded. Such oracular structures are tautological, self-fulfilling; cause and effect are planted in each other, then separated by a time span only to snap back together when the critical effect happens. Expectancy, when aroused by a need for progressive continuity, is but one system of augury. Progressive art history is like that, dependent on logical sequence. The textbook history of art is largely how puzzles are made of survivable artifacts made to fit structures of expectancies.

By rejecting Peace represented on the Ara Pacis by a personification, one is left with the larger and more variegated concept of peace, more appropriate to the aggregate of Romans and other Italian peoples. The mother of Rome is family love, the love of one's leader and one's nation. Love and War are linked in the sexuality of male and female, while Love and Peace are linked to family life, as good husbandry and good government, as peace settling over the land. The agrarian basis of Roman culture is government as family—Roman history, a history of families. Fertility and procreation figure in the manifest character of Love and Peace, not Love and War. Family love is linked to sacrifice for the family's sake, the wife bears children in pain and gives of her body, the husband labors by the sweat of his brow and gives up his paycheck. Honor and Virtue are the male/female coordinates of the marriage bond: the man honorable, the woman virtuous.

14

THE TRUTH ABOUT VENUS

Can the women I'm calling Tellus be Venus? Karl Galinsky is a strong advocate for the personification in this relief as Venus. He also layered Venushood on the two *aurae,* saying they are "predominately Venus." His visual evidence is the one child holding out an apple and that the *hora* on the left is astride a goose—apple and goose adding up to Venus. But, as I've said, I hope convincingly, the fruit is not an apple, and the bird not a goose. As for literary evidence, Galinsky cites one line written over 400 years earlier in Euripedes *Medea* (431 BC), and one line from Ovid's *Heroides* (16:23) where Venus is mistress of the *Aurae.* This method of identifying the Roman Venus can't avoid mixing her up with the Greek Aphrodite. And using a 400 year old precedent to identify a contemporary image is like explaining, in geological time, an armadillo's scales by holding up a fish with scales.

Horae and *aurae* are playful and often very naughty girls, not mothers. Having found stars in the billowing mantle of Aphrodite pictured on an Attica lekythos, Galinsky identifies the aura on the sea serpent also as Venus, calling her the goddess of the heavens, Urania. While Greek art offers examples of Aphrodite with billowing mantle aboard a goose, for every one of them I can offer an example of Aphrodite with billowing mantle riding a swan, also on an Attic vase [100]—for that matter, when represented as her dark side, she rides a goat. Anyway, the Roman Venus is not the Aphrodite of Euripedes, or the Aphrodite that's pictured on the Attica Lekythos, any more than is Venus Genetrix the Venus of Willendorf.

Galinsky sees the *hora* on the swan as "presiding over humid, fertile soil," and assumes she is also the earth goddess. But beneath that figure is not agricultural soil but a swamp (marsh drainage was one of Augustus' projects for agricultural land restoration). "The woman's breasts are much too full and splendidly modeled to be Tellus'," he says, "but certainly they could be Venus' breasts." Overlooked is that Tellus' breasts on the *Gemma Augustea* are just as ample, and that she was, after all, a lactating young mother. Galinsky then rests content with a contradiction he's left with—his having said that the adolescent-type breasts of the *aurae* could also be Venus' breasts. Those breasts are hardly full and splendidly modeled. Anyway, large and splendid breasts do not make Venuses out of earth mothers.

[100] Aphrodite (Venus) on a swan. Image on an Attica Lekythos.

To be sure, Venus had an abundance of female qualities, but other than being protective of Aeneas and the fleeing Trojans, after first trying to do them in, she was not at all motherly. And I find it difficult to think of the female representations on either side of her as aspects of Venus. They are *aurae* or *horae*, celestial and earthly nymphs—cloud tenders, breezes, moonbeams, garden aromas, swirling pond mist, ocean spray, perfume scents—the aura of places and things. In human form, under certain circumstances, *horae* were Roman harlot priestesses, sex teachers for boys whom the Semites called whores. Most ancients who thought about such things associated Venus, the age-old goddess of kitchen-garden fragrance, with the Greek goddess Aphrodite, who was born near Cythera off the south of Greece, says Hesiod, out of sea foam churned up when Uranus' severed genitals hit the water and thrashed about in it. Venus thus wouldn't have had an infancy and upbringing appropriate to the development of motherly proclivities.

The designations mother, son, father, daughter were so extensively bandied about in ancient Greek and Roman literature as to put one wisely on guard against genetics. Venus was also called, at times, the husband of Vulcan. In the *Iliad,* Homer casts her (as Aphrodite) not only as the sister of Ares but married to Hera's son Hephaestus, while in *The Odyssey* we find her as Ares' lover, and Hephaestus is married to Charis.

Shortly after the publication of Galinsky's provocative 1966 essay, "Venus on a Relief of the Ara Pacis Augustae," I was obliged to test it against the program I'd developed earlier for the reliefs. If my Tellus was Galinsky's Venus, my program would have to be forsaken. That threat agitated me to the point of calling on Professor Galinsky to meet me at high noon on the Campus Martius. But in the mid-1960s, I was not prepared to throw my legion, comprising a lactating mother with twin babies and two adolescent girls, against Galinsky's three Venuses backed by Cupid's deadly arrows that might fell me with fatal lovestrokes on the battlefield. So I retreated back into the thicket of modern art where Manet's *Olympia* had obliged Venus to own up to her true character, and had sent her phantasm back to sea in an undertow. Now I am more prepared. Nonetheless, considerate of Galinsky's bredth of knowledge and my respect for his work, I will call upon Plato for help.

Wanting to be intelligently precise, in his *Symposium* Plato gave names to the two Grecian aspects of Aphrodite. Those aspects will be retained when Aphrodite metamorphosed into the Roman Venus. Plato says:

> No one will deny there are two goddesses of that name. One, the older, sprung not from a mother's womb, but from the heavens. We call her Urania, the heavenly Aphrodite. The younger daughter of Zeus we call Pandemus, the earthly Aphrodite. It thus follows that Love will be known as heavenly or earthly, according to with which goddess one keeps company.

What Plato had in mind, of course, are the two aspects of the woman who, in modern terms and most likely in his day as well, translates as the kind of woman a man takes as a wife (the heavenly woman), in contrast to the kind of women he plays around with or takes as a mistress (the earthy type). The Roman Venus absorbed more of Pandemus than Urania, and Pandemus/Venus soon developed a sordid reputation, that, in my opinion, would keep her off an altar to peace and off a rock tending babies. She was pandemonius (*pan* + *daimon,* the abode of all devils, calling to mind Pandora's deadly box). Hot-headed, vain, and ruthless, her retaliations against women who spurned her as a love goddess were dreadful. Furious with the women of Lemnos for failing to adore her, she caused their genitals to exude a foul odor that repelled their husbands. Perhaps she had some influence over the sea god Posidon, who may have been her foster-father, for, in Euripedes' *Hipplytus*, after fraudulently getting Hippolytus into a compromized situation with his father, Theseus, the young man is killed while riding on a road beside the sea. A sea monster rises suddenly from the water and spooks his horse; his chariot tips over and he is smashed against rocks, Euripedes had Venus proclaim:

> Great is my power and wide my fame among mortals, and also in heaven. All men who look upon the light of the sun are under my sway. I bless those who respect my power, and disappoint those who are not humble before me. Theseus' son Hippolytus is the only inhabitant of this land who declares that I have nothing to do with sex. It is his sinful neglect of me for which I will punish him this very day.

As the Uranian Aphrodite, her peerless birth would make it possible for her to be pictured astride a seahorse if, before washing ashore at Paphos, in Cypress, as "the birth of Aphrodite," she had frolicked for some time at sea while her gorgeous body ripened.

The fall of Uranus' genitals can be taken as well as a fall to earth of his generative powers. In the *Danaid* of Aeschylus, one reads: "Heaven is full of desire to mate with Earth [Uranus with Gaia], and Earth is overcome with desire to find a mate" [explaining why Tellus is usually depicted on her back]. Rain falls from amorous Heaven and impregnates Earth [*tellus*]; the Earth brings forth grains and fodder for the flocks and herds, the gifts of Demeter [Ceres]. From the same moistening marriage rite, tree fruit ripens. "Of these things, I am the cause," Aphrodite says.

A pomegranate wouldn't even hint of Venus, so virginal that her ovaries were most likely seedless and surely no blood would ooze from her immaculate uterus. Still, one must allow for the fact that the word *pomme* is responsible for confusion among old world fruits. The designation was commonly used throughout the ancient Mediterranean for tree-borne fruits of different kinds, like we use the word "fruit," that got lumped into "apple" when translated, as did *triticum*, wheat, when called "corn" (corn kennels are clustered on cobs; the cobs are ears, for they grow on the sides of stalks, like ears on the side of one's head; cereal grains are not ears; they cluster as heads, not ears; each corn kennel sports a single thread that, combined with the others, is called corn silk, while grain heads have tough beards that can stick to your clothing. The persistence of English-speaking scholars calling wheat, corn, is an academic affectation, like calling festoons garlands and breeding bulls oxen. I credit David Catriota, who performed extensive research on the Augustan silver cups in the British Museum, for correctly identifying heads of grain as "bearded wheat," rather than bearded corn, even though elsewhere he holds to the misnomer, "ears of wheat." That said, let me rant on:

The preferred apple of classical lore is the "golden," called *le golden* in France and "golden delicious" in the United States. In the Judgment of Paris context, the golden apple that Paris hands Venus is for her gift to him of Helen of Troy as a wife—to possess her, make love to her, not to impregnate her, as if the apple were a fertility symbol, which it is not and never has been, nature having made pregnancy a trap that lurks behind passion. The three golden apples Venus concealed in Hippomenes' garment to detract Atalanta over the course of their foot race so Hippomenes might win her for his wife, were not to make her fruitful so she would wrinkle, go to seed, and rot. Atalanta was a devotee of Diana, who loved her freedom and disdained the thought of marriage. Having chanced to see Atalanta naked, Hippomenes so desires her that he will risk death should she outrun him. That was the deal. Several young men before him had lost the race and lost their heads—terminal impotency. During the race, when Atalanta teasingly lets Hippomenes take the lead, Venus contrives for Atalanta to lose her own head, her maiden head and her maiden beauty. Each time Atalanta thinks it's time to overtake Hippomenes, Venus tosses an apple in her path. Having her own share of Venus' vanity, Atalanta pauses to pick it up. After being tricked three times, Hippomenes is too far out in front to be overtaken. He wins. Atalanta submits. They fall into a post-race embrace, and in the heat of passion forget to get married. That raises the wrath of Cybele, in her aspect as goddess of marriage and child-birth. She forcibly hitches them up, literally: she harnesses the speedy couple to her chariot (the expression, "to get hitched," is carried into our time).

One of Catullus' poems to his mistress Lesbia (the beautiful, aristocratic, uninhibited lover, Clodia Metelli), written in the first century BC, is a hymn to Diana, the chronic pain in Venus' side. One may gather from Catullus' words that the notion of fertility is moot. Greek and Roman women were plenty fertile. Had there been a god of contraceptives (and there may have been one), that god would have eclipsed any god of fertility as to worship and receipt of sacrifice. It was Catullus-type poetry that spoke to women. Here is Catullus transcribing the young woman's fantasy:

> We are as flowers in a garden, hidden from all men's eyes. No field creatures walk in this place. No plow divides us. Only the gentlest wind and warm rain from a soft cloud, and a quickening sun, nourish us. We are the treasure that many girls and boys desire. But once de-flowered, our virgin's bodies rancid, neither boys nor girls will turn to us again, nor can they arouse our passion.[79]

Before she became infused with the Greek Aphrodite, Venus was the Roman goddess of vegetable and flower gardens—not of plants but of their enticements. Her promotion from garden aroma to perfume and cosmetics was strictly via horticulture—the word that's indebted to *hora,* the culture of *hora* (from *hora* also comes the word *whore,* who exudes Venus' lures). It was the influx of the earthly Aphrodite (Pandemus) that moved Venus from kitchen gardens to inhabit damp and mossy places, like spring heads (the musky sweet *pudenda* of virgins) where aromas are aphrodisiacs—*horae* that drive men senseless. In the Homeric hymn where Aphrodite emerges from the sea, she is dressed and adorned with jewelry by *horae,* like gardens and breezes are adorned with aromas, the sweet smell of crevices that draw in men, the slick labia and pearliness of the shelled oyster. She was carried over the sea by the moist breath of the western wind. Fresh breath is also a *hora,* like Double Mint gum as double pleasure.

The dual Aphrodite, of whom Plato speaks, would become the dual Venus about whom many Romans spoke. Earlier, I quoted Cicero's writing of Verres' personal sack of the Temple of Minerva in Corinth—"sacked not by an enemy who would still retain some sense of religion and the laws of propriety even in war, but by piratical robbers." Then comes this statement implicating the vile vanity of Venus: "Verres, who owed his vows not to Honor or Virtue, but to Venus and Cupid, was the man who dared despoil the temple of Minerva the Virgin."

Venus' character was not lost on Roman intellectuals or sophisticated populace. Like her modern imitators—Olympia, Mae West, Marilyn Monroe, Madonna—she was idolized but not necessarily esteemed. I have analyzed a passage by Pliny where Venus figures. He is writing about trivial laws put on the books by the censor (ca. 169 BC), such as the rule against eating dormice at meals. He asks why there shouldn't have been a law forbidding importation of exotic marble, considering the great expense and perilous sea-crossings endured in order to transport columns crafted of rare stone. Pliny classifies the quest of such luxuries as a vice, especially when done at public expense, as when used temporarily for public functions but ending up privately owned. "Yes", he concludes, "the laws were silent when, in the aedilship of M. Scaurus (58 BC), people saw 360 columns transported to the stage of a temporary theater, used there for scarcely a month for the "delight of the public" and then carted to Scarus' private house for installation in his portico:

> For by what route do vices more commonly make inroads than the route of public interest? By what other path has the use of ivory, gold, and gems entered into private life? Is there anything that we have left exclusively to the gods?[80]

How Venus fits into this document of Roman history is signaled by how I read Pliny's lament on official immorality disguised as public service. The key passage is this:

> Yes, the laws were silent while such massive elements of marble were dragged past the terra-cotta roof ornaments of the temples of the gods. Nor can one assume that Scaurus took by surprise a city which was naïve and unable to see its potential evil.[81]

The thematic undertext for this passage may be the naive, unable-to-see-its-potential-evil shepherd of the *Judgment of Paris.* Blind to the portents behind his choice of Venus as the most beautiful and desirable among the three vain goddesses, Venus, Hera, and Athena, Paris awards the golden apple to Venus, whose bribe was Helen as his wife. The potential evil was, of course, the fall of Troy at the hands of the Greeks that marked the flight of Aeneas and the beginning of Roman history. The woman Paris abandoned for Helen was Oenone, a nature nymph. The contrast between her and Venus fits neatly to Pliny's contrast of terra-cotta with exotic marble. Venus represented the vanity of voluptuousness—ravishing marbles only gods could have created—while Oenone was like earth's clay that is worked by humans.

One also finds in Pliny's text a specific reference to Venus in uncomplimentary words. He recalls an earlier event featuring an orator by the name of L. Crassus, who first had marble in his house on the Palatine. In the course of an argument about its propriety, his house was given the name Palatine Venus. Pliny then writes of others who were criticized in their time for using expensive, imported marble. He winds up this discourse on indulgence saying, "Such facts and events prove that today we are better men, for who today has such columns in his atrium?" Suetonius gives a contrasting report on Augustus' taste, that Augustus lived always in modest quarters: "His house on the Palatine was conspicuous neither for its size nor its decoration, since the porticos in it were short and had columns of volcanic stone quarried from the Alban mountain, while the rooms lacked marble of any sort."[82]

Digs at Venus must have been a commonplace for decades. In the second century BC, the comic playwright, Plautus, whose ribald skits still delighted audiences in Julio-Claudian times, wrote, "If a man wants to meet a liar or a braggart, he should go to the temple of Venus Cloacina."[83] This temple, more like a shrine, stood at the northeast end of the Forum.The world *cloacina* refers or course to Rome's sewage canal, the *cloaca*, a fitting simile for the whore's vestibule into which men spew waisted semen and brag over copiousness like tellers of fish stories.

As love in general rather than specifically sexual love, Venus was embedded nonetheless in the material conception of motherhood, as the goddess who caused wives to submit. One of the most relevant passages promoting her association with procreation is by Lucretius:

> Mother of the Aeneadae, life-giving Venus, who fills the ship-conveying sea, the cereal producing lands, since every sort of living thing conceived through her springs forth and sees the light of day.

> For her the winds take flight, the earth puts forth sweet flowers, the oceans smile, the calmed sky shines.[84]

Lucretius does not substitute Venus for Tellus, for Venus is love as the force of procreation, not its production (conceived through, not by, her); it remains for Earth to produce. Lucretius calls Earth the universal mother. In great detail he explains how she gave birth and why the earth is called Mother. His understanding of fecundity is syncretic. Without Venus' urgings, Earth would not conceive.

Long ago Venus had moved off the farm. Like any farm and hamlet girl, after experiencing the sights and glamour of Rome's urban life, she wasn't about to return to waft her aroma over cottage gardens ("You ain't gonna git her back on the farm, once she's seen Paree"—a U. S. Midwestern version, as ancient as my youth). Venus was not the sort of goddess to sit placidly on a crumbly rock outcropping and tend babies, or have anything to do with livestock or such banal vegetative matter as acorns. Nonetheless, for all her frivolities and vanity, she was useful for political purposes as an appropriate goddess to be made the mother of all Romans, a role Julius Caesar created for her. With the genes of Anchises fathering Aeneas, Caesar grounded the Julian family in the body of Venus Genetrix. The benevolent side of her dual venality figures importantly in Augustus' theogony.

> For Venus alone can make men happy with tranquil peace. Mars sinks often upon your bosom, overcome with love's eternal pain. While he thus lies, pouring out sweet conversation, he asks for the Romans a placid peace (Lucretius).[85]

Venus figures in Virgil's account of her attempt to induce Vulcan to forge weapons and arm the Trojans. Venus wraps her arms around her quarry, moving him to passion, so he will help Aeneas win the war. She casts her plea as a mother begging for her son. She regrets that she'd failed to arm the Trojans. In her vanity, she'd not realized that Jupiter was guiding their victories while she deployed her amorous wiles to foster his defeat. Now, to recover status with Aeneas, she uses her charms to seduce Vulcan; she manipulates him, pretends she hadn't aided the Trojans with weapons because she did not want to burden him with blacksmithery toil for a lost cause. She envelopes her victim in her snowy arms and sends passion to his marrow bones, hugs him this way and that in her swan's down embrace, while Vulcan's wife looks on but without jealousy, confident in her own loveliness.

The importance of Mars comes to the forefront when considering the Ara Pacis' significance, its place in the Campus Martius, and Mars in the lineage of Augustus. Mars' love for Venus took a bizarre form as the coupling of a left-hand horse (female) with a right hand horse (male)—the left an unlucky side in augury. During Roman New Year festivals, the climactic ceremony was a race of two-horse chariots held on the Ides of March (the fifteenth). The right-hand horse of the winning team was sacrificed to Mars. Half its blood was delivered to the Vestals, the other half poured over the hearth of the Pontifex Maximus, which signed for Vesta (surely the pouring was but a symbolic dribbling, not a blood bath).

The Roman festivals of Venus *verticordia*, described by Ovid, were linked to the festival of Fortuna *virilis*. Women of all stations could partake of these ceremonies, prostitutes included, for at issue was the virility of men and the sexual performance capability of women. The primary duty that Venus *verticordia* demanded of women was that they be sexually available to men. The first rite performed at her festival was for women to wash her personification and adorn it with jewels and flowers. While they themselves bathed, the women, wearing wreaths of myrtle, burned incense and drank cocetum made of milk, honey, and crushed poppies, a drink served to apprehensive brides in order to relax them on their bridal night.

15

THE REALITY BASIS FOR MYTHS

At no point when delving into Roman religion can one escape the sexual implications of ancient myths and rituals. All are phantasms in search of answers to mysteries of origins, the "From where did we come?" syndrome and the enigma of passions that one cannot control: flushes of love, erotic pulsations, erections, urges to seduce and urges to submit, and the pleasure-pain of hymenal sacrifice.

Mars' sacred animals, the woodpecker and the wolf, were tap rooted in Roman history, the woodpecker associated at a psychic deep strata with jabs of the thrusting spear, the wolf with ferocity and courage, the sure delivery of the thrusting member that the groom would need to enter his bride in manly fashion ("pecker" is still a synonym for the male member). While Roman marriage ceremonies differed in ritual, in preparation for one of the most formal types, the bride's hair was divided into six locks, the divisions make with the point of a spear, the marital contract sealed when the groom took the bride's right hand in his, the bride then embraced by her mother but torn away, abducted, and escorted to the groom's house by three young boys most likely personifying Venus' *amores*, there to be carried over the threshold so she wouldn't stumble and prematurely fall, thence to the marriage bed where her brave husband awaited. In rituals that followed closer on Greek traditions than the old Roman, the bride would greet the groom, saying, "If you are Uranus, I am Gaia." It was up to the groom to prove that, though Uranus, he wasn't a castrate, and that his member would rain semen, not water.[119]

Although Ceres, too, was associated in some circles with marriage, it was not as the bride's body that she would be seeded, but as her daughter's, just as rice seeds are tossed nowadays at newly-weds (according to the teachings of the second-century Greek anatomist, Galen, the woman's ovaries contained seeds, while male semen, like fertilizing rain, only stimulated the seeds to sprout). The social commentator Servius, saying that Ceres favors weddings, quotes the celebrated Republican love poet, Gaius Calvus, saying that Ceres "taught the sacred laws [of procreation] and joined loving bodies in weddings." Here again, one finds Ceres as a teacher, as she was of agriculture, while it's the bride's body as Tellus that is furrowed and productively energized by the groom. For that act, Venus is responsible. And from that moment on, she has no interest in a virgin bride who'd become a woman.[86]

Reality tends to organize itself around myths as much, if not more, than myths imitate reality. Myths are short, pithy stories with familiar structures that allow the narrative to be easily grasped, like morals, fates, and aspirations—catechism stories, fairy tales, and psychoanalytic dreams. Having been filtered through generations and adapted to successive cultures, ancient stories remain rooted in real-life strata. Old Greek and Roman myths infiltrate histories. Durable, like all human foibles, they repeat in the Italian Renaissance, again during the French revolution, and again in modern moral rhetoric. Cicero would feel quite at home in France's Chambre des Députies, the rostrum backed by a tapestry of Raphael's *Socrates and Plato Received by Great Men of All Ages*, or in England's Parliment or the hall of the United States Senate, and the Choice of Paris will never be erased by Miss America contests and the line-ups of prostitutes in a brothel or girls along a dating bar. Myths pass from one generation to another, modified from time to time and place to place, to explain origins and control social beliefs about causes and effects that fit to variable cultures. Myths translate their realty base, making reality cognizable through slogans and persisting patterns of human behavior. In that respect, reality and its mythical coating are two aspect of an integrated system of belief, forming a single psychic entity in the mind, like the fusion of description with interpretation. The reality base tends to be universal in that it is not made by humans but by such realities as the sun, moon, storms, earthquakes, floods, and so on. When subjected to artful telling—altered to be convincing (the mission of pure rhetoric)—imitations of mythical interpretations of the reality base are from time to time re-motivated to serve a didactic purpose, such as fables as moralizing tales and horror stories to restrain wayward children and wives. The life of the myth is then perpetuated by the art of the myth, but only as long as the reality base, upon which the myth was built, is sustained.

The perpetuation of a myth depends on periodic celebrations, such as those entered on the Roman Calendar of Feasts—today's Passovers, Christmases, Thanksgiving Days. Venus hovers in the eastern sky as the new moon, her virginity renewed monthly. Myths fall out of their motivated belief system when the reality base is dissolved or reduced to banalities, as when Haley's comet is identified as nothing but a dirty ice ball hurling through space with no sense of direction, or when the Wizard of Oz is exposed as an intimidated professor who fantasized his power. Secularization can be defined as the process by which myths are demythified, their subject matter rationalized and washed away by erosive waves of empiricism. Secularization comes about when human industry modernizes to an extent when daily life and economics can no longer be attributed to the work of gods, when Ceres no longer enhances grain yields out of benevolence and receipt of sacrifices. Rather it's fertilizers, seed selection, and weed control that crowns the farmer's fields with wheaten wreaths. It doesn't take much of an advance in industrial planning to realize that gods do not exist in the real world, or that augury can substitute for planning. Nonetheless, we still have long range weather forcasts and the Chicago Futures Market; we race two-year-old horses and adolescent homing pigeons in futurities.

It's to the reality base of the Tellus relief imagery that my attention keeps returning. Every aspect of it points not to poetry that dresses it up but to the reality of Roman life that bares its nakedness. With that is mind, I will now explore the myths of Tellus and Ceres in order to mine what lies beneath their mythical layers. My process is a style of undressing, knowing that beneath clothing there is naked truth.

This chapter will now consolidate Greco-Roman folk beliefs in order to fashion one grand mythical narrative and bring it to bear on the Tellus panel as representing Tellus (*tellus*) as land (*terris*) before agriculture and before the advent of history—as the state of the beginning out of which came origins, such as the origin of Rome. My explication will follow the shift from the mythical theogony of Hesiod and Homer to the rational theogony of the sixth-century BC Xenophanes of Colophon, who I single out to represent an intellectual movement that emerged on the fringes of Greece and settled primarily in Sicily and southern Italy. This movement opposed the mystical explanation of the world's beginnings as battles between personifications, with a god as a cosmic force for every event and element—earth, sky, moon, sun, water, and so on—down to gods of doors, hinges, and latches. Xenophanes and his colleagues proposed a three-part schema to replace the older theogonies: personified elements replaced by physical realities, with the rationalizing process a transition from god-driven cultures to secularization.

This tripartite schema consisted of the origin of the world, the origin of humans, and the origin of cities. The origin of cities was already part of the Roman belief system. It shows itself on the Ara Pacis relief panels that are dedicated to Romulus as responsible for the origin of Rome and to Aeneas for bringing his lineage to Italy, propagating those who would be Romans. Structurally these events were associated with a tripartite schema that is inherently vertical, ascending through phases: first the earth (Tellus), then the people (the processionals), then the city (Roma), as a schema of progressive generations. Implicit, too, is the structure of process: the beginning, development, and result, combining to explain how something comes about. This tripartite structure can be summed up as the original meaning of the Greek word *phusis*.[87] Interestingly, Plato planned a book based entirely on *phusis*, which would trace the origin of the world to the origin of mankind, then to the origin of Athens.

Tripartite structures are as common as colds, but I can't resist associating the notion of *phusis* with the need for people to locate themselves in space and time by scaling back from the present moment through generations that began with the foundational act of creation and moved on to the present. I recognize this sort of scaling as the pervasive schema of the Ara Pacis reliefs. One starts with Tellus on the left flank of the east façade—the foundation, the *terra firma*, the *prima firma*, upon which the movement of *phusis* starts, with *phusis* understood as nature in process as the first Greek intellectuals understood it. From the origin of the earth, one moves around to the west façade, to the origin of Romans (Romulus and Aeneas) at the founding place of Rome, then back to the east facade, to Roma as the city. In short, the four panels put nature in process (the Lupercal panel, the Aeneas panel) between the primal and timeless state of Tellus, and the the achieved city, Roma, implying "for all time." This progress and its result are not accomplished by an automatism of *phusis*, but rather by rational effort, meaning human industry through generations as represented by the procession on the shrine's south and north friezes. By definition, a procession is a movement: the picturing of parents with children, while perhaps recording an event, represents the perpetual motion of Rome assured by successive generations. The procession moves toward Augustus, and if Augustus is indeed holding the *lituus*, as Chief Augur his act would be prognostication favoring the future of Rome. If pouring a libation, his act represents the achieved state of Rome that book-ends history between him and Aeneas.

Should the foregoing make sense, then an interpretation of the Tellus panel as Ceres, or any other female deity, would render any program for the overall iconography out of joint. If the Tellus panel represents fertility, fecundity, and prosperity based on agriculture, which it certainly cannot, considering the evidence I've presented to nullify that assumption, then the panel would be as isolated iconographically as it is by virtue of its symmetry. For Ceres cannot represent the origin of anything other than agriculture, which comes about much later than the origins of the earth and of humans. Tellus is the condition of the beginning before anything had an origin.

In what context of ancient history did one distinguish between myth and fact, such that the distinction might bear on the Tellus panel, and by extension on the whole meaning of the Ara Pacis? Where does one find a maternal figure seated on a rock with an infant or two, nymphs, a swan, a sea horse, a marsh, a stream, along with acorns, poppies, pomegranates, irises, and maybe even a poisonous plant? Where would we find these linked and registered in the common mind? I will relate a story in which they all figure, and in so doing interject reality bases upon which I believe the various motifs of the stories are incited into becoming at times metaphorical and at other times symbolic while at all times real.

During the period of Roman culture into which Augustus and the

Ara Pacis fits, Virgil and Ovid promulgated the most popular narratives of the origin of humankind that, centuries earlier, were foisted on the Grecian world by Homer and Hesiod—the latter born and raised as a farmer; his writings as accumulative and concentrated folk beliefs of generations before him. Hesiod's period on earth was long after the Trojan War, so he and Homer would have absorbed into their writing several centuries of oral traditions before their consolidation as a basis for understanding the nature of reality before science and mathematics. Some scholars claim that Homer was not an individual, that the books attributed to him, the *Illiad* and the *Odyssey*, were compilations from different parts of the Greek world brought into epic format by accretions and collective efforts. If so, and I believe it was so, the Homeric books represent a universality of beliefs rather than the imaginative creation of one man. This universality of beliefs figured as well, I propose, but in a more limited format, in how the Ara Pacis was programmed and subsequently perceived by an aggregate populace.

Particles of the Hesiod and Homer myths show up in Virgil, Horace, and Ovid's texts, and also in various contexts of Augustus' time, including the enactment of sacrifices, cult rituals, and even marriage ceremonies when the bride is referred to as Gaia and the bridegroom as Uranus. But underlying the aggregate of origin myths and just plain folk tales that explain things would have been a core, an encompassing scenario, that I assume to have been ancient stories of origins transformed from Grecian to Roman formats, such as Persephone into Proserpina, Aphrodite into Venus, Gaia into Tellus, and so on. I will tell the stories as I believe they would have been known to the Roman commoner, to whom the Ara Pacis imagery was addressed.

In what context of ancient history did one begin to distinguish between myths and facts, with the meaning of myths confined to the behavior and actions of gods? To repeat, where do we find a maternal figure seated on a rock, an infant or two, nymphs and *aurae*, a seahorse, a marsh, a stream, the sea, acorns, poppies, pomegranates, irises, and maybe even a poisonous plant? Where would we find these meaningfully fitted together before the advent of agriculture, taken to mean as well the origin of civilization? How would these phantasms have registered in the people's mind during an era when gods supplied explanations for everything that existed or happened?

All beginnings start with gods, and all gods dwell in fables. The most popular narration of the origin of agriculture—a sequence of events any person back then would have been able to retell—started with the first Golden Age when, disrupted by a fall-out among gods who were offspring from the marriage of Uranus and the earth-body, Gaia. Uranus had his pleasures with Gaia, impregnating her time and again (read, plowed and seeded her many times). She gave birth to the Titans, six male and six female. But after those issuings, Uranus refused to allow Gaia to bring forth more children. The unborn piled up inside her (the Roman sacrifices of pregnant sows, ewes, and cows would figure here: specifically, Aeneas' sacrifice of a white pregnant sow as depicted on the Ara Pacis shrine). To prevent additional pregnancies, Gaia called upon her youngest son, Cronos, for help. As the first oedipal act, Cronos castrated his father with a sickle—a crop-cutting agricultural tool (read, castration of fallen enemies so they wouldn't breed new enemies in the afterworld, as done well into modern history with a small knife in the shape of a sickle, equivalent to cutting off seed heads, the male organ, even then referred to as a head—*caput*). Thus Heaven and Earth became separate (the first divorce). One may conclude from this that Earth would thereafter be self-seeding, while sky could just send down rain, like urine in golden showers (golden droplets from the oak trees—from Jupiter, the Roman Zeus, who is sometimes thought to be Uranus incarnate—or as a belting, punishing rain that gullies and swamps Earth, grooves her body with streams and rivers. Anyone who has parked a car under an oak tree will have experienced on the hood and winshield sticky golden droplets that oak leaves secrete from basal leaf stems). Because Earth was a real body, not just surface, sky was all around her and could even permeate her from the underside (as underground river-flows).

Once castrated, Uranus lost his power over Gaia. Her gestated children were born as a brood (like the brood-sow that delivers litters). Cronos then married his sister Rhea. She gives birth to many of the Greek gods. But knowing he would one day be supplanted by one of them, Cronos swallows the children as they are born, to Rhea's distress. When she gives birth to Zeus (hereafter Jupiter), she slips a cloth-wrapped stone into her husband's mouth. Thinking it was a very hard child, he swallows it without chewing. Rhea then hides the baby somewhere on the island of Crete. When Jupiter grows up, he forces Cronos to disgorge the rock and all the children he had swallowed. Then, with the aid of the other Titans, Chronos wages war against Jupiter and his brothers. But they are overwhelmed and locked up in the caves of Tartarus, in what is now southern Spain (Virgil locates them under Mount Etna). Their rage and efforts to escape take the form of vengeance against Earth (Tellus), as earthquakes shaking her and volcanoes spewing forth hot anger. This earthshaking and rupturing causes Pluto to fear the Titan's wrath will crack Tellus' surface and expose his dark underworld to light. So he sets out on his chariot, pulled by black horses, to survey the earth's body and check for damage.

Meanwhile, on Mount Eryx, Venus is playing with mischievous Cupid. She spots Pluto. She tells Cupid to select his straightest, most keenly pointed arrow, and shoot Pluto as he drives by (Venus had good reason for this: she knew of Ceres' beautiful daughter, Proserpina, who showed signs of following her mother by not marrying. By then, Earth had been re-deified in dual aspects. Tellus was the earth's corporeal body and natural produce, while Ceres had become the goddess of agriculture. Venus had taken over Aphrodite's charms, becoming goddess of love and its consequence, marriage. Venus had been angry with the haughty Diana and Minerva, who rejected love and marriage, and figured that Proserpina would foolishly heed their ways. She apparently saw in Pluto an opportunity for both a forced marriage and good riddance to the carefree maiden).

At the moment Cupid takes aim, Pluto's carriage is passing through the vale of Enn where there is a lake bounded by woods and moist ground covered with wild flowers, a place where spring is eternal ("spring"—either the season, an unpolluted source, or a virgin girl—is for Venus an opportune condition for virginities to be taken). Down there with her virginal companions, Proserpina is gathering lilies in her basket (a virgin womb). Pluto is hit with Cupid's arrow. Having spied Proserpina, he falls instantly in love with her. He descends and grabs her up. In her fright, she drops her basket, her flowers spill to the ground (she is de-flowered).

Pluto carries Proserpina tucked under his free arm to where he reaches the river Cyane (read *cycnus*, or *cicinus*, as swan, hence Swan River or Swan Lake). He is refused crossing. Furious over that impudence, Pluto strikes the riverbank with his trident (read Roman three-pronged cultivating fork). The earth opens up (read yields to him; but Tellus, not Ceres, is the yielding body) and he passes underground with Proserpina (read plants her in Tellus' furrowed soil).

Missing her daughter, Ceres sets out to search for her (Tellus of course knew where Proserpina was, because she had been forced by Pluto to open up, just as Gaia had known where the children seeded in her by Uranus were). When Aurora (dawn) comes forth in the morning and Hesperus (evening) lets the stars out, they notice Ceres still searching. After an exhaustive hunt, Ceres tires, changes herself into an old woman (no longer fecund) and sits down on a rock where she remains for nine days and nine nights (the rock is where Eleusis now stands, and from where, it is often written, knowledge of agriculture spread to the rest of the world). Ceres is spotted by a girl out gathering acorns and berries (this was a pre-agriculture place). This girl is the daughter of a humble food-gathering family living nearby, the family of Celeus. When she approaches Ceres, who looks so old and wearied, she calls her "Mother." The girl's father then approaches and implores Ceres to come to the house for food and rest.

Ceres goes with them. Along the way she gathers up poppies (pre-agricultural seedy flowers from Tellus' body). Arriving at the cottage, she finds the wife of Celeus in great distress: her infant son is gravely ill. Ceres kisses the child on the mouth (read nourishes him) and the child recovers. The wife prepares a meal of curds, cream, apples, and honey in the comb (all pre-agricultural foods). With no one noticing, Ceres juices poppy petals and puts them in the infant's milk (to sedate him). And after darkness, when the household is asleep, she moves to the infant's cradle and moulds its body all over (read, kneads bread), then takes him up and lays him on the hot ashes of the fireplace (read, puts the loaf into the oven).

The mother, having awakened, rushes up and extracts the infant from the heat (read, no knowledge yet of bread baking). At that moment Ceres assumes her god-like form and chastises the mother, saying, "You have been cruel in your fondness to your son (read, eaten him, because she loved bread), whereas I would have made him immortal (for gods do not eat mortal-type food); nevertheless, as a human, he shall be great and useful" (greatness and usefulness were not qualities of pre-agricultural men, for the gods did everything necessary and the ideal virtue was passivity and humility). Ceres then adds, "He shall teach men the use of the plow and the rewards labor can win from the cultivated soil" (note that her reference to soil is not to herself, for soil is Tellus).

Ceres wraps a cloud around herself, mounts her chariot, and rides off. She continues her search from land to land, changing horses to dragons when crossing seas (easy enough, considering the shape of sea-horses). Making full circle, she comes back to where her search had begun, by the banks of the river Cyne and the place where Pluto entered Earth's body. A river nymph at that place would like to tell Ceres what she knows, but she fears Pluto (for rivers must cope with the underground as they emerge from and seep into it). This nymph had taken up the girdle that Proserpina dropped when struggling. Imperceptibly, she wafts it to the feet of Ceres (back then, the girdle was not just to trim one's belly for aesthetic reasons, but to tighten the abdomen to retain fertility, as plant germs are tightly encased by cotyledons, and otherwise to outwardly display that one is not pregnant. Much threshing is required to get the girdling shell off seeds—called winnowing). Having dropped her girdle, Proserpina is vulnerable.

Ceres lays blame on the land (Tellus). She admonishes it, calls it ungrateful for having been endowed with fertility and clothed with herbage, yet had opened up to take in her daughter. Ceres vows to withhold seeds until Proserpina is returned. Across the land, animal husbandry fails, livestock dies; plows broke down in the furrows; crops cannot be planted. The growing cycle is thrown off—too much rain, too much sun; thistles and brambles overtake the fields (Ceres had no power over seeds of wild plants—not over wild barley or wild oats, brambles, or thistles; those belonged, by nature, to Tellus). Untended gardens and fields are invaded by weeds (as are untended women and children who are intruded upon by bad company or bad seed. The expression, "sowing wild oats," lingers as sex before intended to be reproductive).

A natural fountain named Arethusa intercedes on Tellus' behalf. Arethusa says, "Goddess, don't blame the land [again, Ceres is distinct from Tellus] for it opened unwillingly to yield passage [was raped]." Arethusa then defies Venus. She tells Ceres how she became a fountain, that she was a woodland nymph of great beauty and did not seek marriage but had developed skill at hunting (as had Diana and Atalanta, both incurring Venus' jealousy and rage). She discloses that, on returning from a hunt perspiring, she had bathed in a stream so clear you might count pebbles at the bottom (a reference to her virginal purity). She was noticed by the stream-god Alpheus, who desired her and pursued her when she fled. As he was about to overtake her, she called out to Diana who came to her aid by wrapping her in a cloudy mist. As she stood in the mist, a cold sweat came over her. Moisture flowed down her long hair and formed a pool at her feet. She became a fountain.

The river-god, Alpheus, then sees her as a fountain of pure water and attempts to mingle his stream with hers (rivers then, in comparison to streams, were taken metaphorically as slow and dirty, like dirty old men lusting after virgins). Diana again intervenes. She clefts the ground (Tellus, perennially cleaved) and the fountain nymph plunges underground. Passing through the Underworld, Arethusa sees Proserpina as the bride of Pluto and queen of the realm of the dead.

On hearing this sad tale from Arethusa, a furious and saddened Ceres sets out for Heaven to complain to Jupiter, who agrees to intervene but only if, during her time in the underworld, Proserpina had not eaten anything; otherwise the Fates will forbid her being released (had she eaten she would have become mortal). Mercury, accompanied by the goddess of spring (probably Flora), is sent to Hades to negotiate Proserpina's release. But wily Pluto had already offered Proserpina a pomegranate, and she had sucked red pulp from a few seeds.

A compromise is reached allowing Proserpina to pass half the year with her mother (the growing season) and half with Pluto (over-wintering). The fate of her daughter settled, Ceres restores earth (Tellus) that had taken in her daughter; agriculture is again possible. Mindful of her promise to the infant, Tripholemus, of the pre-agriculture family, when the boy grows up she takes him in her chariot drawn by winged dragons and passes through all lands imparting seed and teaching the principles of agriculture. In gratitude, Tripholemus erects a temple in her name, Ceres in Eleusis, and establishes her worship under the name of the Eleusianian mysteries. The rituals performed for Ceres surpass all other Greek celebrations, as they will for the early Romans, who were, for the most part, farmers.

16

THE CLOSING ARGUMENT

The four relief panels on the Ara Pacis shrine convey the history of Rome, with Tellus as the primal land, then to the west facade, to Mars and the twins, across the west portal to Aeneas, then back to the east facade, to modern Rome personified as Roma. On the exterior south frieze, Augustus performs a ritual. If repeating Aeneas' sacrificial act, he is pouring a libation onto an altar.

To make sacrifice is to humble oneself to what transcends the self as a higher order, taker to giver. The Latin word *religio* recognizes an external power that hosts by its grace the presence of humans, infusing them with awe, as associated with sacred groves and springs, virginal places, and the abodes of spirits. Having arrived at one such abode, I find it as good any place to bring my text to a close.

In the *Aeneid,* King Evander tours Aeneas around archaic Rome founded on the Palatine Hill, speaking of the Sacred Grove, where Romulus took shelter, as Rome's first location. He shows Aeneas the grove and the rocky crag overhanging the grotto, the Lupercal, where Romulus and Remus were suckled by the nurse-wolf. "Some god," he says, "it is not sure what god, lived in this grove." Virgil moves the narrative on to the Capital, which he is quick to say is now (in Augustus' day) all golden, but in the old days was wild and tangled with underbrush—"awesome even then," King Evander says, "back when a strangeness filled country folk with dread." So primitive was ancient Rome that Virgil has the king offer Aeneas a place to sleep on a mattress of strewn leaves covered with a bearskin.

The old kings were *rex sacrotae*, kings of sacred things, of the family hearth and home, groves, springs, and fields. They safeguarded boundaries, drove off wolves that savaged flocks and rampaging wild pigs from gardens. They defended against crop pillage by marauding hordes. Nature was awesome, its mechanics unknown. Man had no control over it in those days before the oxen-driven plow and before wind and water mills had been invented, before the felling axe, the wire saw, and the long bow and throwing spear that could kill beasts at a distance. One yielded to natural forces as to the divine; by divine grace, nature yielded harvests. All advances in the technology of agriculture were acts of aggression against nature to force her to produce more than her natural gifts, the aggression measured against primordial humility as the natural state of the human—the infants on Tellus' lap, the tranquil bull, the nibbling lamb, and plants going to seed after submitting their virginal state to reproduction.

Belief systems that fed the program for the Ara Pacis were stories we call myths (defined as events broght about by gods)—simple, repeatable structures promoted by storytellers and carried about in one's head. Stories that flow most easily through history are the kind that entertain and are structured by morals, anxieties, and fears, that have at their base enough reality to convert suspended belief into a figurative discourse. Most myths are defense mechanisms, lessons one cannot forget. With the advent of book writing and widespread literacy, myths became literature; in time, the poetic voice was challenged by prose that suffocated myths under blankets of reality—prose nurtured by history and history derranged by poetry. Still, neither natural nor human history can wholly replace mythology, because history unfolds with regard to myths and within mythological structures. Truth falters when assaulted by myths. Lacking structure, truths blow around in the wind until collected by ideologies and other integrating fancies. People behave less according to facts than to beliefs.

Personages represented on the south and north wall friezes were true to life in the eyes of beholders, collectively a social class. Yet the historical and allegorical panel images were to be understood by citizens of all classes. One can only imagine the subjects' true-to-life vividness as seen when the reliefs were painted in bright colors. From our remoteness and custom of seeing (and preferring) ancient art and architecture as ruins, the intense reality of the imagery is lost behind veils of archeological imagination.

The Roman will to reality was a powerful force that set the Roman mind apart from the Greek. Poetry was of little use for those who were obliged to face daily the reality of making a human-type life in the natural world (for that matter, of minor use for interpreting Roman imagery). The Greek geographer Strabo, who, from 44 BC through Augustus' reign, made several visits to Rome, admired the Romans for having created an earthly state comparable to the heavenly one, for having fused religious with secular life and myths with reality. The Syrian geographer Posidonius—Cicero's teacher and an influence on Lucretius and Virgil—wrote of the Roman Empire as having established kinship of all humanity. As had Lucretius, Posidonius had studied the causes and effects of natural forces, like tides and volcanoes, and tried to reconcile nature as animated by divine reason yet with the increasingly effective principles of human industry that was driving the social and economic progress of Roman industry and culture.

Over this brief discourse on modes of representation I've referred to the Aeneas and Mars panels as pictorial. They picture events lifted from a narrative—two parts of the same story. Augustus had promoted the worship of Mars as father of Romulus, founder of Rome and builder of the first city on the Palatine hill. In 42 BC, Augustus vowed a temple to Mars in vengeance of Julius Caesar's assassination. In 20 BC, he ordered that a temple of Mars Ultor—"avenger"—be built in the Forum, the temple dedicated in 2 BC. Ovid provides a detailed description of the Forum named after Augustus. Even though Mars, central in the pediment of his temple, looks out over the forum, Ovid imagines him as if looking at the temple:

> Mars, strong in armor, looks upon the temple pediment and rejoices that unvanquished gods occupy the places of honor. At the entranceways he sees arms of all sorts from all the lands conquered by his soldier [Augustus, no doubt].

This much of Ovid's description coincides with the Ara Pacis image of Roma seated on the arms and armor of defeated enemies. He continues:

> On one side he sees Aeneas with his precious burden [referring to Aeneas carrying his father Anchises from burning Troy], and about him the many ancestors of the Julian house. On the other side, Romulus with the arms of the enemy chief he conquered with his own hand (the *optima spolia*).

Here we have a parallel to the left and right Ara Pacis panels picturing Aeneas in one and Mars/Romulus in the other, as well as the "many ancestors" represented by Augustus' extended family members on the north and south walls. The concluding sentences to Ovid's adulation of the Augustan Forum also keys to the fact that the "peace" of the Ara Pacis is entirely Augustus'. Ovid says, "Mars gazes upon the temple and reads the name Augustus. Then the monument seems to him even greater" (thus the god is admiring the man).

Ovid's description reinforces how the Ara Pacis programmers conceived the interaction of the east and west panels. But it also helps to clarify that the Aeneas and Mars panels evoke stories while the Tellus and Roma panels are self-contained; not surprisingly, each is symmetrical within its own frame and to each other across the entrance; both are stable states of the universe: at its beginning and after a tour around the shrine, taking in Mars and Aeneas, at its present. It is appropriate then that these two panels are at the east entrance, for east is the place of the sun's daily beginning and the dawn of each new age—the rise and setting of the sun having been known since the origin of humans as the constant on which one can depend.

One can assume that the programmers followed story lines from Virgil's *Aeneid*. With his aged and lame father, Anchises, on his back and his son Julus by the hand, Aeneas flees burning Troy, bringing as well the Penates and Lares, the simple household and field gods in the form of statuettes. The Delian oracle tells him to seek the original land of the Trojan race. On his first voyage, having assembled a fleet, Juno, the goddess of Carthage, a city the Trojans are prophesied to destroy, incites wind-god Aeolus to stir up the sea. But Neptune resists in Aeneas' favor and calms the waves (it is not unreasonable to assume that this event is at least subliminally recorded in the Carthage copy of the Tellus relief).

En route, Aeneas stops at Carthage, where Juno and Venus have conspired to bring his travels to a halt by causing Queen Dido to fall in love with him. But Aeneas' will is driven not by amorous desires but by the augury.

Jupiter demands that Aeneas set sail, which he does, confessing to distraught Dido that he has no other choice. She commits suicide in anger and grief. On making landfall, Aeneas consults the Cumean Sibyl who forewarns him of perils he will undergo before reaching Latium (Italy). She takes him down into the Underworld where he will see those *who will be reincarnated to build the new history of Rome*. He sees Dido, but she is not all impressed by his excuse that he had to leave her against his will. He sees his father Anchises, by that time deceased, *and of course he sees Augustus*. Back above ground, the ordeals unfold while on Olympus the gods debate the conflicts like senators during wars.

The prophecy that reaffirms the birth of Aeneas from Venus—Anchises the father, whom Jupiter struck with a bolt of lightning, rendering him lame, for having boasted of his seduction of the goddess (although most likely Venus did the seducing by transforming herself into a human, an old Jupiterian trick, considering Jupiter's affairs with earthling maidens Leda and Europa)—that prophecy Virgil made up to flatter Caesar, and thus Augustus, and to imbue the Claudian bloodline with divinity.

Venus appeals to Jupiter on behalf of Aeneas:

> My lord who rule
> The lives of men and gods now and forever,
> And bring them all to heal with you bright bolt,
> What in the world could my Aeneas do,
> What could the Trojans do, so to offend you
> That after suffering all those deaths they find
> The whole world closed to them, because of Italy?
> Surely from these the Romans are to come
> In the course of years, renewing Teucer's line,
> To rule the sea and all the lands about it.

Jupiter tells Venus that Aeneas will see Lavinian's walls go up, and will pass three summers and three winters in Latium. Then his son Iulus (Julus) will hold power for thirty years, after transforming his capital to nearby Alba Longa, where for three centuries that kingdom will be ruled by Hector's race (Trojans):

> Until the queen and priestess Ilia [Rhea Silva],
> Pregnant by Mars, will bear twin sons to him.
> Afterward, happy in the tawny pelt
> His nurse, the she-wolf wears, young Romulus
> Will take the leadership, build walls of Mars,
> And call by his own name Romans.
> For these I set no limit, world or time.
> But make the gift of empire without end.
> Juno, indeed, whose bitterness now fills
> With fear and torment sea and earth and sky,
> Will mend her ways, and favor them as I do,
> Lords of the world, the toga-bearing Romans.

Jupiter mentions the royal house that will bring an end to its enemies.

> From that comely line
> The Trojan Caesar comes, to circumscribe
> Empire with Ocean, fame with heavenly stars.
> Julius his name, from Iulus handed down…

Thus Julius Caesar is inserted into the royal line, the family of Iulus (Julus), the Julians. That Aeneas, son of Anchises, was born of Athena, Caesar's divine status is assured. The prophecy ends with:

> And grim with iron frames, the Gates of War
> Will then be shut: inside, unholy Furor.[88]

The prophecy narrates both the role of Aeneas and Romulus (referring now to the west panels on the Ara Pacis), and ends with the Janus gates being shut and peace settling over Italy (the east panels, featuring peaceful Earth and Roma on a heap of trophies that may signify the demise of all enemies and thus the end of war). So it is possible, as has been suggested, that Augustus on the south wall may be holding the *lituus*, the augur's wand, and that the act he's performing is not a sacrifice but an augury.

Virgil established the role of Aeneas in Roman history, and through fictional descendants gave history a real Julius Caesar and a real Augustus:

> Here is Caesar
> and all the line of Julus that will come
> beneath the mighty curve of heaven. This,
> this is the man you heard so often promised—
> Augustus Caesar, son of a god, who will
> renew a golden age in Latium,
> in fields where Saturn once was king, and stretch
> his rule beyond the Garamantes and
> the Indians.

Although dedicated to divinity and featuring propitiatiary sacrifices, the Ara Pacis was also a grand secular monument bolstered by the origin of the Roman people as having a blood infusion of deity; the gods acknowledged on the altar but materialized as humans, augured acts portrayed by history from the primordial state of Italy (Tellus) to the exalted present of Augustan Rome (Roma).

In *Tiberius* 47, Suetonius maintains that Tiberius was not only pathologically mean but that during his reign no major buildings were erected. While some were, including several triumphal arches, as Niels Hannestad correctly says, most of the building resources must have gone into finishing Augustus' public works program.[88] Hannestad also points out that while Tiberius was a loyal and dedicated civil servant, he had no Virgil, Horace, or Livy to embroider his principate, to which I might add that the fictional origin of royal blood was wearing thin. Tiberius depended on publicizing Augustan virtues and keeping Augustus in the public mind.

The *ara Pietatis*, although decreed by the Senate as early as AD 22, was not completed until the Claudian reign. So nothing stands in the way of saying that the *ara Pacis Augustae* was not completed *as we see it now* until the reign of Tiberius. Neither the architectural nor sculptural style can deny that it was, nor can the iconography. The Tiberian Ara Pacis, having incorporated the altars of 13 and 9 BC, was designed and built to support the fragile and politically troubled reign of Tiberius, which was known more for treason tribunals than for grand civic and religious building projects. Augustus' ghost held his successor's empire together.

That ghost would pale as ensuing decades drained off the Julian blood. Mussolini's effort to reinstate the Augustan authority two millennia later was as futile as a dunk in the Fountain of Youth. What is left to remember Augustus by is nonetheless the *Ara Pacis Augustae*, which I have neither destroyed nor even modified but merely reassembled chronologically in order to get to the bottom of what was troubling me, and to compel that structure to finally leave me in peace.

finem

ADDENDUM

For readers not familiar with the historical events leading up to the *ara Pacis Augustae*, I will briefly lay them out. My coverage will be as abbreviated as Julius Caesar's famous *veni, vidi, vici* (I came, I saw, I conquered), but for this book's function it will have to do. And in so doing, I will offer my opinion of what was the Augustan Peace as a chapter in Roman history.

The story of Octavian becoming Augustus is of course well known to specialists and familiar to the general reader who has imbibed the murder of Caesar and the saga of Antony and Cleopatra as featured by Shakespeare in *Julius Caesar* and *Antony and Cleopatra*. Less well known is that Caesar preceded Antony in Cleopatra's bed by a few years when in Egypt after bringing about the defeat of his one-time partner, but later political rival, Pompeius Magnus (Pompey the Great).

That seminal event in ancient Roman history came about in this way. In the year 50 BC, Julius Caesar was preoccupied with problems in Gaul, particularly Cisalpius Gaul (now upper Italy) that controlled overland access to Rome from the north. Back in Rome, taking advantage of Caesar's absence, Pompey was amassing personal power over the Senate and provincial governors, eclipsing Caesar's sun. Alarmed by this conspiratorial situation—he had his own designs on home rule—Caesar defied the Senate by violating a constitutional imperative that holders of a provincial command voluntarily forfeit their *imperium* (the right to command troops) when leaving his assigned province. Caesar crossed the Rubicon, a narrow river separating Italy from Gaul, yet retained command of his army. That act of insurrection prompted the Senate to declare war against him, which may have been something Caesar had maneuvered into happening. Caesar's response was to march on Rome and assault the Senate with a military coup.

The suddenness of Caesar's action caught Pompey off guard and unprepared, his designs on imperial rule incomplete. He hastily gathered what forces he could and fled Rome, thinking he could forge an army at a distance, return to overthrow Caesar, and be honored with a great triumphal procession with Caesar 's head on a pole. The first-century AD Geek historian and biographer, Plutarch, quotes Pompey saying he could raise an army just by stamping his feet on Italian soil, but when reality replaced fantasy, Pompey's boast proved gaseous.[88] Caesar could press eighty thousand men into action while Pompey had to settle for what he could scrape together. A large part of his military command was immovable from Spain.

Caesar had been away from Rome for almost ten years. After reestablishing his status by threatening oppositional senators while convincing others to back him, he was elected *consul* for the year 48 BC (a *consul* was the supreme magistrate at Rome and commander of the army when on campaign). Comfortable then with senatorial backup—the Senate had about one thousand members—Caesar set out to neutralize Pompey's forces that were camped all along the Adriatic coast of northern Greece, a bit south of what is now Durres in Albania, and mustering and training for Pompey's counter-invasion.

In what is known as the Battle of Pharsalus, with Caesar's highly experienced field commanders displaying exceptional skill in battlefield strategy, Pompey was defeated. He escaped by sea, taking with him his wife and a number of close relatives, hoping to find refuge in Egypt. But he never set foot on land. In the Nile's delta, in a small off-loaded boat, his own guards, sensing their fate should Caesar be not far behind, and that Pompey's head might bring them forgiveness in Octavian's eyes, set upon their defeated leader and murdered him with his distraught family obliged to look on.

On arriving in Alexandria, Caesar got caught up in a conflict between the young pharaoh, Ptolemy XIII, and his sister Cleopatra, who was twenty-two at the time and had been deposed from her throne by her brother. Fifty-year old Caesar had enough military power on hand to unseat Ptolemy XIII and put Cleopatra back on it. She would rule jointly with her younger brother, Ptolemy XIV. So in more ways than one, Cleopatra reigned over Egypt at Caesar's pleasure, and soon at Antony's.[89] After enjoying a romantic Nile cruise with her (that tryst not verifiable), Caesar left her pregnant and set out to deal with problems in North Africa (Mauritania) and bring a final defeat to Pompeians at Thapsus on the Tunisian coastline south of Sousse.

Caesar returned to Rome in 47 BC to take charge of an unruly home front.

He made bold moves to put an end to republican government, which by tradition was in the hands of the aristocracy. He assumed the title *emperator* and moved to implant supreme power within his own family, having in mind a dynasty. Ruthlessly he expelled disloyal senators and governors; his loyal generals pursued those who managed to flee by ship, some with contingencies of the army and navy under their command. In 46 BC, his legions defeated the senatorial forces in Africa; by the following year's end he had subdued the Pompeian forces still marooned in Spain. His power over the government continued to expand until a few generals and senators, alarmed by his driving ambition, conspired in 44 BC to bring it to a halt. So not one of them could be accused of the fatal dagger thrust, several assailants assembled in the Senate house and collectively murdered him. Twenty-three dagger wounds were counted on his body.[90]

Brutus and Cassius, who led the insurrection, were allowed to avoid reprisal by being granted governorships of eastern provinces far from the city. In time, when they realized their deed had not brought normalcy to the government but made them outcasts and subject to capital punishment, each raised a small army to secure his defense. Meanwhile, Marc Antony, who'd been Caesar's co-*consul*, managed, with the help of Caesar's protégé, Marcus Lepidus, to neutralize factional outbreaks of pro- and anti-sentiment over Caesar's demise. But the murder brought Octavian, the future Augustus, into the picture. On hearing that Caesar had adopted him, Octavian, then only nineteen (born in 63 BC) and in Macedonia participating in strategic planning for the projected campaign against the Parthians, came to Rome, arriving a few weeks after the assassination. Ecstatic crowds and soldiers still feeling loyalty to Caesar welcomed him with such outpourings of passion that the Senate was obliged to respect him as Caesar's heir, the assignment having bestowed upon Octavius the name C. Julius Caesar Octavianus. That aligned him with the royalty extending back through Caesar and Aeneas to Romulus.

Antony had not moved aggressively to take command of the Senate, so he was caught as unprepared for Octavian's return as Pompey had been for Caesar's. It was said that he refused to hand over Caesar's papers (with which he had tampered) and that he and Lepidus had already dipped into Caesar's family fortune that was to pass to Octavian. For himself, Antony had obtained Caesar's power-position as governor of the province of Cisalpine Gaul, the gateway to Italy from the north from where Caesar had launched his invasion southward to Rome. While preoccupied with transferring his legions from Macedonia where he'd previously been in command, Antony's absence from Rome allowed

Octavian to raise doubts about his loyalty—his not having taken immediate action to avenge Caesar's death. Antony had convinced the Senate to grant Brutus and Cassius amnesty and keep them on quasi-diplomatic missions, even though they were in de facto exile east of the Adriatic. That effort at diplomacy was valid, considering that the conspiracy to murder Caesar had been confined to a small faction within the Senate.

Octavian's offensive against Antony was a mistake, for Antony had supporters in the Senate as well, and he commanded a huge military force. If threatened, he was positioned to sever Rome's supply routes from Spain and Gaul and descend on Rome, as Caesar had done when routing Pompey. But Fortuna was with Octavian; two of Antony's legions en route to repositioning in Gaul shifted loyalty and joined Augustus' forces. And a sudden turnabout by a majority in the Senate resulted in orders that Octavian collaborate with Antony's enemies in the north and deploy senatorial military forces to exterminate him. This mandate was not implemented, but the Senate's action put Augustus in command of the entire Roman army.

The mandate was not unanimous. When Antony's future brightened by a number of governors and field generals declaring for him, Octavian, at the time some distance away and taking a cue, perhaps, from Caesar's action when frustrated by the Senate, turned his legions about and marched on Rome. He forced the Senate to elect him as *consul*. Confronted then with Octavian's heightened status and a deteriorating loyalty of his own military commanders who sensed their vulnerability, Antony was left with no choice but to meet with Octavian for negotiations—which he did, in October 43 BC, on an island in mid-river near Bologna. Lepidus, who was then a governor, acted as arbitrator. The result was the creation of the Second Triumvirate by which, having formed a commission, the three men would regulate the state.

According to the second-century Appian of Alexandria, who'd practiced as a lawyer in Rome and written narratives of the various Roman conquests, shortly after the Triumvirate was formed, Octavian, Antony, and Lepidus drew up a list of enemies to be exterminated. Appian may have exaggerated the number of victims, but the essence of his report rings true:

> As soon as they were on their own, the three drew up a list of those who were to die. They proscribed, both then and later, those of whom they were suspicious because of their ability to subvert, as well as their personal enemies, trading each other for the lives of their own relatives and friends.

> They decreed death and confiscation of property for about 300 senators and 2,000 knights, among them their own brothers and uncles, as well as senior officers serving under them who had cause to offend them. On departing the conference table for Rome, they decided to postpone most of the killings, but as a warning they secretly sent out assassins to execute twelve (some say seventeen) of the most important victims, including Cicero.

With Antony and Lepidius' support, Octavian had his way as to avenging the murder of Caesar. His and Antony's land and naval forces pursued Brutus and Cassius and defeated them in the battle of Philippi in 42 BC, the two assassins committing suicide.

Over the ensuing years, Octavian and Antony were preoccupied with external and internecine battles while Octavian also struggled with land grants for discharged soldiers, disgruntled post-Caesar had-beens and would-have-beens, and senatorial elbowing and squabbling as the change of leaders reshuffled the deck of power positions. For reasons not entirely clear, perhaps because he opposed Octavian's authority in the west, Octavian and Antony deprived Lepidus of his provincial governorship, leaving him relatively powerless. In 36 BC, Octavian would force him into retirement. By then, Octavian was flouting his title "Imperator" and acting as the Roman army's unrivaled commander. Over these same years, Antony was not faring well militarily. Octavian took advantage of his colleague's misfortunes in battles to deny reinforcements and finally to see that Antony was degraded from a governing to a diplomatic position and effectively disowned by the Senate.

By 32 BC, the narrowing-down triumvirate had come to an end. His power in decline, Antony took up with Cleopatra, then thirty-two, and established himself in a position of power over Egypt. Concerned about Rome's dependency on Egypt for grain, as much as on Sardinia and Crete, as well as distress over Antony's gifts of imperial territory to Cleopatra—fearing that his titular control over Egypt's exports could unbalance Rome's economy—the senatorial majority looked to Octavian for a solution. By that time, Octavian was in command of Rome's land forces, while the brilliant admiral Agrippa, who was loyal to Octavian, commanded the navy. The Senate voted to declare war on Cleopatra for having violated Egypt's status as a trading client of Rome. To avoid the stigma of civil strife—the assassination of Caesar lingering on many minds—Antony was not designated as the enemy.

In 31 BC, Antony and Cleopatra's naval forces came up against Agrippa's. The better part of Antony's fleet was destroyed in the Gulf of Ambracie at Actium (a promontory on the western shore of Greece). On land, Octavian's infantry and cavalry strategically outmaneuvered Antony's forces and cut them off from supplies. After a few battles—for the most part Romans against Romans—Octavian pushed the couple and their decimated armies back to Egypt, sailing on remnants of their fleet that had managed to evade Agrippa and remain afloat. Antony and Cleopatra hoped to regroup there. But when their commanders realized they could not defend Egypt against Octavian's approach, they and their legions deserted. The distraught couple committed suicide.

Most of Antony's soldiers and sailors were granted amnesty. Those who were Roman citizens were repatriated as members of Octavian's army. To guarantee that Cleopatra's son, Caesarion (after whom caesarian births are known), would never claim royalty as Julius Caesar's son, Octavian had him put to death. He then weakened the pharaoh's throne, annexed Egypt to the Roman Empire, and assigned it to his personal rule.

The nineteen-year-old Octavian was now thirty-three and unopposed. Aware of Caesar's downfall for having asserted an excess of personal power, the wiser Octavian pushed through a modified constitution, and, rather than accept dictatorial authority, he opted for a vote of the Senate to award him control of Gaul, Spain, and Syria, the three provinces to which Rome looked for natural resources and where the major portion of the Roman army was stationed. By that arrangement, Octavian would effectively control the military defense of the Empire while allowing the Senate to manage, but not dictate, financial and economic affairs, Octavian having retained the right of veto.

When newly named Augustus (the revered one, or having heightened qualities), Octavian was positioned to rule the Empire until his death, which came forty years later The Augustan era was one of relative peace and prosperity, with peace at last understood as a concept and a way of life rather than the absence of war. Expansion of international trade resulted in mutual dependencies and, in times of crisis, mutual aid. Disputes could, for the most part, be settled through diplomacy rather than by taking up arms. Of course with thousands of coastal miles to patrol, and piracy still a leading industry, battles on land and sea wouldn't entirely let up, nor would palace intrigues, slave revolts, and mutinies.

The Augustan Peace did not come about as a moral success. Only when military campaigning became unprofitable did the motivation for waging war wind down. Peace was driven by a shift in economics. Peace was good business. Fortunes made as importers, war contractors and provincial tax collectors built a wealthy class among Rome's checkered population, lifting a patrician layer above the masses, like sky above earth. But as time passed, and the geographical economy expanded, war-making to take loot and slaves generated inherent contradictions. Great victories meant returning soldiers who couldn't compete as small farmers with industrialized farms operated by businessmen in control of crop prices, markets and distribution systems. Decimated foreign nations did not make good exporters of Rome's essential imports.

An excess of slaves brought to Rome by victorious generals swelled the urban mob. Crime was rampant, and lawmaking a senatorial passion, as if laws alone could quell the misery of the masses. Horace poked fun at laws forcing the majority to observe rules of conduct that were meant for the minority, such as the alcohol control law stipulating the amount to be drunk at a banquet—the temperate man thus obliged to drink more than he wants, the drinking man less, jibed Horace. Prisons and detention camps were not workable institutions. Jails were solely to hold prisoners until physically punished or executed. Notions of reforming criminals or shipping back useless slaves were probably not on anyone's mind. Criminals and excess slaves were introduced into the entertainment industry. Roman war games were deadly. Losers died. Public executions were ritualized as public slaughters. Gladiatorial combats were live-shows. Pictorial representations of combat, victors and victims, were transformed into virtual reality.

Wars worked against international business—caused hatred of Romans and Italians. Sulla had defiled and decimated Athens to the despair of many thousands of Greeks who lived in distant lands but remained loyal to their racial center. In Asia, vengeful natives, inspired to revolt against Rome by Mithridates VI of Pontus, slaughtered some 80,000 Italian residents. People remember such events decades later. ***(While writing notes that made their way into these pages, Japan's emperor was in China coping with the Chinese people's memory of atrocities from a half-century ago. In last week's Herald Tribune—21 October 1992—one reads a sub-header "Hate Hurts Business, German Company Says").*** War messed up trade routes and trade relations, put distant trade partners and resource centers in jeopardy. Military expeditions eventually overworked the shipbuilding industry and deflected the economic purpose of the merchant marine: in the mid-third century BC war against the Parthians in Sicily, Rome is said to have lost 700 ships and their crews. Ships back then were relatively small, were both rowed and wind driven; shipbuilding lumber and mast poles had to be imported because Italy had been divested of quality pine forests. Economies muscled by import and exports across seas depend on stable money. After international currencies replaced the weight-value of gold and silver (Augustus was a major contributor to that change), the heavy costs of campaigning stimulated a false monetary base. War also bred piracy, local uprisings and revolts in colonies, inflated the value of silver mined abroad, undercut international banking and lending, opened up commerce in corruption. Stability depended on uniformity. Standard coinage, standard weights and measures, differed not a bit from Augustus' creation of a standing army and navy. Before then, armies and armadas were raised only for specific campaigns.

For too long the Roman government had depended on spoils of sacked foreign cities to finance the Empire's budget. Over the decades when pillage helped support the national economy, the sack of Tarentum in 209 BC alone gained 83,000 pounds of gold and an inestimable amount of silver and precious stones. But successive pillages undermined Rome's capability to support an economy through business, manufacture, and trade; the purchase of rare and precious objects brought to Rome as loot and sold at auction or private treaty drained excess wealth of the rich from the capital needs of industry. An over-importation of slaves contributed to massive unemployment among citizens and returning military men. Many of the newly imported slaves were literate, educated, sophisticated artisans and professionals, not just field workers and factory bodies associated with mines, quarries, factories and the oar-deck of ships (the stereotype of the African slave trade). When absorbed at minimal expense into Rome's businesses and industries, educated slaves displaced clerks and managers who required salaries. Mines, timberlands, agricultural acres, port and manufacturing facilities, taken over by victorious Roman generals, were sold to Roman speculators or directly to industrial diversifiers. While serving to redistribute wealth among the provinces, this exit of money from Rome diluted employment of peninsular Romans.

Taxation would seem a likely substitute for plunder, but was not easy to establish. Taxation was bad politics. The proletariat, small farmers, fishermen, and the mass of urban and rural-village poor lived at subsistence level and couldn't be tapped anyway. Most Romans and Italians lived without excess funds; only patricians, senators, high officials and professionals had wealth beyond need. Taxation of citizens would involve accountants, auditors, and paper, but paper had not been invented: writing was done on cheaply produced erasable slates or wax-coated boards. Few could afford papyrus scrolls imported from Egypt. Government expense collecting taxes from the peninsular populace would be most likely greater than the taxes collected. Low-income people couldn't pay, merchants would cheat, and the wealthy and the government officials would be obliged to disclose their finances! By Senate decree in 167 BC, the very idea of taxation of Roman citizens was annulled—not by a benevolent Senate to help the populace or boost the retail market but to prevent the same mess taxation has created in modern Italy, where 4 to 5 million citizens are tax evaders.

Rome's dependence on colonial taxation to support the government, and line the pockets of the rich beyond gainful income, was economically perilous. To enhance profits for home investors, tax collectors routinely looted the provinces of financial resources, reducing moneys that more effectively would have supported Roman exports and industrial expansion. Provincials, coerced to pay tribute, larded tax coffers and protection money. Extortion was an industry. The Mafia, as such profiteers are called today, was highly organized throughout the Empire, especially in Sicily. High profits made by tax collecting syndicates, when distributed among investors in Rome, threw market economies into disarray as supply-and-demand lost efficacy of balance. In keeping up this brace of practices, the capital greed of the metropolitan and provincial patricians was comparable in monetary rapacity to generals hauling booty and slaves to Rome to fetch income when auctioned.

The alternative to pillage was to rebuild destroyed nations and establish trade relations, what today is called post-war reconstruction. A handy example of an economically motivated war is Rome's assault on Sicily. Romans traded extensively over a half-century with Sicily when the kingdom of Syracuse was under the competent reign of Hieron II, but when his successors in 215 BC showed signs of shifting trade in favor of Carthage, Rome sent Marcellus and a mighty military legion to prevent it. The vast population of Syracuse was butchered and the city sacked to bare walls. Marcellus overdid it but his campaign was based on economic planning that was still in the hunting and gathering phase of civilization, not on warring instinct as the innate, irresistible urge of Romans to rape and plunder. Roman wars were not instinctual, not even ideological, like "holy wars" or "wars in name of freedom" but, like most modern ones, were waged as economic necessities, financed by tributes, indemnities, defense emoluments—

by what are called today war reparation payments, weapons-sale agreements, reconstruction contracts, mutual defense funds, and interest on foreign loans for restoration of trade.

At the time the Roman Senate decided on the Augustan Altar of Peace, Rome had not been massively at war abroad for fifteen years, and seventy-five years had passed since a major civil strife was settled by military action on Italian soil. Battles were fought here and there, but far from Rome; few back at home evn knew they were going on. How could the Roman citizens of 13 BC be weary of war and pining for peace at last? There were millions of Roman citizens at the time—not many of them affected negatively by war. The Augustan Peace was a settled-down, becalmed government and economy, coming after many years of political upheaval, intrigues, assassinations and corruption—not that they wouldn't continue. The peacemakers realized that political and social stability, with wholesome international relations, was good business. They were the patricians, corporate agrarians, manufacturers, bankers, merchants and traders, not "the Roman people" generalized as if there were no differences among them—and certainly not the Roman poets.

Despair was largely an urban malady. What the bulk of the general public wanted were stable prices, cheap wheat, fresh water, police and fire protection, luxuries like the wealthy had, entertainment and spectacles. The urban masses wanted housing, social welfare, and public games where people and wild animals would suffer a lot more than they did. Augustus gave them huge theaters—one held forty thousand people—with gladiatorial combats, staged animal hunts, at times with lions against convicted criminals and ill-equipped slaves—the lions winning often enough. Along with listing his senatorial honors, his public acclaim, and having thrice closed the Janus doors, Augustus also boasts in *his Res Gestae* that he'd entertained his people at his own expense with eight gladiatorial games featuring ten thousand combatants. He produced twenty-six animal games with thirty-five hundred animals killed in total. The first hippopotamus and rhinocerous seen by the populace were trotted around the arena and then set upon and wound-by-wound slaughtered (Dio, 51.12). To promote the dedication of the Forum of Augustus, he sponsored a circus in which 260 lions were killed. How many humans we don't know—Augustus didn't count people, only animals, and it is hardly the case that that many animals were hunted for public entertainment without the hunters at risk. For the same event, on the opposite side of the Tiber, he had a vast body of water adapted to re-enact the sea battle between the Persians and Athenians. The spectacles offered an orgy of sex and violence. After each show, the prostitutes in *lupanaria* (whore stalls) around the amphitheater did brisk business with boys and men pumped up like Priapus' dependable member.

To maintain peace at home, Augustus gave everyone what they wanted. He gave the patrician class places in the Senate, civil positions of power and influence, governorships of provincial cities, praetorships, mayoralties of towns, ministries, opportunities for pleasurable wealth, preferred seats in the amphitheater, and most favorable treatment. In 28 BC he had purged the Senate of unworthy members and replaced them with successful men from influential and moneyed families. Augustus himself was not Roman but Italian out of bourgeois stock, which caused some to resent his powers. Italians did not enjoy the full benefits of the pure Roman citizen. Aware of this subliminal snubbing, pure Roman senators opposed to him either shaped up or were extirpated.

Mass entertainment was staged at great expense. Gladiatorial shows and animal slaughters, condemned prisoners to be torn apart by beasts, were as expensive to produce as Hollywood blockbusters. Lions, bears, and buffaloes are not by nature ferocious. Lions had to be captured in Africa, imported, and trained to hate humans. Bears had to be captured in the North and trained to tear humans apart. Buffaloes and steers and bulls, unlike Spanish fighting bulls that are bred for generations to be instinctually aggressive, will not charge and gore humans by instinct. None of these so-called wild beasts could be made into savage man-eaters without training, not even by starving them: a starved lion quickly weakens. Lions and bears had to be weaned onto human flesh by being fed slave meat over a period of time before they would get a taste for it, and they needed practice to build confidence by killing a few worthless slaves or convicted criminals in dress-rehearsals, if expected to perform in the arena and not run from their opponent or cower in stage-fright when hearing the crowd roar at their entrance. Gladiators, too, were costly to train, their equipment expensive. When the circuses at last declined for a few decades, it was not that a Roman gene for cruel behavior had become ineffectual, but that what the rabble had come to expect had become too expensive to produce.

But for all that one may hold up as examples of Roman cruelty, subsequent global history testifies to the fact that the Romans were not "by nature cruel" (as one reads in the most popular undergraduate art history textbook: Helen Gardner's *Art Through the Ages*). The history of human slaughter by human slaughterers is not genetically specific. Slaughter to gain territory, as ethnic cleansing or in the name of God, puts the human at the top of predatorial species, and without the excuse of instinct. The ancient Roman colosseum is in every major city of the Western World, with contact sports and uniformed gladiators carried off the field in stretchers—slaughter tempered by sublimation. And there you have it: war, pillage, and slavery sublimated into international business: the chairman of the board the commanding general, salesmen making killings, competition substituting for pillage, and employees for slaves. The Augustan Peace did not change human nature. It stablized the Empire's economy. As ancient historian Tacitus said, "Yes, there was peace in those days, but a bloody one."

SELECTED BIBLIOGRAPHY

The following well-written books by noted scholars, accessible to students and the general reader, are recommended for further reading on the phases of Roman history traversed by the addendum.

Andersen, Jr., James, *Roman Architecture and Society* (Baltimore and London, 1997).

Barton, Carlin, *The Sorrows of Ancient Rome* (Princeton, 1993).

Brendel, Otto, *Prolegomena to the Study of Roman Art* (New Haven and London, 1979).

Brilliant, Richard, *Roman Art from the Republic to Constantine* (London, 1974).

Brilliant, Richard, *Visual Narratives. Storytelling in Etruscan and Roman Art* (Ithaca 1984).

Duncan-Jones, Richard, *The Economy of the Roman Empire* (Cambridge, (1974).

Fuhrmann, Manfred, *Cicero and the Roman Republic* (Oxford, 1990).

Galinsky, Karl, *Augustan Culture: An Interpretive Introduction* (New Jersey, 1996).

Grant, Michael, *The Ancient Historians* (New York, 1970).

Grant, Michael, *The Roman Emperors* (New York, 1985).

Hardie, Philip, *Ovid's Poetics of Illusion* (Cambridge, 2002).

Jones, A. H. M., *The Roman Economy:* (Totawa, NJ, 1974).

Kamm, Antony, *The Romans* (London and New York, 1995).

Keppie, Lawrence, *The Making of the Roman Army* (New York, 1984.

Levi, Peter, *Horace: A Life* (New York, 1998).

Nelson, Stephanie, *God and Land: The Metaphysics of Farming in Hesiod and Vergil* (New York and Oxford, 1998).

Oglivie, R. M., *Roman Literature and Society* (London, 1980, 1988).
Starr, Chester, *The Influence of Sea Power on Ancient History* (Cambridge, 1989).
Syme. Sir Ronald. *History in Ovid* (Oxford, 1978).
Tarn, W. W. and Charlesworth, M. P., *From Republic to Empire* (New York, 1965).
Wittaker, C. W., *Frontiers of the Roman Empire: A Social and Economic Study* (Baltimore and London: Johns Hopkins University Press, 1994).
Zanker, Paul, *The Power of Images in the Age of Augustus* (Ann Arbor, 1988).

NOTES

Considering the enormnity of the bibliography on the Ara Pacis, I will not duplicate the effort others have put into listing it. Authors and their publications that I found useful for my purposes are given in the following notes. I have not made a note of every passage from texts by ancient authors that I refer to or quote. Scholars of the period will know the source material, and students should read the entire texts. In some of my notes, I refer the reader to publications that are more expansive on certain matters than I felt necessary to explore in greater depth than I have.

1. For readings on Mussolini's identification with Augustus, see *L'Italia di Augusto e l'Italia di Oggi* (Academie e Biblioteche d'Italy, vol. 11 (Rome, 1937), pp. 207-22; L. Curtius, "Mussolini a la Roma antiqua," *Nuova Antologia* 12 (1934), pp, 487-500. For recent literature see M. Cagnetta, "Il mito di Augusto e la rivoluzione fascista," *Quad-Stor* 3 (1976), pp. 139-81; Diane Conlin, *The Artists of the Ara Pacis* (Chapel Hill, NC: University of North Carolina Press, 1997), pp. 13-21. For a comprehensive coverage of ancient Rome's territorial expansion, see C. W. Whittaker, *Frontiers of the Roman Empire: A Social and Economic Study* (Baltimore and London: Johns Hopkins University Press, 1994).

2. Spiro Kostof, "The Emperor and the Duce: The Planning of the Piazzale Imperatore in Rome," in *Art and Architecture in the Service of Politics*, eds. Henry Millon and Linda Nochlin (Cambridge, MA: MIT Press, 1978), pp. 270-325.

3. The steel and glass structure was demolished in 2001 in preparation for the Meier project. Rumors had it that in 2002, when the left-of-center Amato government lost out to the rightist oriented Berlusconi government,

Berlusconi's undersecretary for Beni Culturali (national cultural patrimony) issued a stop-work order on the Meier project and instructed the architect to draw up an entirely new plan that would retain the look of the glass pavilion. This scandal was reported by jornalists, but I have been informed by Richard Meier's office that it was not true.

4. Gaius Suetonius Tranqui'llus, *De vita Caesarum.* I am using *Lives if the Twelve Caesars,* trans. Robert Graves (New York: Welcome Rain Publishers, 2001), Part II.

5. The basic book on the reconstruction of the Ara Pacis is Guiseppi Moretti, *Ara Pacis Augustae* (Rome 1948). An abridged coverage of the altar's history and description, based on Moretti's book, is Erika Simon, *Ara Pacis Augustae* (Tübingen 1967 and Greenwich, CN, 1967).). For analyses of the imagery, see Karl Galinsky, "Venus, Polysemy, and the Ara Pacis Augustae," *American Journal of Archaeology* 96 (July 1992); John Elsner, "Cult and Sculpture: Sacrifice in the Ara Pacis Augustae," *Journal of Roman Studies* LXXXI (1991); Nancy Thompson De Grummond, "Pax Augusta and the Horae on the Ara Pacis Augustae," *American Journal of Archaeology* 94 (October 1990); 1990; E. La Rocca et al., *Ara Pacis Augustae: in occasione del restoro del fronte orientale* (Rome 1983); Babette Stanley Spaeth "Demeter/Ceres in the Ara Pacis and the Carthage Relief," *American Journal of Archaeology* 90 (1986), pp. 210ff. E. Simon, *Augustus, Kunst und Leben in Rom um die Zeitenwende* (Munich 1987); S; Settis, "Die Ara Pacis," in *Kaiser Augustus in die verlorene Republik* (1988); D. E. E. Kleiner, "The Great Friezes of the Ara Pacis Augustae, Greek Sources, Roman Derivatives and Augustan Social Policy," *Mélange de l'Ecole Française de Rome, Antiquité,* XC (1978) pp. 753-785; Richard Brilliant, *Visual Narratives. Storytelling in Etruscan and Roman Art* (Ithaca 1984); Peter J. Holliday, Time, History, and Ritual on the Ara Pacis Augustae, *Art Bulletin* LXXII, No. 4 (December 1990). For bibliographical comprehensiveness to 1986 see G. Köppel, "Die historischen Reliefs der römischen Kaiserzeit," *Bonner Jahrbuch* 187 (1987), 101-157. Mario Torelli, *Typology & Structure of Roman Historical Reliefs* (Ann Arbor: University of Michigan Press, 1992) is the most completely thought out and documented study of the Ara Pacis and related monuments. These resources will be cited in other notes.

6. For the identification of more than one workshop, see B. Ashmole, *Architect and Sculptor in Ancient Greece* (New York, 1972).

7. Otto Brendel, *Prolegomena to a Study of Roman Art,* ed. Jerome J. Pollitt

(New Haven and London: Yale University Press, 1979), pp. 70-72.

8. Marcus Vitruvius Pollio, *De architectura.* Book I, ii, 2. I am using the Loeb Classical Library edition, edited and translated by Frank Granger (Cambridge, MA and London: Harvard University, 1944 and later). This edition is based on the oldest manuscript, the Harleian 2767 in the British Museum.

9. For these examples and quotations in context see Alison Burford *Craftsmen in Greek and Roman Society* (London, 1972), and Diane Conlin, *The Artists of the Ara Pacis* (Chapel Hill, NC: University of North Carolina Press, 1997), pp. 34-42. Conlin makes good use of Burford's material while adding new and important information. For examples of the Roman Senate exercising control over certain architecture functions, see Colin's text on pp. 40-43. A book that came to my attention too late for consideration in my text, that deals extensively with ancient Roman design and building processes, including building codes, is Andrea Scheitauer, *Kaiserliche Bautätigkeit in Rom, Das Echo in der anttiken Literatur* (Stuttgart: Steiner, 2000).

10. J. Bundgaard, "The Building Contract from Lebadeia, *Classica et mediaevalia. Revue danoise de philologie et d'histoire,* 8 (1946), p. 27. Cited by Conlin, *The Artists of the Ara Pacis,* p. 39.

11. Vitruvius, *De architectura,* Book III, 4.

12. This monument was constructed at the expense of C. Domitius Ahenobarbus, a senator who commanded a naval squadron for Antony, explaining why the other three sides have reliefs of sea-deities. For a summary of opinions about the date and purpose of this monument, see Mario Torelli, *Typology and Structure of Roman Historical Reliefs* (Ann Arbor: University of Michigan Press, 1982) pp. 1-15. First published as "Typographia e Iconologia: Arco de Portogallo, Ara Pacis, Ara Providentiae. Templum Solis," *Ostracka. Rivista di antichita* 1 (1992), pp. 105-31.

13. David Castriota, *The Ara Pacis Augustae and the Image of Abundance in Later Greek and Early Imperial Art* (Princeton: Princeton University Press, 1995), pp, 33-37. Castriota looked to the Ara Pacis for the platform and podium that he hypothesized. One must be cautious to not reverse the direction and read his hypothetical construction as an influence of Pergamene altars on the Ara Pacis.

14. The title *princeps* was fairly common—applied to the principal of a company as applied today as a public school principal or a principal in an architecture firm. A good example from ancient Roman times is Q. Olius

Princeps, a *redemptor operum publicorum*, a contractor for public constructions. See James C. Anderson, *Roman Architecture and Society* (Baltimore and London: Johns Hopkins Press, 1997), p. 109.

15. *Res Gestae Augusti* 12.2. [Aram Fortunae Reducis ante aedés Honoris et Virtutis ad portum [Capenam pro reduti meo se]natus consacravit in que ponti[fices et virgins Vestales anni]versarium facere [iussit eo die, quo consullibus Q. Lu[c]retio et [M. Vinici]o in urbem ex [Syria redieram, et diem Augusttali]a ex [c]o[gnomine nost]ro appellavit. [Ex senatus auctori]tate pars praeto[rum e]t tribornorum [plebi cum consule Q.] Lu[c]retio et principibus viris [o]bviam mihi missa e[st in Campa]niam, qui honos ad hoc tempus nemini praeter me es[t] dec[retus. Cu[m exHispa]nia Gal[lique, rebus in iis p[rovincis prosp[e]re [gest]is. R[oman redi] Ti. Ne[r]one P. Qui[ntilio consullibu]s, arum [Pacis A]u[gust[ae senatus pro]redi[t]u meo co[nsacrandam censuit] ad cam[pum Martium, in qua ma]gistratus et sac[erdotes virginesque V]esta[les anniversarium sacrific]ium facer[e iussit.]

Here follows the compressed text the paragraph pertaining only to the Ara Pacis: Cum ex Hispania Galliaque, rebus in iis provinces prospere gestis, Roma redim Ti. Nerone P. Quintilio consulibus, aram Pacis Augustae senatus pro reditu meo consacrandam censuit ad campum Martium, in qua magistrates et sacerdotes virginesque Vestales anniversarium sacrificium facere iussit.

The text I've quoted also speaks of a second altar, the *ara Fortunae Reducis* (*Fortuna Redux*, or Fortunate Return), to which I will turn later on. The *ara Fortuna Reducis* and the *ara Pacis Augustae* were associated with the safe return (*reditus*) of Augustus after success firming up provincial rule and quelling conflicts.

16. Gaius Suetonius Tranqui'llus, *De vita Caesarum* (Life of Augustus), trans. Michael Graves, p. 101. The Vestals' perpetual state of virginity, akin to Diana and her troop and the chastity of nuns in convents, testified to unbroken guardianship of the renewal process, a sustained holding out of promise (hence virginity), a function rooted in the duty of women to be vigilant, to guard what would guarantee a rightful heir. The Vestals' function as guardians alludes to the womb as private and secret, as receptacle and container of what was to issue in pure form at the right time: a legitimate document or legitimate child. For a detailed discussion of the Vestals, see Dumézil, *Archaic Roman Religion*, trans. Philip Krapp (Baltimore and London: Johns Hopkins University Press, 1966, vol. 2, pp. 585-87. First published as *La*

Religion romaine archaïque auivi d'une appendice sur la religion des Etrusques (Paris, 1966).

17. Faint support for saying the monument was destroyed by fire is the presence of charring on some of the excavated blocks. But because the entire altar complex was of stone, it's hardly possible that it had been destroyed by fire.

18. Publius Ovidius Naso (Ovid), *Fasti* I, 709-22. On the Roman calendar of feasts, see A. Degrassi, *Fasti Anni Numani et Juliani, Inscriptiones Italiae* XIII.2 (Rome, 1963). Torelli, *Typology & Structure of Roman Historical Reliefs.* For the definition of *feriae* as a particular type of feast day, see Dumézil, *Archaic Roman Religion,* vol. 2, pp. 560-565. The Roman Calendar of Feasts was an official calendar compiled by pontiffs listing religious festivals and games. Days were marked with letters to set-off non-festival from festival days; indications were given for how the days were to be observed. The letter "C", for example, standing for *comitialis,* meant that public assemblies were permitted on that sacred day. *Feraie* designated a day when no one worked and when no other public festivals would take place. Such "feasts" included days when the wealthy prepared meals for the poor, as still today in church potluck dinners and food kitchens for the homeless. People of means were expected to provide for those with less means, so all would feast equally.

19. Virgil had extracted a promise from Varius that he would burn the unfinished manuscript after his death but Augustus confiscated it and had it published after editing by Virgil's literary executors Varius and Tucca. The extent of their editing is not known, and some classicists hold that no changes were actually made.

20. Paul Zanker, *The Power of Images in the Age of Augustus* (Ann Arbor: University of Michigan Press, 1988), p. 83.

21. Publius [or Gaius] Cornelius Tacitus, *Annals.* I.2. Cf. Tacitus, *The Annals of Imperial Rome,* tr. Michael Graves (London: Penquin Group, 1956 and later).

22. Theodore Mommsen, *Res Gestae divi Augusti ex Monumentus Ancyrano et Apolloniensi* (Berlin, 1883). See also Fairly, "Monumentum Ancyranum" (with Latin text, translation and commentary), in *Translations and Reprints from the Original Sources of European History,* vol. V, no. 1 (University of Pennsylvania, 1898); David M. Robinson, The *Res Gestae Divi Augusti,* as Recorded on the Monumentum Antiochenum, " *American Journal*

of Philology, vol. XLV11 (1926), pp. 1-54; Paul Brunt and John M. Moore, *Res Gestae Divi Augusti: The Achievement of the Devine Augustus* (Oxford: Oxford University Press, 1967); Victor Erenberg and Arnold H. M. Jones *Documents Illustrating the Reigns of Augustus and Tiberius* (Oxford: Oxford University Press, 1976); Jean Cagé, "*Res gestae divi Augusti exmonumentis Ancyrano et Antiocheo latinus Ancyrano et Apolloniensi Graecis* (Paris: Société des belles lettres, 1977); Rex Wallace, *Res Gestae divi Augusti* (Wauconda, IL: Bolchazy-Carducci Publishers, 2000).

23. Friedrich von Duhn, "Uber einige Basreliefs und ein romisches Bauwerk der ersten Kaiserzeit," *Miscellenea Capitolina* (1879), pp. 11-16.

24. Eugèn Petersen, "Ara Pacis Augustae," *Sonderschrift des Oesterreichen Arcaelogischen Instituts*, vol. 2 (Vienna, 1902), pp. 224-228.

25. Vitruvius Pollio, *De architectura*, Book IV, ix. Cf. *Pollio Vitruvius, The Ten Books of Architecture*, tr. Morris Hicky Morgan (New York: Dover, 1960), ch. ix, p. 125.

26. In Book III, 5, Vitruvius points out that this is not a feature found in Roman temple architecture. An extreme example in modern architecture is the new Bibliothèque Mitterand in Paris, which is fashioned as an enormous base, or podium, on which the four high-rise buildings are placed. The street level slopes; an enormously wide set of steps follows the street downhill. The base of the library complex, consisting of these stairs and open top surface, is public space. In the case of most Greek religious and government buildings, the stepped base is found on all four sides. The reason usually given is so the building can be accessed from all sides. I prefer the reason that I've given here. Roman temples and buildings in the Etruscan tradition tended to be more emphatically frontal, with steps only in the front. And that style eventually extended to most of the Hellenic provinces, and is still the case in most public buildings, especially those that are federal, as symbolically on a firm foundation. Among numerous examples are the Temple of Portunus in Rome, the early first century Temple of Augustus and Livia in Vienna, and the Sbeitla three-temple Capitallium of the mid-second century. For a fine discussion of this architectural transition between public and private space, see William L. McDonald, *The Architecture of the Roman Empire* (New Haven and London, Yale University Press, 1986), vol. II, pp. 66-73.

27. See the appendix to Petersen, "Ara Pacis Augustae," pp. 224-28. Also, E. La Rocca et al., *Ara Pacis Augustae: in occasione del restoro del fronte orientale* (Rome, 1883), pp. 63-65. Most scholars of the Ara Pacis call the festoons

"garlands," ineptly derived from the German *Girlande*. In the English language garlands are of fresh flowers, not autumn fruits as found in festoons, and garlands encircle a neck or a column, rather than drape between attachments as festoons do.

28. Among Roman art scholars the identification of the participants on the two friezes is for the most part established, with some disagreement on a few of them. For a more complete inventory than I have given, see Mario Torelli, *Typology and Structure of Roman Historical Reliefs*, pp. 47-50; Diana E. E. Kleiner, "The Great Friezes of the Ara Pacis Augustae: Greek Sources, Roman Derivatives and Augustan Social Policy," *Mélanges de l'École française de Rome. Antiquité*, 90 (1978), pp. 753-85; R. Syme, "Neglected Children on the Ara Pacis," *American Journal of Archaeology* 88 (1984), pp. 583-89; Paul Zanker, The *Power of Images in the Age of Augustus*, trans. A. Shapiro (Ann Arbor, 1988), p. 121. Diane Conlin has photographed and given detailed descriptions of every personage in *The Artists of the Ara Pacis*, cited above.

29. E. Welin, "Die beiden Festtage der Ara Pacis Augustae," *Dragma Martino P. Nilsson, Acta Inst. Regni Succiae*, ser. 2.1 (Lund, 1939), pp. 500-513. See Torelli's discussion of this wording in *Typology and Structure*, p. 30. Ovid's books for January through June survived.

30. Quintus Horatius Flaccus, *Odes*, Book 4:5. I–4. Trans. W. G. Shepherd, *Horace: The Complete Odes and Epodes with the Centennial Hymn* (New York, 1983), p. 179.

31. Cassius Dio (Dio Cassius), T*he Roman History: The Reign of Augustus*, trans., Ian Scott-Vilvert (London: Penquin, 1987), Book 54.25.

32. Dio, Book 56.34. On the importance of archived portraits see Polybius, *The Histories* VII, trans. W. R. Paton (Loeb Library Editions), pp. 53-54. Polybius was Greek but in the mid-second century BC in exile in Rome.

33. On the great variety of sacrificial rituals, see Georges Dumézil, *Archaic Roman Religion*, vol. 2, part 4, ch. 1, "Sacra Publica," pp. 553-75.

34. Claimed most recently by Barbete Stanley Spaeth, *The Roman Goddess Ceres* (Austin: University of Texas Press, 1996), p. 126, where on reads, "The interior face of the wall is an imitation in stone of a temporary altar precinct; a wooden fence in the lower zone, "etc. For a claim that the marble walls "carefully reproduce in marble" the wooden boarding and the *anguli* of the augural *templum*, see Torelli, *Typology and Structure*, p. 129, and Richard Brilliant, *Roman Art* (London: Phaidon, 1974), p. 20, where one reads, "The Ara Pacis Augustae preserves in marble part of its original wooden

form." An intriguing comment on the interior wall surfaces is Paul Zanker saying, "On the interior of the Ara Pacis, a scared precinct is suggested by a construction of planks and scaffold." Zanker refers to this condition as "an illusion of reality," which would refer to a wooden structure as real, but perhaps Zanker means reality as compared to the fantasy of the bucrania and swags. Zanker, *The Power of Images*, p. 117.

To my knowledge, the only surviving wood carvings associated with a shrine were found preserved in a deep oxygenless bog at the sanctuary of Sequana at the source of the Seine near Dijon. The shrine was probably Celtic.

35. See John Pollini, "Ahenobarbi, Appuleii and Some Others on the Ara Pacis," *American Journal of Archaeology* 90 (October 1986), pp. 453-460, especially pp. 457-459.

The title, Pontifex, had a long and complex practical usage before becoming a religious one. It designated at times a bridge builder and at times a custodian of a bridge. Far back in Roman history, a bridge crossing the Tiber joined Latium and Etruria. Built in wood, this bridge could be destroyed easily by Roman defenders, burned or dismantled, to bring any invasion to a halt on the opposite bank. When at last the early Romans weakened Etruria's military power and felt secure that Etruscans no longer threatened, this bridge was rebuilt in stone. This happened in the mid-390s BC. The stone bridge rested on piles, so it is referred to as the Pons Sublicus, but the word *sublicus*, a modifier, is confused in modern scholarship with a proper name: *pons sublicus* simply means a bridge built on wooden piles. This bridge was put under control of a priest who then was called the *pontifex*, meaning bridge-builder, or one who looks after a bridge (that information from Suetonius, but refuted by Plutarch). The prefix *pon*, as in *pontifex*, also prefixes the Italian word *ponte* for 'bridge', the French word *pont*, meaning 'bridge', and the French *ponctuation* for word bridging. The word *pon* supports an array of terms denoting bridges and bridging, pontoons, platforms, and scaffolds. And *fex* (as *fiss* in current Italian or "fix" in English, as in "fixative", the word originating, perhaps, from the Latin *facere*, to make, or to fashion) runs the gamut of meaning from "stabilizing" or "fixing in place", to "fix" and "repair". In a religious context, the *pontifex* bridged from deity to laity, just as the Catholic pontiff, holding the keys of Saint Peter, bridges from Earth to Heaven: he controls the draw-bridge, so to speak.

36. See A. Borbein, "Die Ara Pacis Augustae: Geschichtliche

Wirklichkeit und Programm," *Jahrbuch des Deutschen Archäologischen Instituts,* 90 (1975), pp. 242-66, esp. pp. 260-61; John Pollini, *Studies in Augustan Historical Reliefs.* Ph.D. dissertation (Berkeley, University of California. University microfilms No. 7904581, 1978), pp. 123-26. Also, Pollini, "Ahenobarbi, Apulei and Some Others on the Ara Pacis, p.458 and note 51.

37. For these historical dates and the evidence, see S. Settis, *Kaiser Augustus und die verlorene Republik* (Mainz, 1988), p. 401; Simon, *Ara Pacis Augustae* (1967), p. 8; Elsner "Cult and Sculpture: Sacrifice in the Ara Pacis," *Journal of Roman Studies* LXXXI (1991), pp. 51-52. Charles Rose prefers the 9 BC date: "Princes and Barbarians on the Ara Pacis," *American Journal of Archaeology* 94 (July 1990), p. 463. Reprinted in E. D'Ambra, *Roman Art in Context. An Anthology* ((Englewood Cliffs, NJ, 1993), pp. 53-74. For a summary of opinions on which of the two dates is represented by the processional friezes, see R. Billows, "The Religious Processions on the Ara Pacis Augustae," *Journal of Roman Archeology* 6 (1993), pp. 80-92.

Kleiner, in *Roman Sculpture* (1992), p. 90, writes: "The foundation stone of the altar was laid on 4 July 13 BC, and a great ceremony was held on that day with a solemn sacrifice to the state gods and to the goddess Pax herself. The altar was completed and dedicated three and a half years later on 30 January 9 BC." I find it impossible to accept Kleiner's belief that on one single day of the year there occurred Augustus' return, the Senate's vote, the altar precinct's constitution, and a vast ceremony with procession and sacrificial feast. Cassius Dio, who is reasonably trustworthy as to reportage, says that Augustus entered the city unnanounced at night, as was his custom. On the following day, he convened the Senate but was suffering bronchitis and had someone else speak for him. He also attended to several duties over the next few days. Dio does not mention any sort of festivity taking place at the time (Dio, Book 54.25). No documentary evidence supports Kleiner's imaginative facts. Moreover, as I mentioned elsewhere, Pax, to whom Kleiner refers as a goddess, was not a goddess until so deified during the reign of Hadrian.

38. Zanker, *The Power of Images*, p. 21.

39. Karl Galinsky, *Augustan Culture: An Interpretive Introduction* (Princeton: Princeton University Press, 1996), p. 142.

40. Ovid, *Fasti* I, pp. 709-22.

41. Dumézil, *Archaic Roman Religion*, p. 240.

42. Torelli, *Typology and Structure*, p. 64, suggests that the dedication date for the *ara Pacis* was made to coincide with Livia's birthday.

44. R. Ross Holloway, *The Archaeology of Early Rome and Etruria* (New York: Routledge, 1994, 1996), pp. 128-3.

45. Cf. M. W. C. Hassall, "Altars, curses, and other epigraphic evidence," in *Temples, Churches, and Religion: Recent Research in Roman Britain with a Gazetteer of Romano-Celtic Temples in Continental Europe*, ed. W. Rodwell (Oxford: British Archeological Report 77), pp. 79-89. See also, D. Kleiner, *Roman Group Portraiture: The Funerary Reliefs of the Late Republic and Early Empire* (New York, 1977).

47. Suetonius. *Augustus*, vii.

48. I am going by Rudolfo Lanciani's "Note from Rome," of December 12th, 1901 published in *The Athenaeum*, vol. 3869, pp. 848-9 (London, 1901).

49. See Zanker, *The Power of Images*, p. 86. Zanker writes: From Suetonius we learn that the golden offerings had the form of tripods (Suetonius, *Augustus* 52). These must have been very large and ornate, an impressive visual testimony to the piety of the dictator. The spectacular gesture of melting down so much sculpture was, incidentally, a convenient opportunity for Octavian to get rid of some statues of himself spouting self-assured gestures that did not fit in with his gradually evolving new style and image." While Zanker's impression of what the melted-down sculptures looked like sounds fair, we have no evidence of their look. The tripod, supporting imagery and often elaborated with vegetative material, emerged during Augustus' reign as a symbol of hope and piety, but was rooted in Greek traditions.

50. For example, the stairway bases at the Temple of Augustus on which the Monumentum Antiochenum was carved. David M. Robinson, "The Res Gestae Divi Augusti as Recorded on the Monumentum Antiochenum", *The American Journal of Philology*, XLVII, No. 1 (1926), p. 22, note 17. Robinson's team of excavators found most of the Temple's rinceau, architrave, frieze, all four pediment corners, parts of the walls and columns, acroteria and other parts. The srchitectural order was Corinthian, with a two-story circular colonnade. The building stone was was found to be limestone, not marble, as others had earlier assumed.

51. Richard Brilliant, *Roman Art from the Republic to Constantine* (London: Phaidon Press, 1974), p. 241.

52. Torelli, *Typology and Structure* , p. 66.

53. Brilliant, *Roman Art from the Republic to Constantine,* pp. 197, 234. In one sense, Brilliant's words suggest that I may be wrong in saying that the small frieze zones of the Ara Pacis are from a different and perhaps earlier altar, but my point here is not related to that issue. Its only too obvious that altar barriers at either end and the back side of the table top could be lifted off and put on any other altar with a top sized for the barriers to fit, or the table top and the podium sized to fit the barriers, were the barriers of special importance. This issue does not affect my belief that the Ara Pacis, as reconstructed, is Tiberian. In no way can anyone on stylistic grounds say it had to be Augustan. Even Brilliant admits (p. 239) that "not everything in the Ara Pacis is dependant on immediate Greek sources; the paratactically composed frieze which decorates the altar proper within the precinct closely follows the model developed a generation before in the ceremonial relief from the Temple of Apollo Sosianus."

One can say that the small frieze is later and thus "influenced" by the Sosianus relief, but only if one first says that the small frieze dates later, which can be no more certain than saying the Sosianus relief came later. In my opinion, the small frieze could be earlier than the Sosianus relief. And besides, one of them needn't have had any affect on the other. There must have been hundreds of such reliefs in Rome.I might add that in my design work for the great mosque in Riyadh, I used Kufic (15th-century) script all the way around the interior of the mosque, carved in travertine, while using an adaptation of Farsi (modern) script for the mosaic band that forms the collar of the dome's drum. The use of the two scripts was meant to reinforce the long history of Islam. I was not being stylistically eclectic (see the supplementary reproductions at the end of this text).

As Otto Brendel pointed out in *Prolegomena to the Study of Roman Art,* p. 9, Greek art exhibits a distinctive and self-contained character. "What makes the case of Roman art so baffling," he wrote, "is that we are confronted with a significant main branch of ancient art, of long tradition and productivity, yet surprisingly deficient in those exclusive, constant, and definitive traits which differentiate most other ancients art from each other like so many different languages." This seems especially puzzling, Brendel adds, "because the Roman accomplishments in other fields are both distinctive and outstanding." Brendel is referring to Roman art lacking constant and definitive traits of the kind that move through several centuries of Greek art. He compares that to other aspects of Roman culture, such as engineering, warfare technology, social planning, and building technology, all precisely defined Roman accomplishments.

Yet a stylistic connection between the "small friezes" on the altar and the "large friezes" on the shrine has been asserted by several authors. The connection is seen by Simon, *Ara Pacis Augustae,* pp. 31-33. See also H. Kähler, "Die Ara Pacis und die augusteische Friedensee," *Jahrbuch des Deutschen Archäologischen Instituts* (1954), pp. 67-100. In a rather labyrinthine explanation of the relationship of this frieze to the outer one, Elsner, in "Cult and Sculpture," p. 56, connects the bull depicted in the altar frieze with the bull in the Tellus relief. I find that unacceptable. Moreover, on pp. 63ff, he associates the bull with the "ox that plows the earth for man," a line he found in Virgil's *The Georgics.* Not distinquishing between a bull and an ox is a common error in academic writing. Oxen are not bulls but castrated males and non-milking cows bred as dray animals. The non-gendered name for the bovine species is "cattle"—always plural—not "cows." One herds cattle but brings in and milks cows. Unless bred to be milked and to produce calves, cows used as oxen were often spayed. Cows give birth to calves and are kept in production either for milk, calf-bearing, or both. As the saying goes, a cow is a calf until it has a calf, then it's a cow. A cow must produce a calf in order to become a milk producer, and must be bred every year to stay "fresh," for cow udders come fresh only when about to deliver a calf, and are kept fresh by daily milking (like midwives). As second and subsequent breedings are made, a few weeks before the cow delivers its calf, the cow's udder is dried off by milkers' taking progressively less milk from her over a period of days. After drying, the cows "comes fresh" after calving. A heifer is a female calf ready for breeding or pregnant for the first time; she becomes a cow when suckled after calving A bull is male and is "entire," that is, with testicles. A bullock is a weaned or yearling, bull, the adolescent counterpart of the heifer. It becomes a bull when secondary sexual characteristics mature. Oxen are bred from different types of bovine stock than are cows and breeding-bulls—bred for docility and strength, not for meat or milk. Virgil has advice on this in *The Georgics* III, where he recommends that cows selected to calve oxen be rough in appearance, with a course head, roomy flanks, everything built on a large scale, "more like a bull to look at," he says. (Oxen were often the metaphor then, as today, for people who are stubborn, dull, stupid, but mighty strong). The frequent citation of Virgil to substantiate the sacrifice of "oxen" is an error. Virgil says "bullocks," not "oxen." Bulls cannot be used as oxen, for two bulls cannot be coupled in harness without fighting; bulls are unmanageable in the proximity of a cow in heat. Oxen were not used as sacrificial animals, as often said, while calves, heifers, cows, bullocks, and bulls were. Cows and heifers were often sacrificed when pregnant, but one must keep in mind that heifers and cows are pregnant a good part of their lives. Bovine gestation is ten months. After delivering a calf, cows are serviced by the herd bull within weeks. Most sacrificed cows were pregnant whether or not it was intended that the sacrificial cow be pregnant.

Male sheep and pigs were typically castrated in Roman times as today. One cannot keep two or more boars with sows or piglets, for the boars will kill each other. Bulls and boars must be maintained in isolated, separate quarters during the non-breeding season. Male sheep, if not castrated, will isolate clusters of ewes into private herds; two or more rams cannot be kept in the same sheep pen or small herd. If fertility figured in the sacrifice at all, it would have been "entire" piglets of either sex, boars or sows; "entire" lambs of either sex, rams or ewes. Like cows, ewes and sows are pregnant three-quarters of their lifetime. A good breeding bull, ram, or boar and a productive cow, ewe, or brood-sow were valuable animals selected for breeding quality. So mature bulls, cows, ewes, rams, boars, and sows would not have been indiscriminately sacrificed. Farmers were well paid for the animals when not donating them as good public relations to promote one's products. Priests were selective; only superior animals were worthy of state sacrifices.

The tendency to be pious when thinking about religious rites, especially of sacrifice, suppresses the fact that most public religious ceremonies were meant to bring people together. Religion is both personal and social, but for most people at any time it is purely social. Scholars tend to make religion more religious than it is, as when saying that the Vestal Virgins saved the ashes of the unborn calves for special services, as if the Vestal Virgins were scattered throughout the Roman World rather than just in Rome. To burn a pregnant cow down to ashes during a single public ceremony would take a fire as great in dimensions as the entire Ara Pacis shrine.

Unborn lambs, calves, and piglets have been a delicacy since the Paleolithic era and went out of fashion in the United States only during my lifetime. The sacrificed animals, probably bled, the blood drained ceremonially and certain organs or entrails burned, with the meat eaten by the celebrants at the festival associated with the sacrifice. One need not assume that the sacrificial rites were much different than Christians taking communion and then having an early Sunday dinner. Sacrifice was the Roman form of Mass followed by festivities when everyone ate sacitified butcher's meat.

54. Torelli, *Typology and Structure*, pp. 29, 66, 60, note 71.

55. The propaganda value of the Roman building program under Augustus and his successors is thoroughly detailed in Zanker's *Power of Images*. Of comparable value is Andrea Scheithauer, *Kaiserliche Bautatigkeit in Rom. Das Echo in der antiken Literatur* (Stuttgart: Steiner, 2000). I suggest that the history of Roman architecture as to propaganda was not the same as the history of architecture as to principles of design and construction. One must be cautious however, in failing to understand that the artists of the Ara Pacis were not propagandists. They dealt with problems of art, not of politics.

56. Vitruvius, *De architectura*. Book IV, Ch. IX. Quoted from Pollio Vitruvius, *The Ten Books of Architecture*, tr. Morris Hicky Morgan (New York: Dover, 1960).

57. To my knowledge, no one has come up with a less farfetched explanation for the double entrance than saying precedent may be found in certain Greek structures such as the *Altar of the Twelve Gods* (*Altar of Pity*) in Athens' agora, which dates five hundred and fifty years before the Ara Pacis. That proposition fails to take into account that only a minute fraction of ancient architecture has been reconstructed for the modern eye, and that during the Augustan Age no one seen the *Altar of the Twelve Gods*. Centuries before the Ara Pacis, that altar had been reduced to rubble. This assignment of the Altar of the Twelve Gods in the Athenian Agora as the prototype for the *ara Pacis Augustae* has been made often, initially by H. A. Thompson, "The Altar of Pity in the Athenian Agora," *Hesperia* 21 (1952), pp. 60-82, and more recently by Zanker, *The Power of Images*, p. 160, who says, "The modest proportions of the Ara Pacis Augustae reproduces those of the Altar of the Twelve Gods in the Athenian Agora of the fifth century BC." For the same opinion, see Diane. E. E. Kleiner, *Roman Sculpture* (1992), p. 756. This assumption should be laid to rest. Protesting the Altar of the Twelve Gods as a prototype for the Ara Pacis is Torelli, *Typology and Structure*, p. 57, note 12, with whom I agree.

As for which of the east or west sides is the front of the shrine, one should take into account only the altar, not the walls. Nancy Thompson de Grummond, "Pax Augusta and the Horae on the Ara Pacis Augustae," *American Journal of Archeology* 94 (October 1990), p. 666, supposing, I think erroneously, that the personification of Tellus on the east wall is Pax, says, in so many words, that if the image is Pax she should be on the front, that is, on the west side, because the priest would go up the steps to the altar. Confused here is that the "main" entrance to the precinct is from the east, while the altar faces to the east. Moreover, priests mount an altar from the back of it, and when officiating, face the same direction as the altar.

58. A denarius of C. Antistius Vetus. Zanker, *Power of Images*, p. 85, discusses this imagery in context. Torelli, *Typology and Structure*, pp. 31-32, lists several coins depicting a Janus shrine and others depicting an ara Pacis, assumed to be the *ara Pacis Augustae* (p. 32). All will be found in H. Mattingly, *Coins of the Roman Empire in the British Museum.* 4 vols (London 1923-36); for Janus, vol I, p. 215, nos. 111-113, pls. 141.1; pp 299ff, nos. 156-67, pls 42.6-7; pp 238f, nos 198-204, pls. 43.8-9; pp. 243f, nos. 225-33, pls. 44.5-6. For the *ara Pacis Augustae*, see pp. 271f, nos. 360-65. Most of these coins are reproduced in my text. See also, Marvin Tameamko, *Monumental Coins: Buildings and Structures on Ancient Coinage* (Iola, WI: Krause Publications, 1999).

59. For Simon's conjecture that the *ara Pacis Augustae* is a replica of Janus Geminus, a new gate of the enlarged Augustan Rome resembling the gate of the Palatine Rome, see E. Simon, *Ara Pacis Augustae* (Tübeingen, 1967). For Torelli's extensive discussion of Janus Quirinus as the pattern for the *ara Pacis Augustae*, see his *Typology and Structure*, pp. 30-32.

60. Torelli, *Typology and Structure*, pp. 30-31.

61. Torelli, *Typology and Structure*, p. 31.

62. My thanks to Marvin Tameanko for this information given to me in personal correspondence.

63. Galinsky, *Augustan Culture*, pp. 142, 144.

64.An excellent study of the plants and birds in Pomeiian wall paintings is Wlihelmina F. Jachemski, *The Gardens of Pompeii* (New Rochelle, 1979).

65. Brendel, *Prolegommena to a Book on Roman Art*, p. 188.

66. Elsner, Review of David Castriota, *The Ara Pacis Augustae and the Image of Abundance in Later Greek and Early Roman Imperial Art* (Internet: *Bryn Mawr Classical Review* 95.09.05).

67. Minot Kerr, "Contexts for the Ara Pacis", [www.reed,edu/mkerr/paper/apacis97.htm].

68. For identification of the Tellus figure as "either Italia or Ceres" see Eugène Strong, "Terra Mater or Italia," *Journal of Roman Studies* 27, Part I (1937) 114-126. A. W. Van Buren was perhaps the first to interpret the image as Italia, *Journal of Roman Studies* III (1913). Jean Bayet, *Mélange d'architecture*

et d'histoire (1931), pp 64ff., argues for Italia. See more up to date summaries of the literature in Spaeth, "Demeter/Ceres in the Ara Pacis and the Carthage Relief," *American Journal of Archaeology* 90 (1986), p. 210, who suggests that the figure is Ceres. Brilliant, *Roman Art*, p. 204, refers to the figure as "Tellus or Italia." Kleiner, in *Roman Sculpture*, identifies the figure as Tellus Italiae.

69. Phyllis Lehman identified an Augustan age relief with Nilotic motifs. Phyllis Williams Lehman, *Roman Wall Paintings from Boscoreale* (Cambridge, 1953). See a reproduction in R. Paribeni, "Nuovi monumenti del Museo Nazionale Romano," *Bollettina d'arte* XII, 1918, pp. 53ff. and fig. 5. Others have recognized an Alexandrian, oe Eastern Greek, hand in the Tellus relief.

70. For a fascinating account of the persistence of the Judgment of Paris imagery, see Hubert Damisch, *The Judgment of Paris*, trans. John Goodman (Chicago and London: Chicago University Press, 1996). First published as *Le Judgement de Paris: Iconology analytique 1* (Paris: Flammarion, 1992).

71. Harold Fuchs, *Augustus und der antike Friedensgedanke*, No 3 of W. Jaeger, *Neue Philologische Untersuchungen* (Berlin 1926), p. 191 and n. 3. An earlier proposal that the figure was Pax was made by V. Gardthausen, *Der Altar des Kaiserfriedens: Ara Pacis Augustae* (Leipzig 1908). For another early opinion by A. Diederick, *Mutter Erde* (Berlin, 1926), pp. 80f.

72. Arnoldo Momigliano, "The Peace of the Ara Pacis," J*ournal of the Warburg and Courtauld Institute* 5 (1924b), pp. 228-229. E. Strong, *Roman Sculpture* (1907), p. 43; Strong, "Terra Mater or Italia," *Journal of Roman Studies* 27, pp. 114-126.

73. Nancy Thompson De Grummond, "Pax Augusta and the Horae on the Ara Pacis Augustae," *American Journal of Archaeology* 94 (October 1990); p. 666-669. The description of the Tellus panel that De Grummond makes is cited by her from G. Hafner, *The Art of Rome, Etrurian and Magna Graecia* (New York, 1969), p. 192. Hafner's description is flawed. The closest anyone has gotten to a likeness of Pax is an assumption by E. Simon, *Augustus, Kunst und Leben in Rom um die Zeitenwende* (Munich 1986), p. 30. See also E. Simon, *Eirene und Pax, Friedensgöttinnen in der Antike*, Bd. 24,3 (Wiesbaden and Stuttgart, 1988). On the iconography of Eirene and Pax, see G.G. Belloni, "Expressioni iconographiche di 'Eirene e di Pax'," in M. Sordi, ed. *La pace nel mondo antico* (Milan 1985), pp. 127-45.

74. Babette Stanley Spaeth, *The Roman Goddess Ceres* (Austin: University of Texas Press, 1996), p. 127. Spaeth identifies woman on the panel as Ceres,

and says that she wears a*corona spicea* of wheat stalks and poppy capsules, adding that these can be detected only when carefully viewing the relief and not in photographs. My own direct examination of the relief did not confirm either wheat or poppies, or even a wreath: I saw the tightly curled-knot hair-do extending across the woman's forehead, similar to what one sees in women's hair styles in Pom[peiian paintings. Spaeth directs our attention to L. Berczelly, "Ilia and the Divine Twins," *ActaAArtHist* 5:89-149. 1985, p. 116, no. 101, where the wreath is called a crown of flowers, and to Simon, *Ara Pacis Augustae* (1967), where it is called a wreath of fruit. Simon does not agree that the wreath is a *corona spicea*, while also denying that the woman is Ceres. See also, Spaeth, "The Goddess Ceres in the Ara Pacis Augustae and the Carthage Relief," *American Journal of Archaeology* 98 (1994), pp. 65-100.

75. G. K. Galinsky, "Venus, Polysemy, and the Ara Pacis Augustae," *American Journal of Archaeology* 96 (July 1992), pp. 457-475, where his views are updated from his 1960s essay. He writes that the image is "Venus...the figure most emblematic of Pax" and that all aspects of the relief fit to "Venus a great deal better than Pax." See also, A. Booth, "Venus on the Ara Pacis," *Latomus* 25 (1966), pp. 871-79.

76. S. Weinstock, "Pax and the Ara Pacis," *Journal of Roman Studies* 50 (1960). pp. 44-58.

77. K. Hanell, "Das Opfer des Augustus an der Ara Pacis," *Op. Rom.* 2 (1960), pp. 33 ff.

78. Galinsky, "Venus on a Relief of the Ara Pacis Augustae," and "Venus, Polysemy, and the Ara Pacis Augustae," both essays cited above.

79. One must distinquish between official and public meanings to the identity and behavior of the Roman gods, and not take them so seriously. Catullus' message is rendered as poetry in Greek form, addressed not to poetry lovers but to the people as social commentary. He represents a generation of writers who were educated, articulate, risk-taking social critics. To get at the underlying message of such veiled poems, I will cite one poem, but not translated as poetry. It has to do with the behavior of Julius Caesar and his chief engineer Mamurra during the invasion of Gaul:

> Sex-crazed Mamurra and his bedroom brother, Caesar, make a fine pair of debauchees. It's no wonder they have the same disease. No medicine can cure the symptoms of this entreeched foulness. Pretentious litérateurs, degenerate twins, companions sharing one sofa, they compete with each other fucking the same girls and share

the same ungodly itch.

80. Pliny, *Natural History* XXXVI, 4-8.

81. Pliny's commentary dates a century later than the event he recounts, but such scandals tend to persist in the public memory. The contrast of Italy's native terra cotta with imported Greek marbles goes back to what I mentioned earlier as to Cato's complaints recorded by Livy, XXXIV, 4, 3-4, over the erosion of old Roman values, the abandonment of terra cotta as a building material in favor of marble, representing an intrusion of foreign luxury.

82. Suetonius, *Augustus* LXXII, 1-3. Cf. Pollitt, The *Art of Rome*, pp. 111-12. Pollitt offers several other examples.

The stone referred to was peperino, known as Alban stone. It came into use in the third century BC. The vast marble quarries of Carrara were not opened until the first century BC, although some white marble had been quarried off and on. Suetonius records Augustus' boast that he had dignified Rome, leaving in marble what he had found in stone.

83. Plautus. Quoted and discussed by Pollitt, *The Art of Ancient Rome*, pp. 48-49.

84. Lucretius, *De rerum natura*, Book I, vv. 1-25. I am paraphrasing in this and other of Lucretius' statements from T. Jackson's translation (Oxford, 1929).

86 Lucretius, *De rerum natura*, Book V.

87. I owe this notion of *phusis* to Tzvetan Tovdorov's *Théories du symbole* (Paris: Editions du Seuil, 1977). English translation by Catherine Porter, *Theories of the Symbol* (Ithaca: Cornell University Press, 1982).

88. Niels Hannestad, *Roman Art and Imperial Policy* (Arthus University Press, 1988), p. 94.

SUPPLEMENTAL ILLUSTRATIONS

The King Khaled mosque at Riyadh. Design and fabrication by Vesti Design International: Wayne Andersen, principal designer; Leslie Chabot, project manager; Edmund Avasian and Brian Clarke, associate designers. *Exterior features*: doors, decorative travertine band. *Interior features: top to bottom:* dome, stained glass skylights, ring skylights, calligraphic mosaic ring band, stained glass windows, calligraphic travertine wall band, travertine and ceramic mihrab, doors and etched glass windows, stained glass windows, carpet.

Exterior carved wood doors and intermittent stained glass windows.

Stone carver at work on the KKIA mirhab elements at the Carrara workshop. Note the hammer at the lower left that would hardly be different from hammers used by the ancient Romans. The only tool used here the Romans did not have is the pneumatic chisel. The tradition among the carvers at this shop was to make a daily hat out of the morning newspaper. This is the same studio, with the same master carvers, where Henry Moore's late marble sculptures were carved, including the altar now in Christopher Wren's church, London.

Below: Wayne Andersen, with Edmund Avasian, verifying the stone carving dimensions.

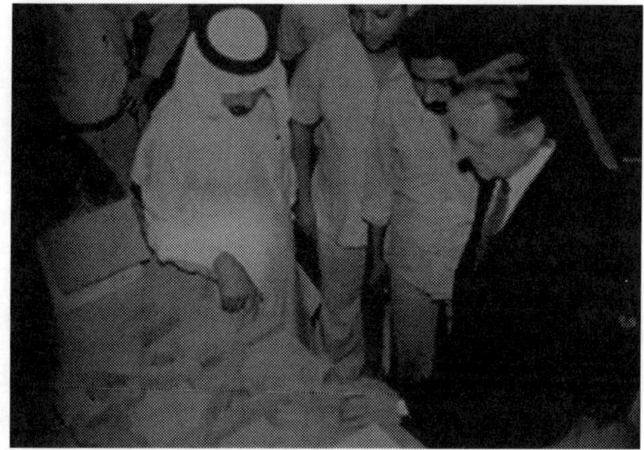

Above: Andersen in Jeddah, discussing door carving designs with Egyptian carvers (with Saudi translator).``

Andersen with Edmund Avasian at the Cararra quarry workshop, finalizing design details of the mirhab elements

The mirhab in the King Khaled mosque at Riyadh.
Wayne Andersen/Vesti Design International,
architects. Edmund Avasian, designer.